View from the Surgery

Dr Ken B. Moody

View
from the
Surgery

Matador
9 De Montfort Mews
Leicester LE1 7FW, UK
Tel: (+44) 116 255 9311 / 9312
Email: books@troubador.co.uk
Web: www.troubador.co.uk/matador

ISBN 978 1906510 039

Cover photo: Paul Mellon
"An apple a day keeps the patients at bay."

Typeset in 11pt Stempel Garamond by Troubador Publishing Ltd, Leicester, UK
Printed in the UK by the MPG Books Group

Matador is an imprint of Troubador Publishing Ltd

Dedicated to Cara, James and Tom,
and Dr Moody's long-suffering patients.

CONTENTS

Out and About

FOREWORD

Turning a series of articles, written over several years, into a book is a trickier job than it would first appear. These articles vary from the deeply moving and reflective to those of great levity and even, occasionally, of questionable plausibility. Tears still roll down my cheeks when I read some of them, and I don't count myself a particularly emotional fellow. The style and quality of Dr Moody's writing changed somewhat as the years elapsed. He seemed to write increasingly fluently and candidly. Never dull or serious, his earlier articles were a little less tongue-in-cheek and somewhat shorter and it could easily be argued that they just got better and better. The chapters herein were not assembled in any particular or chronological order and more insightful readers might spot the earlier from the later ones. I know of at least one ongoing PhD looking at this very subject.

Thanks must go to Fiona Pagett who approached him in the first place with the invitation to record his experiences in the *Peeblesshire News* and *Border Telegraph*. It took more than one request (and reminder) before he removed the stethoscope and took to his typewriter one evening each week to document memorable and amusing stories and events. Dr Moody agreed to write his column, *View from the Surgery,* on the understanding that neither Fiona nor the editor, Atholl Innes, should expect dry, informative lessons for patients' "tea-time" reading. He went so far as to say that should he ever be found concluding a piece with the recommendation that a reader "should see your own GP first thing Monday morning" he would cease being a scribe forthwith. If that were the case, he felt he would: "be obliged to offer grovelling apologies to my beleaguered colleagues whom I would have undoubtedly burdened further with extra work from the already flooded market of newspaper doctors who sell themselves down the river by regurgitating commonly known facts and playing on people's anxieties." (Such candour, righteous indignation, clichés, medical imagery and long sentences are typical of the man!)

The plan for a twice-monthly trickle of 300-word articles cascaded into weekly 900-word epistles. The initial 3-month contract burst like a dam.

Journalists on the paper tried not to voice their objections too loudly as the "Doc Column" grew ever broader (in dimension and in range) and moved to the centre pages. Perhaps they were only too aware that they might find themselves, one day, on his examination couch.

Late evenings of good wine and searching questions led eventually to Dr Moody admitting to me that some of the patients mentioned had names and details altered to protect their anonymity. He claimed he was torn between the accuracy expected of a clinician and finding material that would make for a good story. He asked patients' permission where appropriate but said that, even if he missed a few, those recognising themselves would be tickled pink, though many had already gone to "the great waiting room in the sky."

I have no doubt that this book is unique. It will not sit comfortably on university or academic bookshelves, as it is not directed specifically at a medical readership, nor is it likely to induce sleep. There are no alphabetical lists, incomprehensible Latin terms and no high-resolution photographs of human innards (thankfully!). It breaks no new ground in any field of research nor even in the doctor-patient relationship. I suspect general practice boffins will raise shaggy eyebrows at some of the practises and remedies Dr Moody adopts and at his strategies for coping with the challenges of rural general practice. It is also unique in that patients (for that is what we all ultimately are!) will find his lack of pretence, his obvious humanity and his sense of humour most refreshing.

This is no reference book either. If you are in need of urgent medical advice do not waste precious minutes leafing through these pages. There is a further danger too that you will be distracted from more serious issues. If, instead, you are in desperate need of cheering up, I suggest you are holding the right book.

One of the joys I got from compiling and editing these articles was that I took different meanings from excerpts and phrases, each time I read them. Whether this is what Dr Moody intended is another matter, but I believe the wisdom and insight he displays transcends the moment or even the generation from which he writes. He and his work are timeless. He is rather conservative by nature and traditional in outlook, and I notice there is practically no reference to political or historical events. Yet he is modern enough to accept change, eventually or under duress, and seeks what is ultimately best for his patients. What more could one ask and expect of their doctor?

His column always has a photograph or image, appropriate to the subject matter. I know it is often great fun for him choosing these pictures, and articles sometimes are in fact written after one has been selected.

I was keen to involve his long-term colleague and friend Dr Bodie Aiken in the preparation of this book. Bodie, however, professed a chronic shyness and reticence, belied by his years working with the public, and declined to "interfere", as he put it. He was aware of his junior colleague's column but declared he rarely read it for fear of what "the whipper-snapper might be saying aboot me now." When Bodie retired from medical practice an article was dedicated to him. The picture featured was of a benign looking dinosaur. Whether Bodie found this endearing or offensive remains unknown for he never once referred to it.

My interviews with Ken were lengthy and tremendously entertaining. In addition, his sharp intellect and singular insight into psychology and human nature are worthy of more serious and weighty medical tomes. He once said, though, that he would rather be remembered for spreading a little light-heartedness than spreading medical knowledge "that would only be proven as bunkum the following year."

Dr Moody seemed bemused at first that I should wish to share his witticisms and observations with an audience outside his native South of Scotland, as "these are God's chosen people and I know how they think, drink and breathe. Why in tarnation would others be interested in what this old duffer has to say?" I daresay we don't know the answer to this but perhaps after reading what follows you may find a good reason.

When asked for a comment that would sum up his motivation for writing a humorous account of his career, without hesitation he declared: "Laughter is the best medicine and medicine the best laughter." He seems to see it more or less his Hippocratic duty to amuse readers, patients and colleagues, and who are we to stop him?

This book is in places heart-rendingly poignant and elsewhere side-splittingly funny. It is my keen desire that what you read in these pages is a real tonic. It certainly was for me.

David Carvel
Biggar 2007

CASE HISTORIES

TURF DECISIONS

"You're only newly out of hospital, so take it easy," I urged Terry Cotter-Potts one Friday afternoon. "Sure, Dr Ken, I'll just be messing about in my paradise, my garden of weedin', this weekend." Recovery from a heart attack should involve a scheduled exercise programme but I knew Terry long enough to know that this jokey dismissal in itself was cause for concern. Maintaining his three-acre plot and bringing it up to the standard expected of a serious contender for the *Groundsmen, Rakesmen And Seedsmen Society (GRASS)* annual competition perhaps even led to his coronary. His employer kindly, but perhaps ironically, had given him as much "gardening leave" as he needed but assured him he was not being put out to pasture quite yet.

Many of my patients frequently refer to, and take enormous pride in, their gardens. The dedication and love may be the same whether they need less than an hour each week to tend their compact hanging garden of the Borders or require several full-time gardeners to maintain the Babylonian ancient version.

Gardening, I believe, is wrongly regarded as a middle-aged pastime. It takes and needs all sorts and ages. Nowadays television channels are devoted to the green things surrounding our houses and a new species of human seems to have been cultivated, namely the celebrity gardener. He or she is invariably chipper and knowledgeable. But beware, one day you may return home to discover your garden has had the fateful "total make over." Even our garden centres now resemble supermarkets and you should be prepared to queue for a parking space on a Sunday afternoon. It's all rather a long way from the corner shop with its shelf of seeds and from the days when sets of tools were passed from father to son.

I quite enjoy glancing at a patient's garden when I'm summoned to a house call. I think it gives rather a lot away about the householder. While most people proudly fiddle and potter with their green fingers, in a street or terrace there is often a "sore thumb" sticking out (which metaphorically would be purple rather than green, I suppose!) Weeds, thistles and grass there may be waist-high, trees wildly overgrown and car radiators or boat hulls might lie scattered around too. Predictably, the dwelling itself will not be appearing in this month's *Utterly Gorgeous Houses* glossy magazine either. I've never been too keen on gardens turned over to chuckies especially when weeds grow freely through. Such a compromise may suggest other problems with the owner, such as illness, though doctors try to be more exact with our assessments of patients rather then make formal diagnoses from the rusty gate. (Though a diagnosis of simple laziness in fact may turn out to be accurate.) Neighbours, of course, famously argue about hedges and tree heights but poor relations between semi-detached house owners may be obvious when their shared postage stamp of a lawn is cut only to the halfway margin. Quite why a young person cannot take a few extra minutes to pull a weed or mow the lawn for an elderly neighbour one can only wonder.

Garden ornaments are often a cause for amusement. I actually quite like a partially hidden green man or a well placed weathered sundial but am less keen on armies of industrious gnomes, legions of oversized butterflies on stalks or forests of reproduction classical sculptures.

Garden ponds can be rather attractive but are one of the commonest causes of tragedy for exploring, inquisitive children out of the sight, even momentarily, of distracted adults. As pleasant as gardens are they can be seriously dangerous places. Tree felling and roof tile replacement should be left to those used to doing such tasks. People over the age of sixty really should not go up ladders, particularly after leisurely liquid lunches. Despite this, many feel obliged to prune and pollard the fruit trees or paint the peeling eaves annually. Most avid gardeners have a shed full of power tools, including: chainsaws, mulchers, hedge cutters and leaf blowers. Even extension cables and the obligatory lawnmower can be dangerous, especially if cables get severed without a power breaker in place. Wee ones again are at risk when not seen or heard above the din. Tree swings with frayed ropes a generation old, barbecue paraphernalia or the smouldering autumn bonfire are further hazards.

Like Botanists, doctors have a passing knowledge and sound authoritative when employing Latin terminology. It is useful to distinguish between the two fields as I suspect you would rather suffer a growth of *myosotis* (forget-me-nots) then myositis (painful inflammation of the muscles) and would rather culture *Foeniculum vulgare* (fennel) in your herb garden than *acne vulgaris* on your chin. Interestingly though, lichen can grow both between your branches and your toes!

You've got to take it easy Terry, otherwise you may find yourself pushing up the daisies (*Bellis perennis*). I too love chopping wood for the stove, tearing out the dead growth and loading the compost heap. But just sit in your garden this weekend, this winter, Terry. Read the papers and survey the great work you've already achieved.

LOOKING A GIFT-HORSE

Some of us might count ourselves fortunate to receive a cheque through the post. Perhaps more so when it is unexpected and for a considerable sum. Most, I suspect, would check the provenance and validity of it and recognise that it might have been issued in error.

I knew a man who was the recipient of such a cheque. Eck Wynne had never been one to count himself lucky but he really felt, that day, that his horse had won by two lengths. Around the time of his father's death a certain bank sent him a five-figure sum. His father's estate co-incidentally was in the process of being wound up but, as there were hardly two beans to rub together, this cheque was, frankly, a little improbable. Never one to stall at an opportunity, Eck felt he had been given a free rein to spend and squander, fritter and wager. He raised more than one glass to his father's memory and I suspect others did the same, perhaps bemusedly grateful for the benevolence of an old man they had never met. Eck must have known that the money had been sent in error but was happy to adopt the principle that "finders keepers." The bank to his surprise took a less philosophical view and asked, initially in a polite fashion, if they might have it back. "It wasn't there to be returned," he related to me ruefully in surgery, "how could I possibly give them it back?"

Eck never married and his only relation was his elderly mother. She was a dignified lady and I recall her equine and balletic ceramic figurines lined along the mantelpiece. She would defy anyone to ever spot a fleck of dust on them. Mrs Wynne knew her late husband's financial affairs better than he did himself and would undoubtedly have questioned the receipt of such a considerable sum. Eck tried hard to keep news of his supposed good fortune from his mother, but she suspected something was awry when she learned of his new-found popularity at the local inn. After the first few letters from the bank were ignored, this large financial institution started to rear in anger. Solicitors became involved and Eck himself eventually realised he would need to mount some form of defence to prevent things turning nasty. His lawyer did not argue that the windfall was anything other than "erroneous" but tried to contend that, if Eck fecklessly spent the sum and had no income of note, he was not in a position to return it. His low moods were obvious to all. Soon, in a blinkered like fashion, he could see or talk of nothing else, other than this insurmountable mountain of debt. Sadly Mrs Wynne was pulled down into the depths of misery with him, and turned from being a most gracious and amicable lady to being a dejected, nervous wreck. Feeling saddled with her son's debt she saw it as her dubious duty to help as best she could. From her own limited resources, she pulled together a fraction of the demanded sum to appease "the beasts" snapping at his heels, but still they came calling.

Eck reached the point he could not leave his house or even make the simplest decisions. Mrs Wynne felt the capital just had to be realised and the only option, as she saw it, was to sell her quaint little cottage. She moved into the spare room of her son's rather modest dwelling. At last, after years of grief and stress, the bailiffs whinnied and backed off. The stable door was finally closed on the matter but sadly, the horse had already bolted; the damage done.

It really spoke volumes for her love and support of her son, but I knew she did not approve of the mess in which they found themselves. "Mess" would also be the word I might use to describe the state of Eck's abode. He had never been the most fastidious and organized of individuals and the sitting room was lit by a single naked bulb. Packing cases were stacked wall to wall. The gas had been disconnected and the single bar electric heater was simply inadequate. Early one winter morning, Mrs Wynne tripped over a flex on the way to the bathroom. She fell heavily striking her head against the corner of a tea chest. She never regained consciousness and died the following week in hospital, from a traumatic brain haemorrhage. Guilt was something Eck could shovel by the cartload, and this was the final straw. No one saw him after the funeral and his body was found the following week in the small outbuilding behind the house. Verdict: suicide by hanging.

Some would argue Eck and his mother were the victims of his own folly; others that if the bank had been less negligent in their actions, none of this would have happened.

What should not even have been a life-changing sum of money was in fact a life-ruining one, twice over.

Eck looked the gift-horse right down to its tonsils. Unfortunately it bit, and bit very hard.

UNBEARABLE BEHAVIOUR?

"You'll have to do something about him now (expletives laboriously deleted), he's running riot again," roared an irate father down the phone. He had returned home and his 7-year-old son was apparently acting up, once again. Mr Ursine and his wife had "had enough this time" and I was being told that I had to do something, that evening. The call was the verbal equivalent of being picked up by the scruff of the neck and shaken vigorously.

The family had moved to this neck of the woods the year before, and I last encountered them in surgery the previous month. They attended to complain about the lad's "uncontrollable and unbearable behaviour." They previously attended my poor colleague, Dr Bodie Aiken, and seemingly "got no help there." Like me, Bodie assured them he would request a further health visitor's assessment. I remember Bodie recounting the mauling he got from Dad. It all seemed as if we were to blame.

At our meeting Mum, a rather timid little woman, catalogued graphically young Teddy's misdemeanours, which apparently included taking lumps out of his elder sister. He did indeed have impressive jaw muscles which, at that time, were employed supporting the broadest grin I'd seen since Pooh discovered his latest cache of honey. Mum would still be listing his "wicked ways" to this day if I had not interrupted, suggesting that I got the picture. Dad, a large grizzled sort of fellow, sat there, arms folded correcting or embellishing every detail of mum's narration.

It emerged that it was every health professional's impression that the parenting skills, or lack thereof, were the issue. (It took no sleuth to determine that of this sleuth!) A trainee doctor in their previous practice, however, had apparently felt otherwise and signed a letter to this effect. This validated the parents' view that there "must be something wrong with him." Mum constantly criticised the child and Dad threatened, or perhaps more than threatened, violence. They did not play with, engage or even hug him, and he was frequently contrasted with his "perfect" sister. He was in fact no problem at school or at Cubs, but because these organisations said as much they were deemed as: "useless"; "not taking the problem seriously" or "lying so as not to ruin their own reputations." Teddy therefore was frequently removed by his dissatisfied parents and was known to every playgroup and school in the area.

It was strongly felt that he was indeed a boisterous wee lad but did not have attention-deficit disorder or any other diagnosable or treatable condition. (Though the odd treat for good behaviour might have been a start!)

"It's all about benefits you know," a social worker informed me. The family were in receipt of benefits on the basis of the letter written several years ago. Days before this phone call I had been asked to complete a report by way of update and the parents, exercising their rights, had read my response. My comments were based largely on detailed reports completed by colleagues but also on my own observations.

People can act like a certain creature with a sore head and become rather angry when their benefits are threatened. I can appreciate that, whether deserving of them or not, such a loss can make a significant difference to a household's income.

People are often in denial and may go to great lengths to avoid acknowledging that a problem is, at least in part, of their own making. In this case, professionals had been perceived as letting them down and not caring. Even if Teddy's folks did accept that their parenting abilities were less than perfect would they have accepted help, as this may have meant losing face and probably money too? Some situations are "lose-lose." I was seen as the villain, or one of several, in Ursine eyes. Other than fraudulently supporting them in their benefits appeal, I'm sure I would have been out of favour whatever I did.

I've got myself to live with, they've got Teddy.

Of father and son, I know whose behaviour I found less bearable.

LITTLE ANGELS

Old Jean Ettick knew she needed to go into hospital but was worried about leaving her daughter. "But who'll look after her, Dr Ken?" she sobbed. "She cannot be left alone." Fran was now 50 but, having Down syndrome, had been reliant on her parents all these years. Since her dad, John, died some three years ago, Fran's sole carer had been Mrs Ettick.

Down (or Down's) syndrome was first described by John Langdon Down in 1866. It is a genetic disorder where, rather than there being a pair of number 21 chromosomes, there are three. Trisomy 21 is the technical term. It is by far the commonest genetic abnormality that occurs in nature and is seen in all races and in all species.

The typical characteristics are: reduced intellectual capacity; short stature; obesity and distinguishing facial, nasal and ear features. Down children can be particularly cute and adults, I think, often retain a certain childlike quality.

Estimates are that Down syndrome occurs in the human population in about 1 in 800 births, and in an even greater number of conceptions. Many miscarriages are early losses from genetic or other abnormalities; "Nature's harvesting."

In Jean's day, antenatal screening was no more hi-tech than an experienced doctor examining the pregnant belly. It was only when young Fran was not developing or growing at the rate of her contemporaries that it was discovered she had "Mongolism." This archaic and rather unkind label was based on the observation that affected individuals seemed to resemble those from the country nestled between China and Russia.

Ultrasound is now offered during the fourth month of pregnancy. Such an increasingly detailed scan, coupled with a blood test, detects the majority of unborn Down babies. Unfortunately the blood test itself only provides a "high" or "low" risk assessment. This naturally causes enormous anxiety; especially when you consider that only 5% of the "high risk" group indeed carry Down syndrome babies. Those with this stated "high risk" are offered a further blood test and then amniocentesis or Chorionic Villous Sampling (CVS), if indicated. Both of these tests are invasive; therefore there is a small risk of subsequent miscarriage, and for some this is unacceptable. These results are absolute and a mother can be told whether the baby she carries has this or another genetic disorder. An appreciable number of women choose to have no antenatal testing whatsoever, claiming that regardless of the results they would proceed with their pregnancies. I respect them for such a stance but trust they are armed with correct advice, information and support. Most women (and their partners) on discovery of Trisomy 21 or other serious genetic disorder, choose to terminate their pregnancy. Despite the increasingly sophisticated tests, babies continue to be born unexpectedly with Trisomy 21. It was the way it was in the old days, and certainly when Fran was born half a century ago.

Fran's childhood had been a happy one. As is typical with Down children and adults, they are contented and placid individuals. On the physical side though, heart defects are relatively common. Fran had a minor valve problem but never needed surgery. Down syndrome is associated with a greater risk of leukaemia, dementia and thyroid problems in later life and I try to see such patients at least once each year, for blood tests and a general examination.

The saddest aspect of having a family member with Down syndrome is undoubtedly society's attitude. I knew of one vocal community group that fought tooth and nail against the plan for a small facility for eight Down adults. It is true that most cannot live independent lives and, often being born to older parents, will outlive them. Why residents of a street should feel their wellbeing or house value might be compromised by the presence of such peaceable and non-threatening people, I'll never know. I've yet to read of a Down person being subject to an ASBO. I confess to a mischievous amusement when I discovered the arch objectors, having won their case (disgracefully in my opinion), found their new, "normal" neighbours were frequently before the Sheriff for their less than neighbourly behaviour.

Formerly, under Scots Law, people with Down syndrome did not have the right to inherit land, property or title. One large Borders estate fell into ruin because the two "unrightful" heirs both had this genetic condition. It may be true that they would not necessarily have had the wherewithal to manage the estate or its business, but such is the role of the power of attorney and of Trusts.

Sadly, old Jean never did return home; her cancer was more advanced than realised. It seems she would have been more troubled by her failing health than she was prepared to admit. She simply didn't want to be separated from her only daughter.

Fran could not fathom where her mum had gone. Would it have been better for Jean to have died at home? Perhaps. Fran could have been with her to the end and seen her passing for herself. To Fran: "the doctors took mum away and it should have been God."

Fran died in a care facility little over four months later, she never really settled in.

I believe she died of a broken heart.

AUNT JEAN

I lost my aunt last week. Not through some careless omission or simple oversight (she would have appreciated this irreverent aside) but by her moving into death's beckoning embrace.

Aunt Jean, my father's younger sister, had a malignancy diagnosed less than a year ago. She chose to undergo (or rather endure) the chemotherapy and other treatment offered. Despite coping reasonable well with this, her abdominal tumour advanced and her bowel obstructed to a degree where cure and survival were out of the question. Her stay in the hospice was a little protracted but her strong heart and lungs eventually, like the rest of her, succumbed. She was victim to her own terrible variant of what, in fact, is only one of many conditions we choose to lump together under the convenient and rather simplistic umbrella of "cancer."

She liked to read this column (or so she claimed!) She enjoyed pawky humour and said the names of the "characters" were her favourite bit. Quite why everyday actual names of patients such as: Art Cinque; Kay Oss or Vanessa Peacock (used with their full permission, of course) should have been singled out for comment, I'm not sure. Perhaps when writing one should just let the facts and people speak for themselves; truth being stranger than fiction, as was once said.

Aunt Jean was always there; birthdays, weddings, Christmas, christenings, funerals and often on no special occasion at all. She was the voice on the phone, the first to congratulate, the first to commiserate and the last to criticise.

She was a great traveller too. Canada was her particular

destination of choice. Perhaps the easygoing, friendly, faintly old-fashioned ways of that people were qualities she recognised and was attracted to. She never married but rumours within the family were that she almost wed a librarian from Alberta, but none of us ever dared ask.

The day I shall perhaps remember most fondly was her seventieth birthday. Being, we suspect, a frustrated aviator, she had in conversation mentioned that her last unachieved ambition was to take quietly to clear skies in a hot air balloon. The family chipped in and enclosed within an appropriate birthday card a one-way ticket, leaving from a local field to wherever the gentle breeze might choose. She spoke passionately afterwards about the flight and her bird's eye view of the town and county from where she and our family originated. It had been more than she imagined it to be, she said, her dream fulfilled (even paradoxically having been brought back down to earth with a bump!)

Aunt Jean's name will not appear in the history books. Wars were not started or averted by her efforts. The arts and science will have to progress through the genius of others. Her obituary will not even appear in the national newspapers, save for a few formal lines listed alphabetically under surname. But she did change the world I believe; my world, my family's world and that of those close to her. She was a humble, warm, humorous and, most of all, Godly lady.

She never accepted or admitted she was dying, even latterly. Whether it was her eternal optimism or simply denial we'll never know, but that was how she chose it to be.

We broke the news to her youngest great-nephew, who knew and loved her as much as the rest of us did. He looked at us, shrugged and then burst into tears. Even a seasoned old codger like me found this innocent, unpretentious gesture rather moving. Hers was not a tragic death in the truest sense. She had seen her three-score and ten and lived life happily and fully.

The funeral was quite simple. No pomp or circumstance, no austerity. Some tears, some laughter then each their separate ways, taking their own memories and thoughts back to everyday life. For me, back to the surgery, touched once again by death but this time just a little bit closer to home. Reminded, if ever it were needed, of the loss loved ones feel when the end comes, however expected and ultimately welcome it might be.

Thank you for being who you were. I'll miss you Aunt Jean. God bless.

THE EMPTY CHAIR

"Am I going mad doctor, as I find myself talking to him all the time?" Mrs Pine lost her husband Don just two months before. She had been prepared for his death, but now that he was gone she had more questions than ever and hadn't been prepared for widowhood as much as she had expected or imagined.

It was almost a year to the day since Don first attended surgery with jaundice. Contrary to his hope that it was a persisting tan from their holiday, it soon emerged that bowel cancer had already spread to his liver. They faced his illness courageously and bravely. Surgery and chemotherapy were tolerated as well as could be expected but his oncologists shook their heads when asked if further treatment would make any difference. His wish had been to remain at home until the end and our invaluable district nurses helped make this possible. Pain had been the most difficult symptom to control and his stubborn nature often prevented him from admitting when it broke through. This same nature, though, probably helped him see a few more weeks and, best of all, his first grandchild.

Elle sat there sobbing, remembering and recalling with me the lighter sides of Don's illness and passage through to death. He had seen middle age and had survived longer than statistics or specialists predicted, but nonetheless she felt cheated and robbed. Even now she puts out two mugs as the kettle boils and leaves his mail unopened for a few days. She still cries, screams and sits in a darkened room, though was a little ashamed to say so for some reason. The hardest thing, she said, was sitting in the living room with his empty chair there. She declines dinner party invitations and avoids shopping when couples are likely to bump into her. The bed seems bigger, the car sits in the driveway, his wine remains untouched and the photos stare out from every mantelpiece. But it is the vacant seat that gives her a lump in the throat every time she looks at it. In fact, it is a bit shabby but only Tess, his dog, is allowed to sit on it now and she still pricks up her ears in the hope that this is him returning, whenever a noise comes from outside.

Psychologists and counsellors talk of the *bereavement process*. It may seem a bit formulaic to think of such a staged process, but it is usually fairly consistent across cultures and circumstances.

Often one initially feels *stunned*. Clearly in the case of sudden, unforeseen deaths (particularly suicides and homicides) this is at its strongest and often blurs with the so-called second stage, that of *numbness*. People can enter a vacuum where their life is on "pause" and they seem quite removed from what is going on around them, or even the pain suffered by other family members and friends. There is a loss of appetite for all things, whether practical requirements like food or previous interests. Others, during this time, may simply go into "organisational mode" and make detailed funeral arrangements and address diligently all personal and financial loose ends. Sometimes it is suggested that they should sit down and let others see to such practical issues, but such reason is rarely accepted. There then often follows a period of either *anger* or *guilt*. This may be anger that medical staff failed to adequately warn/detect/explain/ treat the late person's condition. Some points, of course, may be valid and, in truth, after some patients' deaths I wonder if things indeed could have been done any differently (hindsight being the wonderful medical tool that it is.) The alternative, guilt element, at this stage may manifest itself when the bereaved feels she could have been a better loved-one, should have said or done something differently (either during the final illness or before) or even that she should have gone first "by rights." It has long been my observation that couples who have been very close for decades often die within a few weeks or months, simply because they literally couldn't live without each other.

The final stage of this assumed bereavement process is that of *acceptance*. It is unusual for someone not to eventually (regardless of how tragic or even negligent the death may have been) accept that he is gone and will not be returning. Those left behind realise they have to manage and get on with their own lives, being there for others too.

Some people rapidly progress through all these stages. Sometimes grieving actually starts long before death occurs, even as early as when serious illness is diagnosed. Others get stuck along the way either not allowing themselves, or not being allowed, to grieve properly. Immersing oneself in work or other activities may be a possible diversion, but if used as a form of escape only delays the grieving process.

My job as a doctor is not to tell people what to do or how to mourn, but to offer support and reassurance that feelings of hollowness or talking to the deceased are well within "normality." I am also there to occasionally prescribe sedation in the early stages of bereavement.

Sometimes clinical depression emerges and doctors are in the privileged and objective position to recognise this. Interestingly, in the months after the death of a close relation, people will consult with myriad minor ailments of their own that they harboured while more serious issues were addressed. "My back is killing me doctor, but I was lifting and straining for months while Don was so poorly."

Bereaved people can find solace in their faith and religion. The worst one could do is question, mock or impose one's own views at this vulnerable time. Whether a medium truly did relay that, "Don is happy where he is and wants you to get on with things," matters little. If comfort is gained, then so be it.

"We, in the surgery, miss him Elle, but I know not half as much as you do."

LEOPARDS AND THEIR SPOTS

"Do you think he'll ever change, Dr Ken?" asked Bracken Blaeu, as hopefully and naively as ever. Her man, with the paunch, can fairly pack a punch. Her regular Monday morning visits are the walking (and photographic) evidence of all that is bad about excessive alcohol consumption in one whose emotional outbursts are not confined to verbal diatribes, stony silences or even the nearest wall. I don't count myself an authority when it comes to issues of domestic violence and have no first-hand experience. (I am glad to say Mrs Moody restricts herself to meting out only the occasional tongue-lashing!) But if asked, as I was here, I would have to say that generally, over a lifetime, people do not change very much, if at all. If a person is boorish, unreliable or aggressive or on the more positive side: civil, considerate or decent, then it is likely if you should bump into him forty years later, that is how you will find him still. If a man raises his fists (or feet, or elbows, or knees for that matter) to his beloved just once, regardless of the supposed provocation, then I would contend that he has declared himself a type. A type who will not change. A type who will resort to the same inarticulate, Neanderthal means and probably will have little recollection until the next time. Worse still, it may be systematic assault in a sober and calculating way. Apologies (real or otherwise) no doubt, will flow. "It was the alcohol, the week at work, the football result" (delete as inappropriate.)

People on the whole do not change. What I mean is, adults rarely can or do truly alter their personalities. They may adopt a new system of beliefs (or undergo religious conversion) or genuinely learn from past mistakes and experiences, and that is commendable, but underneath beats the same heart. They may have suffered dreadful trauma or abuse themselves and have been scarred by this. The First War was probably the starkest example of this, when countless young men returned home shattered and shell shocked and were "shadows" of their former selves. Others may have skipped through the daisies of good fortune, but once a bully always a bully. It is said that: "you can take the boy out of the country but not the country out of the boy" (or just about any variation around that theme.) I am not cynical enough to believe that people never change or improve themselves, but I merely make the observation, from decades of general practice. I do not know if this is particularly right or left wing philosophy, nor do I care. I am no armchair psychologist; more the swivel chair, creaky leather variety really.

I was once criticised for using the term "wife beater." Perhaps to be more politically correct and non-sexist I should have referred to a "partner abuser" or "spousal assailant." Whatever the acceptable, non-offensive parlance, someone who stoops to such levels is not likely to change, in this or subsequent relationships.

It is not just undesirables who get stuck in their ways. People with alcohol, gambling or other addictions hopefully come to realise that they do not have to be subject to the grip of their addictions forever. The draw for them may always remain, and walking past the pub or casino, or better still taking a different route home, may be the key to avoiding such temptation. I've several patients who won the jackpot or had other "life-changing" (if only they had been!) winnings. People who have gone from the proverbial rags to riches are an interesting, some would say privileged, group. One sour old goat, in an instant freed himself of his mortgage, overdraft, first wife and financial insecurity but is still an unlikeable chap. If anything he has adopted an air of condescension to add to his lack of attractiveness and his friends discovered he was still not going to buy them a round at the pub. Realising they weren't going to be secondary beneficiaries, they took themselves elsewhere.

Personality establishes itself in childhood. If the growing child is subject to neglect or abuse or witnesses dad assaulting mum, the damage is often irreversible and immeasurable (even counting prison years later served.) Tragically, the "sins of the father" indeed seem to visit subsequent generations. We have to give our children better opportunities than many of them currently get. The negative cycle has to be broken. I have enormous respect for foster parents and applaud them for the marvellous work they do. Parenting skills to an extent can be taught but are largely learned by example. Some people though should just not be parents. It is a long way from parental deficiency to abuse but for some it seems a simple slope to slide. Our institutional care facilities historically were woeful and sometimes even worse than the alternative for these vulnerable young people. Even in the better homes, unacceptable numbers of children underachieve academically, and in other regards too. Failure to reach one's potential is about the saddest thing I believe that can happen to someone.

I don't think he'll change, Bracken, and I suspect you know that yourself. You have the number for a refuge where you and the wee ones would be out of harm's reach. I know this is financially and actually much easier said than done and would be the boldest decision you ever make.

Leopards really don't change their spots but I believe their cubs can, before it's too late.

DAYLIGHT ROBBERY

Ted and Violet had enjoyed a long weekend visiting their grandchildren but returned home to chaos. Their modest bungalow had been broken in to, valuables taken and considerable damage done. Violet's late mother's jewellery, including her wedding ring, was gone. Particularly cruelly, dust-free spaces on the mantelpiece marked where silver framed family photos stood. Drawers had been emptied and scattered, vases and figurines smashed. The concept of a gentleman thief deftly and neatly selecting a single necklace and leaving his monogrammed white linen handkerchief is the stuff of pure fiction. As in this case, a rather different and offensive calling card had been left behind. It was utterly heartbreaking for them. Violet and Ted felt violated.

They had never installed an alarm. They feared causing a false alarm, disturbing neighbours in the dead of night, when they might be out of reach, miles away. Furthermore, they had heard that, should you forget to set it and are burgled, the insurance company is quick to invalidate the policy.

The police were as sympathetic and helpful as duty and reality allowed. There had been several break-ins in the neighbourhood recently. The officers for some reason were fairly certain it had occurred early one afternoon. Another "Daylight Robbery" they called it. The window frames and sills were dusted for prints but unfortunately yielded nothing. The culprits had probably worn gloves. Violet, relating her sorry story to me in surgery, had been less than reassured when informed that the house had probably been watched. Furthermore, there were two suspects, named as Rob

Berry and Lars Henry. They were half-brothers, local drug users and small-time dealers, who would do anything to finance their habits. They were indeed known for their work in the community, but unfortunately not of the charitable kind. Contrary to the rhyme, these two magpies did not bring any joy. There was no solid evidence however that they were the perpetrators and this made it even harder to swallow. It would have been easier, Violet said, had it been a criminal gang from the city that randomly selected their house and disappeared, never to be seen again. Instead, she would have to tolerate these suspects entering the shop where she worked, only to pilfer of course.

Ted was five years retired from the police force and had dealings with the lads in question. Their father had also been of his professional acquaintance. Currently this Fagin was studying at Her Majesty's pleasure, also a graduate of the College of Crime, albeit without the pernicious influence of drugs in his curriculum. Violet worried that the housebreaking was some form of revenge, as she remembered particular threats young Lars made following one of his many arrests. Being a local bobby or his family, living in the community, can clearly leave one quite vulnerable.

Lars, though, was not the brightest silver sauceboat in the loot bag. Stealing lawnmowers from neighbours' sheds and raiding charity boxes from High Street shops neither endears oneself to local residents and shopkeepers nor demonstrates any nurturing of a criminal mastermind. Ted doubted Lars would have broken in out of malice. When he got drunk or high he had trouble enough finding his own front door and "couldn't hold a thought for five minutes let alone a grudge." Rob, on the other hand, was a smarter and nastier little man who frequently led Lars (further) astray and was quite happy to flee the scene, on more than one occasion, to leave Lars facing the music.

Six months later a vigilant neighbour, who had installed CCTV, provided the police with very clear images of his own house being burgled by the pair. Even their solicitor shrugged his shoulders in defeat, but they denied breaking in to Ted and Violet's house. Lars' girlfriend now wore a ring suspiciously like Violet's mother's pilfered one, but there was no inscription. The police were confident the lads would "go down this time", but the charges wouldn't include that of Ted and Violet's burglary. It was all too much. Years of enjoying and contributing to the fabric of their community had been quashed by the invasion and cowardly actions of a couple of ne'er-do-wells. They sold up and took a flat by the sea, closer to their family. They took their memories and what mementos had been left, but how sad it was for them to leave in such circumstances.

THE DYING ART OF
CONVERSATION

"We never seem to talk any more, Dr Ken. It's like we've nothing left to say." Faith-Anne Hope was not bemoaning a floundering professional relationship with me but rather was describing yet another symptom of her troubled marriage.

It's always sad when couples find themselves exchanging hardly a word from day to day. It may be because they are simply too busy or that the union has in fact "run its course." They might have less in common than was once assumed or hoped. Sometimes it is a destructive silence that comes from resentment, or anger at a sharp word or thoughtless action. At other times it's from apathy and indifference. You hear of couples who supposedly know each other so well that they are thought to be telepathic. Words seem unnecessary to them but, as telepathy is essentially bunkum, I would put such taciturnity down to intuition more than anything else.

Conversation is a healthy thing. We are inherently social beings. While some people are undoubtedly more fluent and articulate than others, these particular skills are not necessary to have a good blether with one another. Women are said to be better talkers than men by having better developed brains, at the speech centre (left frontal lobe) of the brain at least. Baby girls are almost universally earlier talkers than boys, and arguably just never stop.

There really are people though who just don't know when to quit talking. I don't really mean the sort who use twenty words when two words will do or old soldiers and their war reminiscences.

I mean utter bores who go off at such tangents with irrelevancies aplenty. They usually display a complete self-absorption and lack of interest in you, the sorry listener, or any other party; those who would cause the poor proverbial donkey to lose both front and hind limbs. I appreciate that some psychiatric conditions may resemble this description and that such verbal incontinence may indicate a deep unhappiness or insecurity. The difference though is that, when treated (and I don't mean with a sock inserted between the teeth during a rare pause!), there should be a return to one's former self.

A conversation should be more than just one-way. A dialogue is not necessarily just between two people (that would be a duologue of course!) and should be an exchange and interaction of comments and thoughts. I recall a patient, Vera Bose, who decided to move house. She gave her main reason for leaving as being that, despite "speaking to people all the time," she had never been invited in by anyone for a cup of tea. Perhaps the reason was that "friends" would worry they could not get rid of her again! She may yet have to learn that conversation is all about speaking *with* people rather than speaking *to* them, and certainly not speaking *at* them, as she tended to do.

We live in the Communication Age. Technology is ever better at giving us the facilities to keep in touch. Despite this, we prefer to email and text due to lack of time and the convenience of it. Abbreviated words and predictive text iron out any remaining sincerity and character from our communications. We hardly ever seem to pick up the telephone for a chat or write a letter, especially not by hand.

Then there is the champion conversation-stopper of them all. Mrs Moody and I felt obliged to purchase a television set for one of the royal weddings (I forget which one.) Other than the odd state funeral and any film featuring Alastair Sim, we tend not to watch terribly much on the goggle-box. If we have the evening to ourselves I will throw a log on the fire and we'll sit back and watch the dancing shadows while nursing a glass of something smooth and pleasant. I won't pretend that I never snore after dinner, have my nose stuck in a journal or get obsessed with a sticky cryptic crossword clue, and it sometimes requires a lobbed slipper to get my attention. I confess, I sometimes grunt disinterestedly when Mrs M details her coffee-morning purchases, news about friends of friends or the latest celebrity tittle-tattle. Occasionally I'll feign interest, which conceivably she may do for my likes and tastes. Even after all these years we still have much in common but appreciate and respect our differences.

"I'm no expert Mrs Hope but it sounds like the two of you may need a mediator to help with your problems. Speak to your hubbie first, find out what's on his mind and tell him how you feel."

CLASS ACTS

"Teaching and education in general are just not what they used to be, Dr Moody," moaned Wanda Tawse, one of our local teachers. Dr Bodie Aiken says he can recognise a teacher the moment he or she walks into the room. She has the weight of the world on her shoulders and looks as stressed as she describes herself to be. Most teachers will give the same reasons for their considerable stresses. Lack of support from parents and from seniors always feature highly. Erroneous and malicious accusations can have devastating effects on previously confident, committed and competent individuals and I've seen careers come to an abrupt end under such circumstances. In the past, parents would usually accept and agree with the punishment and sanctions meted out to young Dee Grader. Now it seems the little cherub can do no wrong and teachers are rounded on for exerting authority, however proportionate it may be. As in other fields, including my own, responsibility (and more poignantly, blame) is shrugged off in a nonchalant schoolboy fashion and deposited like a pile of jotters at the feet of the relevant establishment; whether: school, health service or ultimately government. We read of schools "failing pupils" when the students themselves have made little effort to participate or learn (other than in less desirable activities!)

In the surgery I meet people who work in a whole variety of occupations but it is perhaps teachers for whom I have the greatest degree of admiration. I feel I could have tried my hand at most things, except Law (I've too great a conscience!) and teaching, for numerous reasons.

Separation and denial of privilege are certainly mature, modern methods of punishment, but seem to have little effect on some. I am undecided about the abolition of appropriate corporal punishment. There is little doubt that the demise of classroom discipline is in part due to the relegation of straps and canes to museums. On the other aching red palm, so to speak, every school seemed to have its psychopath wearing a mortarboard whose cruelty was as legendary as David Copperfield's stepfather, Mr Murdstone. At the other end of the literary spectrum, the likes of Miss Jean Brodie and Mr Chips engender the greatest of respect and a desire for knowledge and learning that is usually lifelong.

Then, there is the great comprehensive versus private education debate. Doctors are often fortunate enough to have the financial ability to have such a choice for their children. GPs, though, see and hear first-hand (as in this consultation) particular problems. We also find ourselves waiting patiently in traffic on the way to a visit, and don't dare to make eye contact with any of the cursing, spitting, littering, smoking herd emanating from the local school (and that's often just the staff!)

In a smaller community such as this, patients are aware where a GP sends his children. If it is to private city schools, it may be interpreted that the local school, however good it actually is, is not adequate for his precious offspring. Always ones to ignore what people *might* think, Mrs Moody and I based our decision on more valid grounds, and of course let the eager learners themselves express their preferences.

It often seems that private schooling produces more articulate and confident young people, however beneficial or otherwise you may feel such confidence to be. Education is about recognising and meeting one's potential, wherever and however this might be achieved. I am aware of how much some parents compromise and sacrifice to ensure a good education for their children. This may be in terms of their own job prospects, time and money, and I admire them for this.

I confess that I would not like to come through the teen years today. Grunge, Goth and other urban cultures of hopelessness prevail. Materialism and unearned wealth with the shallow, talentless, morally vacuous cult of celebrity is sadly what many young people are indoctrinated with and aspire to. Teenage angst and the pressure to take drugs and other risk-laden activities has never been greater. Bullying of course has always existed but suicide rates in young people are tragically increasing. Schools and colleges that are tangled in the sticky tape of bureaucracy and arbitrary targets set by the government of the day are letting down individuals. For example, pupils may be declined entry to a course if they are likely to perform badly, as this would affect overall figures and league table positions. Students get channelled earlier into subjects related to their "chosen" career paths rather than having a broader exposure to subjects. More and more find themselves in further education, often against their actual preferences, only to obtain rather worthless degrees and be saddled with debt for their first few years of work, if they can find any at all.

Good grief, Miss Tawse, you are doing a great job but when I see it like this. I am starting to understand why you are under such pressure and feel so anxious. But I'm afraid, being only a moderate achiever myself, I really don't have many answers.

TRADE ASSOCIATIONS

"My hip'll be the death of me, Dr Ken," moaned the diminutive and ironically named "Lofty" Walker. He was a slater of over thirty years (angular) standing, on roofs for A. Frame & Sons. Like most people in the trades he did not mince his words. He had genuine concerns that he might, indeed, fail to correct his balance quickly enough the next time a grey slate comes loose under his size 6 training shoe.

Many of my patients are in manual work, and it has long been my observation that the joints (particularly of their backs) wear out that bit sooner than those of us cushioned by our office or car upholstery. Common sense dictates that years of kneeling, bending, squatting, stretching, twisting and crawling cannot be good for one's physique. (And I really should acquire a desktidy for my stray pens and paperclips!)

I could count builders, plumbers, joiners, electricians and plasterers and decorators among my patient list. I dare say that a company like Whyte, Vaughn & Mann could, themselves, manage all stages of building a new house or, more pressingly, a new surgery for me. But, more commonly, there is no such "project manager" and it is left to Gus Tomer or me to co-ordinate all relevant trades. It is rather less like conducting an orchestra and somewhat more like herding cats. Poor Gus gets all stressed and finds himself muttering (after twice-the-time-at-twice-over-budget-before-VAT) "never again."

Firstly, tradesmen can be nigh on impossible to contact. Mobile numbers frequently change and Hugh Benz the plumber might be holidaying (again) in the sun.

Thirdly, I've noticed Watt & Dobble, building contractors, rarely admit they are too busy and will stick us, like proverbial plaster, somewhere down their list. It would be far preferable to receive a simple apology to the effect that more has been bitten off than can be chewed (or more wattled more than can be daubed!) but perhaps there is a fear the opposition will be approached and contracted.

Secondly, and as I've just done, if paragraphs and tasks are not ordered and structured correctly, further delays, dismantling and, of course, costs are inevitable.

As much as I dislike to be asked professional questions when I'm minding my own business, after freeing Hugh's ear canals of waxy obstruction, I'll ask when my blocked drains might receive a more industrial version of the same. I would probably draw the line at asking Watty the builder when I can expect my pagoda to be constructed after discussing with him his own erectile delays.

There is then the question of "homers." You know, the jobs that can be fitted in after hours and for which it is hardly worth opening the account ledgers. In the surgery I complete several, more minor, forms and letters each week without charge, so do not see a problem in the trade near equivalent. Call it good will, if you will, though I may receive a pheasant in recompense at Christmas. I suspect I would not have the strength of argument though to convince the tax man about such informal transactions, and confess to paying Sasha Payne, our window cleaner, in cash. It may be somewhat arbitrary, but if a tradesman's bill is less than a round of ale in *The Goose*, I'll pay him in notes and coins. (The Chancellor of course takes his fair shilling from us there too!) For larger jobs I'll ask for a business receipt as I feel fellow taxpayers and I cough up enough, without exempting other workers from such duties.

Some people obviate entirely the need for employing tradesmen, as they are skilled in many manual fields themselves. You will notice that I have not mentioned my own handiwork so far, and this is for good reason. The decision that I should not proceed up the greasy surgical pole was by mutual consent. My superiors and examiners were in agreement that my left and right hands could not achieve such mutuality, and there is little practical use for a non-operating surgeon. My dexterity was adjudged as being somewhere between gauche and clumsy. I continue to darn all my worn socks and to suture simpler wounds (with hand washing between I assure you!) but like the cotton of my feet warmers, this is as far as my surgical skills stretch these days.

I have sympathy for hard-working, all-weather types like Lofty. He has scaled plenty ladders in his time, but not of the career type, and his superannuation contributions may be negligible. It is several years until he reaches pensionable age, so he literally labours on. Joints wear and stiffen, accidents occur, balance, co-ordination and strength diminish and the general effects of age seem to accelerate. I will support him during times of illness and recovery. Who knows, I might even have him round at ours, but performing lighter tasks of course.

Six weeks after a replaced hip joint Lofty was a new man. We just couldn't stop him going up to replace a dodgy joist and a few tiles on our roof, in preparation for winter.

A WAKING NIGHTMARE

"It a nightmare, Dr Ken, I never get a wink of sleep," wept Inez O'Minnack. Though probably not strictly accurate, many patients do complain about how poorly they sleep. I rarely hear patients say they get sufficient sleep, as it seems to be either too much or too little. One of the problems for Inez and her fellow poor sleepers is that many doctors are not very sympathetic towards them. I suspect this has come about as a result of experiences during our training years in hospital. Dogsbodies that we were, our working hours at the Infirmary often totalled over a hundred each week. Naturally such dogsbodies are also dog-tired and we simply grabbed sleep at every given opportunity. Rarely were we able to wake to the cheerful dawn chorus of songbirds in glorious harmony. Instead, it was to the demands of a ringing phone or an incessant pager proclaiming "cardiac arrest," on a ward three-quarters of a mile down the corridor.

Doctors often fail to understand that patients in hospital may have trouble sleeping for good reasons. Some medicines have a stimulating effect on the brain and can cause the most disturbing dreams. Anticipating, or recovering from, surgery can be a very unsettling time and the stress of illness can knock one's sleep pattern for six. Nurses and other staff can be busy on the wards overnight and may speak in tones that are anything other than hushed.

There are great paradoxes about sleep in hospitals. I recall once being woken because a nurse discovered that a patient had not been given his night sedation. It was somewhat frustrating to discover the patient had strayed as far into the Land of Nod as I had been before this nocturnal interruption. Not only that but her intention was to wake the patient to hand him a white pill and bid him goodnight again.

Insomniacs do not get much sympathy from friends and family either. If you are unwise enough to mention your problem, say at a party, you are likely to learn that others have no such problem sleeping. People are somewhat more understanding of disabled people and tend not to say how far they themselves can walk nor tell deaf people how well they can hear.

We now have many medicines for the treatment of insomnia. Contrary to popular belief, such drugs do not give refreshing sleep. They may indeed make you sleep longer, and this in itself could make you feel better, but the brain will be no more refreshed. The hope is that this medication quickly leads to the re-establishing of a decent sleep pattern.

Then there is snoring. Descriptions can be rather amusing when we envisage curtains being sucked in and blown out again, as if in a gale, and ornaments dancing off shuddering shelves. Alcohol and obesity undoubtedly contribute to snoring and the cotton reel sewn on to the back of the pyjama top does not always work. I have known sanity to suffer from such fractured sleep and marriages ultimately to fail.

It is not everyone who has an east and a west wing in their house for such eventualities.

Various pathologies do affect sleep. The condition of sleep apnoea is a serious one. Rather than snoring, the person actually stops breathing for long periods, sometimes many times each night. This puts enormous strain on the heart and can be a serious threat to health. Narcolepsy, not unlike epilepsy, is where people fall asleep instantly, often in dangerous situations and clearly operating machinery or driving is out of the question. Some doctors dedicate their careers to these conditions and suspected sufferers are studied in the "sleep lab." (Where we assume the researchers remain alert!)

It is interesting to hear that some business people have introduced executive "power-napping" into their daily schedules.

While Churchill may have won the war by the more sedate "cat-napping" he is said to have done (I suspect the brandy aided this!) there is no doubt we each have different sleep needs to one other.

Older people do not need as much sleep but some see this as a problem. Tradition or previous habit seems to dictate that they "must" sleep eight or so hours each night. Parents too, like Mrs Wynn-Keye, get frustrated that wee Willie is "up all night and sleeps all day," the irritation really being that he has not yet fitted into what's expected and demanded of him.

Other people, in contrast, are mindful that we sleep some twenty years in a lifetime and feel obliged to deny themselves sleep, fearful they may be missing out on life. Quite what working at fifty-percent efficiency due to fatigue is achieving. I've still to have explained.

Like any other condition, I treat true insomnia on its own merits, tailoring it to individual patients.

One old lady I visited suffered the most disturbing dreams but, incredibly, had failed to make the link with the pile of paperback horror stories on her bedside table. Shift workers may have to find ways of not being disturbed by telephones and kids playing football out on the street during the day.

My favourite anecdote about sleep is of a farmer who told me he tried counting sheep to dose off but felt he ran the risk of waking in a panic, realising he may genuinely have lost one.

Anyway it's late, I'm dead-beat and my cocoa has reached the boil.

(EVERYBODY NEEDS) GOOD NEIGHBOURS

"I just can't take any more of it Dr Ken", sobbed Miss Patience Thinn in surgery one day. I usually have considerable sympathy for people who have bad neighbours and this was no exception. I say "usually" as I remember one time when both warring parties visited me the same week, each claiming mental torture, but when the facts came out in court there was only one perpetrator. We get angry when we hear of people being mugged in the street or being burgled, but to suffer constant noise or abusive behaviour from those through the wall or across the street must be intolerable.

Such "warfare" has led to murder. There was a case a few years ago where a dispute about (or over literally over) a hedge led to a fatal assault. Councils finally seem to be accepting that some neighbours are just so unreasonable and offensive that they and the police sometimes have to take action.

Having a bad neighbour can be like cancer. It eats away at the spirit, causes depression and even suicide and can occupy every waking thought. (Often the source of stress is the very fact of being kept awake of course!) It may not go away either. Vendors are now legally bound to say whether there are ongoing disputes with neighbours or whether those next door are "undesirable." Properties can become "unsellable" and you can find yourself stuck in this purgatory. Even when the rare eviction occurs, it is likely only to lead to misery for another estate or area.

We all have neighbours, whether we dwell on our 2,000 acre Perthshire sporting estate (I've known farmers take shotguns to each other's outbuildings) or live cheek-by-jowl in city high-rises.

I cannot speak impartially as I've been a bad neighbour too. When Mrs Moody and I were tightly packed city dwellers, the noise of our accordion music would occasionally rise when the spirit took us. The lady above would telephone down and graciously ask after out wellbeing, citing some other excuse for calling. We would apologetically take the hint and temper our musical enthusiasm. It is like Aesop's fable of the sun and the wind where gentle persuasion or hinting can often be so much more effective than aggressive confrontation with neighbours, which almost always inflames the situation anyway.

I remember one woman who simply wanted the council to move her to be closer to her friends. She claimed the neighbours were intolerable. It turned out that the entire resident population was elderly and was being "too friendly" by offering to help baby-sit and with the garden etc. She even appealed against the council's decision not to award her any points.

It would be a pretty Utopian society if this was reason enough to move or be moved, wouldn't it?

HOOK, LINE AND SINKER

Rod and Linn Roach had only registered with the practice the previous month. Their medical records, as is often the case, were somewhere between their last practice and ours. Linn attended surgery in a state of some distress, explaining that her father, Gil, had been washed off a pier by a freak wave and tragically drowned. She was devastated, needed to be with her family and clearly required time from her work. Her new employers, she explained, were not particularly understanding and she asked me for a sick line. I sign such certificates on an almost daily basis; treating personal and family illnesses and crises with due compassion and sympathy.

Several weeks later, Linn attended again to say that just as she was preparing to return to work, Rod's mother, Netta, had been mugged. Her assailant cruelly used a cudgel to strike the back of her head. Rod and Linn would both need a further month at least, she felt. I duly extended their lines. She expressed her gratitude through tears and said she found me incredibly understanding. She wondered what they would have done without me. I was sorry to learn that Rod's mum never regained consciousness and the life support machine had to be turned off. The family were gutted at this further loss and it seemed they simply floundered from one crisis to another. Rod and Linn felt lost. They, and the remaining family were, quite simply, all at sea.

During one afternoon surgery, they politely asking me to provide letters of confirmation for the respective causes of death. These, they said, were required by the insurance and other companies, under whom their relatives were insured. They understood they were also entitled to criminal injury compensation, at the higher rate. If the money was there, they opined, they may as well have it. I expressed my regret that I was not in a position to verify these details nor provide such letters as I had no first-hand involvement or knowledge of their late parents. Linn became most upset, asking if I had not seen the suffering they had endured in these last few months. I had indeed witnessed her tears and emotions and listened attentively to the relations about their relations.

As she attempted to retell her tale, contradictions emerged and people she had claimed were deceased could apparently back up her story, if I only phoned them. She was really angling now. When confronted with these red herrings her manner changed as rapidly as my sympathy disappeared, and they darted out the room. Their records arrived the following week after an urgent appeal to the records office. I telephoned their previous GP in Wales; Fishguard, if I remember correctly. He confirmed the couple to be "complete cods" and apologized for not warning me, but hadn't known which waters they were moving to.

Linn had spun me a very elaborate line and tried to reel me in like a plump haddock. She tricked me into providing sick lines by taking a very sick line herself. Whichever angle I look at it, I don't think I would have tackled it any differently. As doctors we may be seen as easy bait by fraudsters, but our primary responsibility is to the sick and ailing. I take people, by and large, at face value. I have not experienced deception in the surgery on such a scale, at least not to my knowledge. Doctors are not schooled in policing and cannot always seek or demand evidence to substantiate patients' stories. If the government wants tighter control and trawling of our patients' nefarious activities it should not be left solely to doctors. Some colleagues even suggest we should not be providing medical certification for employers and other agencies at all.

In smaller communities such as this, many people have relations, living elsewhere in the country, and therefore unknown to us. We cannot verify anything about strangers.

We soon know who our less than honest patients are but most new patients, I would contend, have to be given the benefit of any reasonable doubt.

Rod and Linn were never seen again in the practice. They were, of course, removed from our list, before they had even joined properly.

I felt more pity than resentment that I had listened to her elaborate little story and extended her line each time she tried to pull me in. She might be conscience-free and chuckling all the way to the bank with erroneous benefits payments, I don't know. As criminals go, I suspect they are just little aquatic vertebrates in a big pond but, knowing smaller crimes often lead to larger ones, I have little doubt they will eventually be caught.

There are always a few rotten roe in society but I will not subject suffering or bereaved patients to interrogation for fear of being filleted, as I might have been, had I provided the requested letters. Linn tried to get me hook, line and sinker; but managed only the first two, at best. No one likes being duped and, looking back, I might have picked up earlier on a few clues.

I really should have smelled something fishy from the start.

THE GAMEKEEPER

Gamekeepers are not frequent visitors to the surgery, and Rab Bytte was no exception. The trouble was, Rab was becoming increasingly arthritic and his days on the hillside and in the wood were fewer than the number of acres he covered. He had been the trusted head keeper to the sporting estate of Sir Hector Hodge-Hogg for many years, having served Sir Hector's father, Lord Harry, before that. His master was a short, rotund and prickly sort of fellow but Rab, as with all other mammals, had the measure of him. He knew when to approach and when to steer clear of Sir Hector. (After celebratory dinners at the manor, Rab knew not to sit downwind of him either!)

Rab was a man of few words but what he did say was eminently wise and beyond question. Whisky was his preferred drink but he'd only ever imbibe when invited. Once or twice I was called to pick shot carefully from a visiting gent's behind and would sit afterwards (on the patient's banqueting chair, for he no longer could!) and be enthralled, listening to Rab tell his tales. These were often as long and as tall as the deer fence around the estate. Had he been literate and so inclined, Rab may have made a respectable living in the literary world. A sort of Beatrix Potter meets Richard Adams perhaps. It wouldn't have suited him though. Instead of large advances from publishers, Rab's pay was a pittance. He, his wife Heather and daughter, Bracken had the use of the east gatehouse for as long as they remained useful and in the service of Sir Hector. But Rab and I both knew this may not be for much longer. His slowness and willingness to defer duties to younger, greener keepers was put down to his experience and seniority but, in reality, he was struggling. He no longer had the strength in his hands to grab, by the neck, a sparkling vintage white wine any more than a startled, common grey rabbit.

He had worked the land since his father taught him to deter poachers and trap other pests. His job was the best in the world, he claimed. Gamekeeper to some, Countryside Manager and Wildlife Conservator to others. He maintained the stocks of pheasant and grouse for the visits of "the gentry," half a dozen, or so, times a year.

Sir Hector lived in the city. He was Chief Executive of *Stalker & Gillies*, arguably Europe's largest Hedge Fund Managers; certainly not on the fringes. Money seemed to just fall from the branches, so to speak, like ripe fruit. Down from the city, he'd come, with fellow directors, investment bankers and certain members of parliament. There would be little warning of their arrival, so Rab and Heather kept the drinks cabinets and larders well stocked.

Not unlike these visiting parties their prey, pheasant, though noisy and proud, are not the brightest of creatures. If their drinking receptacles are too wide they tend to drown, so Rab would see to properly filled water troughs and hip-flasks. Without well-maintained boundary fences, there is the danger of the distracted, disorientated creatures wandering onto public highways, being struck by vehicles and disintegrating into swirls of feathers or tweed.

Rab was a conservator of rare and endangered species. If a visitor was drunk or patently irresponsible, with disarming charm, he would disarm the loose cannon. If such persuasion failed, he would speak quietly to Sir Hector. One MP, being a bit too liberal in his outlook, once made inappropriate advances on young Bracken. He was never seen or included in shooting parties thereafter. Each year Rab disposed of the odd rat, dozens of stoats and hundreds of crows. He would argue passionately that such "predator control" was essential, otherwise they would soon malign and dominate the countryside. The things that angered him most were gamekeepers bringing their good name into disrepute, such as by the killing of birds of prey. I remember him weeping at the discovery of the poisoned body of a young eagle owl, many summers ago. He knew who the culprit was and gave evidence against the keeper from a neighbouring estate. It was the hardest thing he ever did and Sir Hector was not best pleased either, but he knew morally that he had taken the right track. Other sources of irritation were pressure groups and "do-gooders," protesting about politically correct topical issues or countryside sports, having little knowledge and "never venturing beyond leafy suburbia." He appreciated its history and tradition, but regarded fox-hunting as rather elitist and the least efficient way of eradicating the ginger vermin, *Vulpes vulpes*. Badgers, though officially protected, he said, are the biggest nuisance of all. One can tear the door off a chicken coop as forcibly as a bear might.

But, years of working in the cold and damp, usually with a rolled-up cigarette dangling from his lips, was starting to take its toll. In addition to his gnarled hands, his knees were worn, his neck stiff and his sight failing. No laird or squire would tolerate his increasing infirmities. The new breed of college-educated keepers is more ambitious, and such graduates would leap stile and brook athletically were word of Rab's predicament to become common-knowledge. He compared himself to the old gun dog, Bullet, he once owned. (That was how she ran in her younger days but ultimately how she fell!) Rab could no longer even trot with the pack, were it required, but he could still direct "the pinstripe boys" to the best birds in the valley.

"I should be put out my misery, once and for all, Dr Ken," he would say, but only half in jest. I did for a while fear he might go to drastic steps but Heather reassured me his deep spiritual belief in the Creator and the land would never allow him to "go before his Master deems it" (and I don't think she meant Sir Hector!)

Bracken became bride to a groom, being a lover of horses herself. Rab and Heather were set to pack their things but, to their delight, were allowed to spend their twilight years on the estate and moved from the east to the west gatehouse.

DOCTOR BASHING

"Between you and me and anyone else who wants to know, Moody's not very good. He got mum's diagnosis wrong and even refuses to give you antibiotics or time off work when you want it. He wouldn't visit me at home when I had earache and has a ghastly dress sense. When I visited him late on Friday afternoon he looked tired and had the audacity to glance at his watch, just as I was about to move onto my second page of problems. Do you know, he even rudely said my toenail didn't need to be seen in an emergency surgery. Well, really. I never did like that wife of his either and he gets paid far too much for what he actually does, it can't be difficult."

Were the slander, innuendo, half-truths and snide nastiness to be removed from Essie Lantt's stage-whispered speech in the Post Office queue, there might be just the odd punctuation mark remaining.

Doctor bashing seems an increasingly popular sport particularly amongst those, I've noticed, not accustomed to exercising either their bodies or minds terribly much. It is also apparent to me that such patients have rarely actually been seriously ill themselves, requiring our particular services.

In smaller towns, where the surgery remains one of the "institutions" in the community, I recognize we may be up for closer scrutiny than our colleagues in the cities. I accept this but do have an increasing contempt for whispering campaigns or broadcast falsehoods designed to undermine and belittle the work we do here.

Occasionally, on the High Street, I overhear such idle chatter. Sometimes it is relayed to me by receptionists, patients and colleagues and occasionally Mr Thugg (Gary) will consider it his duty to inform me that the surgery is "going to the dogs." His given examples give me little reason to agree we are settling down with man's best friends.

I'm no conspiracist, but the government and certain elements of the news media do precipitate some of this negativity. When it was perceived that our representatives negotiated a better deal for us, ignoring the improved services for patients, it seemed time to take us "down a peg or two." Junior ministers lunch with editors and doctors' maximum earning potentials will be quoted as average salaries in the early editions and medical "blunders" and indiscretions will knock stories of medical altruism, genius and discovery off the centre pages.

The medical profession, sadly, is subject to ever more spurious complaints. For a few years, I acted as the "Complaints Partner." Not, I think, because I tend to attract the most criticism but I was simply taking my turn. Constructive, valid criticism is essential to the maintaining and improving of standards but the volume of spurious complaint letters is truly depressing. One man objected to his mother being offered too many blood tests for assessment of her failing kidneys and underactive thyroid gland. In another, Mr Tito Green felt we had not issued, quickly enough, a supportive letter for his wish for a powered golf cart. But the one that I still find hardest to fathom was from a daughter objecting to her father being described in a letter as "an elderly gent." Apparently this was "patronizing and unnecessary." I contended that it was "polite and accurate." Accepting that simple gratitude has been dismissed for indignant expectation by many, the greatest nuisance dealing with letters of this nature is that it detracts from our real work. Where I might have to dedicate an afternoon each month to prepare, reply and even meet the complainers my patient, with newly-developed lung cancer, has to wait another day before I can break the bad news and get cracking with arranging treatment.

If only doctor bashing was limited to verbal assaults. Tragically, many health service workers are on the receiving end of a fist, foot or knife. Emotions can run high in surgery. We might have to admit to errors and unavailable or lost results. We might find ourselves failing to refer, diagnose or treat a case quite as promptly as it, in retrospect, deserved. Patients may be disappointed they were not given the time or attention they felt they needed or were not given other people's test results and details to which they felt entitled. We, too, get frustrated at hospital delays, non-sterility and mistakes but are not ultimately responsible for every event that occurs after a patient joins our list.

One of my former fellow medical students, during an afternoon surgery, was stabbed within an inch of his life (or more accurately, within an inch of his heart.) He was saved only by the actions of a quick thinking colleague. Bottle-wielding alcohol and drug-fueled criminals besiege our Accident and Emergency departments every weekend as children with broken limbs or other genuine needs cower in fear at the language and aggression directed at the skilled nursing and medical staff. Convictions for assaults against paramedics and other emergency service personnel attract greater sentences but doctors currently are seen as no different to other workers, despite our vulnerability.

When Essie Lantt is next in surgery I shall ask her to qualify her very public comments, informing her that at least one of her audience felt strongly enough that I should challenge her.

ST LUKE

Until recently, I tended only to celebrate the feasts of St Andrew and St Nicholas. As these particular days are less than a month apart and being one who appreciates his cultural and spiritual heritage (and the occasional glass of wine does not go amiss!) another High Day or Holy Day had to be found. Perusing a liturgical calendar, I learned that I could in fact choose a saint's day from any day of the year (some have more than one!), but not wishing to lose all meaning and sincerity there seemed only one suitable day.

Besides, it had been rather negligent of me to ignore the significance of the patron saint of my own profession. No-one seems to know exactly when Hippocrates was born or died, some four centuries earlier so St Luke, himself a physician, really is the patron worthy of honour and celebration. The Feast of St Luke falls this year, as in any other, on October 18th.

Luke was born in Antioch, Syria. His name means "bringer of light," with reference, I think, to evangelism rather than to him being an obliging waiter in some ancient cocktail bar. He has been described as the Church's most articulate historian. He was not one of the twelve apostles and indeed probably not even an eyewitness to Christ's ministry but wrote the third of the four Gospels. Not content with just that, he penned the Acts of the Apostles, the accredited sequel to the Gospel story and was closely associated with St Paul. There is considerable overlap in the content of the first four books of the New Testament but Luke's Gospel is the only one to record two particular parables; The Prodigal Son (Chapter 15) and The Good Samaritan (Chapter 10). These are the two which, from my diligent Sunday school studies, always struck me as displaying both the best and worst in human nature. The father of the son, who squandered his inheritance, accepted him back without qualification. We assume the scoundrel returned repentant but wonder too if it was rather just out of desperation. In the story of the Samaritan traveller he, unlike the goodly priest and the Levite before him, stopped to tend the injured man and take him to an inn for recuperation. The lesson being that a neighbour is someone who shows support and concern rather than one who simply shares a postcode, council tax bracket or privet hedge. Even today, many legal systems enshrine "The Good Samaritan law" to protect from liability those who go out of their way to offer well-meaning assistance. These two parables, to me, demonstrate the greatest of compassion and humanity and remain with me as examples of basic human decency.

Luke reached the grand age of 84, "unmarried and without issue," only to suffer the fate of most Evangelists at that time. He was crucified. He met his end in Thebes, Greece, on a gnarled olive tree.

His patronage is not unique to doctors. He must have been a fairly busy and well-liked fellow (or had a predilection for sitting on committees!) as he is also the patron saint of: Italy, Germany, artists, lace workers and sculptors. Not only to these fine bodies of people and nations but also to goldsmiths, butchers, bachelors, brewers and glass-makers. Whether collectively this makes him the patron saint of stag parties is yet to be determined, though he would seem a suitable candidate.

Father George Poulos summed up Luke's relevance and standing in the Christian faith by declaring that: "An appraisal of the contributions to Christianity by St Luke cannot be measured by the number of words he wrote, the miles he travelled in missionary journeys or the number of years he spent in exclusive dedication to the service of Jesus Christ. St Luke, like so many who have given so much to all of us, is not to be appraised only to be honoured."

His contribution to Medicine may not be quite as significant, but Luke lives on in numerous eponymously named hospitals and hospices throughout the world.

I see it as my duty and it will be an honour to raise a glass and remember dear Luke this week.

THE BIG C

Mrs M asked if she had The Big C. She did, in fact.

It's so wretchedly common. They say it strikes one in three and almost everyone knows someone suffering from it. When a patient with an unusual growth, intractable cough or unexplained weight loss attends her doctor, she might not articulate it, but almost certainly has considered the worst. We can hardly even say its name for some superstitious fear it may materialize, so we lighten its solemnity and euphemistically refer to "The Big C." But we should say it, to help overcome this fear, so I will. Cancer. There, I've said it.

Chemicals, radiation, asbestos and other industrial pollutants can give you cancer, even years after exposure. We all know, but many choose to forget, that the biggest identified cause to date is cigarette smoking. But it's not just dangerous habits, occupations and lifestyles that cause it, even clean living, healthy young people are not immune.

The word itself is from the Latin *Cancri*. For astronomers and astrologers, it is a small constellation lying between Gemini and Leo and a water sign, the fourth of the Zodiac. The first observed human cancer was of the female breast. It was appreciated by physicians and surgeons, even in ancient times, that removal of an abnormal mass was to the patient's advantage (unless she succumbed to the surgery itself, of course!) After mastectomy, examination of the newly detached breast showed the malignant growth resembled a crab.

Cancer, or carcinomatosis, is where cells seem to lose all sense of programming and fail to follow the usual pattern of aging, decay and death. Instead, they grow in a chaotic fashion, at the expense of surrounding organs and tissues and ultimately the body itself. The one thing they have in common with normal cells is that they require a blood supply for survival and some forms of treatment seek to destroy or abolish this source of nutrition. Spread within the body to distant sites can occur via the blood or lymph system and even the finest surgeon might inadvertently disseminate cells during an operation. Treatment of course in not necessarily surgical and chemotherapy and/or radiotherapy can be ordeals in themselves and may cause more suffering than the actual tumour. Some patients decline all forms of medical treatment and seek natural remedies. I would support my patient in this course of action if it emerged the disease was too far advanced for more conventional treatment. My fear for those who seek alternative therapies is that, while the relative lack of side effects may be appealing, the evidence of actual benefit is either not established or poorly researched.

Oncologists and other doctors tend not to regard cancer as a single disease. It is really a whole multitude of illnesses and a malignancy can arise from almost any organ in the body (except curiously, the spleen.) Some tumours are aggressive from the start, such as pancreatic cancer, and have a poorer outlook. Other types, such as of the bowel or breast can be chopped out (or resected) and that may indeed be the end of the matter, though the doctor and his patient should maintain a degree of suspicion of recurrence for years afterwards.

How and when a cancer is diagnosed obviously has a bearing on the ultimate outcome. Certain deeper malignancies like ovarian cancer may remain hidden until the later stages. More readily apparent ones, like certain skin growths, may be ignored or misdiagnosed for something more innocent by both patient and doctor alike.

Cancers in children are particularly difficult to deal with from the emotional point of view of all concerned. By and large, their tumours are different from adult ones. Childhood leukaemias however, perhaps more than any other type of malignancy, have had a remarkable improvement in survival rates due to the sophistication of modern treatment.

Patients sometimes attend surgery, shortly after the death of a relative, asking if they can be considered for genetic testing. "Mum died of bowel cancer, as did my aunt and Gran. I'm worried I might be next." As a rule, if relatives develop cancers in their seventies or eighties, it is unlikely that there is a strong genetic link and it may be a simple, but unfortunate, coincidence. However, if a woman in her thirties develops, say, breast cancer her daughters should be very closely monitored throughout life. Genetics departments are inundated with worried relatives but take everybody seriously. At the very least they will take blood samples in the search for rogue genes, that may only be discovered years later, as research pushes back the frontiers.

"I've got cancer" remains one of the most jaw-dropping comments that Mrs Mallaig (Nancy) could ever make to her family and friends. But it really isn't such a one-way ticket to the grave as it once was. In fact, as treatment techniques advance, the chances she'll be cured are greater than ever.

If ever we are going to beat a condition, speaking in hushed tones or declining to even mention its name is not going to help.

LIVING ALONE

"Here's me rattling around all alone in that big house and they say there's a housing crisis, too," bemoaned Mr Todd. He had lived by himself for the last few years and the five spare bedrooms only gathered dust. The children had toddled off to their own places and his wife Anya was now resident in her own heavenly mansion. He had watched with bemusement the price of property rocket around him. He was in the situation where his own residence might have attracted a fair price (well within the range of the smart city set, moving more rurally) but there was nothing and nowhere in the town suitable for him. He needed a ground floor, centrally located, compact and secure dwelling; preferably with a small garden for him to potter around.

The government indeed tells us we are suffering a housing crisis in this country. The population rises and builders seemingly cannot throw up houses quickly enough (despite the incentive of massive profit margins!) Swathes of cheek-by-jowl "newbuilds" appear like mushrooms and are often as substantially built as the average edible toadstool. Rooms are hardly large enough to swing a cat (no animals were harmed in the researching of this article!) and postage stamp gardens are apparently what busy people want, and can be gravelled or monoblocked anyway. Neighbours could practically lean out their respective kitchen windows to shake hands, but the chances are they won't as they are not speaking, having fallen out over some noise or parking issue.

There are certain ironies about this "crisis" in which the nation finds itself. Debt levels have never been higher and yet mortgage lenders make it increasingly easy to borrow beyond our means. Repossessions, consequently, are on the rise and there can be little that is more humiliating to adults and damaging to kids than the arrival of bailiffs over breakfast. We also have the situation where the wrong type of housing gets built. I do not, this time, refer to houses that builders of sturdy Victorian homes would have expressed disbelief, but to the "executive villas" priced well beyond the reach of first time buyers and others on more modest incomes. Home owners seem to delight in the fact house prices rise by some 10% each year but overlook the fact that income is not keeping apace and property is increasingly unaffordable to more and more people. The only real beneficiaries of this situation of course are the banks and other mortgage lenders who continue to announce record billion pound profits. It is also the case that some people own many properties and scoop up all available ones as soon as they appear on the market. I know of one "posh" area of apartments in the city where the building company offers would-be purchasers a facility to let the flat for them, anticipating that the vendors have no plans to reside there themselves. Building primarily for the private rental market like this cannot be a good thing, if others are prevented from getting on the property ladder at all.

But Mr Todd and I were in agreement that what seems to be the biggest problem in the housing market, and perhaps reflective of modern society, is that there are more single households than ever before. Thirty years ago, censuses showed that 1 in 5 dwellings were singly occupied, now it is put at 1 in 3. This, of course, is not the same as saying one in three of us lives alone but that every third house on Avieridge Street is not shared. The reasons for this are multiple but include the fact that people generally live, and maintain their independence, longer. Divorce rates and separations are ever greater and people, if they commit to a relationship at all, generally do so later. Society is more fragmented.

Mr Todd eventually found and moved to sheltered accommodation. He surprised us all though by marrying Mrs Low (Nelly) a widow from a neighbouring street. They were amused that their union meant there was an extra house available in the town, which could only be a good thing.

DR KEN B MOODY

ON DUTY

TIED TO THE SURGERY

YOUR DOCTOR'S DESK

"May I ask what you keep in your desk, Dr Ken?" inquired Mrs Nessie Parker seeing one of my desk drawers slightly ajar. I know people sometimes say or ask silly things during awkward silences, but did she really care what resides within my mahogany, late nineteenth century, half-ton elbow rest? In truth, I am mildly ashamed of its clutter and just a little hesitant to explore it myself, in fear that I am devoured or just chewed up and spat out again.

I politely dismissed her question by suggesting little more than paper and paperclips were stored there but once surgery was over, like any responsible mountaineer, I warned the staff of my intentions and set about dealing with the accumulated mess.

My desk is not much to look at and designed along the standard three drawers deep format with a central void for one's mid-leg joints.

I only ever really use the top drawers. In them I have auroscope earpieces, tongue depressors, a stethoscope and half a dozen rubber stamps. This veritable little collection includes one stamp from my work in the Antipodes that I keep for posterity, others have obsolete telephone numbers or other details. I am always reluctant to bin them having a fear that some fraudster may use one to make false claims. Prescription and sick note pads for use when the printer jams and my trusty Dictaphone with spare tapes sat there too. We once tried voice-recognition software in an attempt to make our poor secretary's life a little more bearable but the programmes never quite managed to interpret my particular brogue and I found myself speaking (with astonishing results) in pigeon English, in the way condescending tourists do when asking for directions abroad.

I have a large steel "obstetric wheel" resembling a lethal frisbee. It was used to calculate when a woman could expect the pelican to arrive with her pink or blue bundle. This wheel probably carried some authority but simply tapping a few buttons on the keyboard gives a quicker answer now. I do tend to use the roll of kids' "I've been good at the doctor's today" stickers. I find children, even when upset, will break between sobs to accept stickers being stuck on to their coats. They will hopefully then not look back on the consultation with total horror. The picture is of a red-nosed, jug-eared, dark-eyed, fuzzy-haired figure of fun. He passes for a clown but if younger children get pleasure remembering me as Coco I'll have no objections.

The middle, less frequently visited, drawers had an even broader range of accumulated stuff. Returned drugs are an inevitable part of general practice. Some people have frank intolerances or dislikes to prescribed products and bring them back at the first opportunity. Sometimes I think they are trying to make a point but more often they see it as the safest form of disposal or have a wish that others may be saved a prescription charge if they can be put to good use. Pharmaceutical laws are tighter these days but we can use unopened "trays" of medicines when appropriate. Unfortunately, I have two full drawers of such returns. On the rare occasions that I do attempt to recycle, I fear patients will catch a glimpse of this stash and comment to the effect that I can't be much of a doctor if I prescribe so many "useless" medicines. These drugs included: (apparently) failed erectile dysfunction products; an alarming variety of indigestion remedies; antibiotics and several blood pressure tablets. The use-by-dates had expired in several cases, so for safety and order's sake I systematically disposed of the lot.

The bottom drawers contained chocolate and a forgotten sandwich, salvaged last week from a rep. There were also numerous (now dodgy) information leaflets, old rotas and practice meeting minutes. I recalled with amusement the issues that used to trouble my colleague, Dr Bodie Aiken, and me and the things that "progress" and change have simply made redundant. There were pharmaceutical adverts for products, which were later withdrawn for safety or marketing reasons. These served as a reminder to me to view newly launched products with suspicion, at least until a time when experience proves their reliability. There was a contraceptive coil device (unused) and numerous sample bottles (mostly unused!) Several bulldog clips of varying sizes, suggesting varying stages of breeding, lurked there too.

Paperclips, pens, old diaries, diploma certificates and demonstration inhalers and insulin pens were scattered throughout as well.

By the end of this trip down memory lane, and with a few black bin bags of waste, I felt better for this "purge." I vowed to be less of a hoarder and to discard things, or store them more efficiently, from now on. It is said that if clothes or shoes in your wardrobe are not used within eighteen months then to the charity shop they should go. The same maxim could apply to desk contents, but surely no self-respecting charity would have need of any of these things?

So, content that nothing living or dead resides within these now cavernous compartments, I only have my car, bookcase and jacket pockets to clear out.

THE MOST ANNOYING
CONSULTATION

"What is the most annoying type of consultation?" This was the title of an article in a recent medical journal. Suggestions were generally those where patients are demanding, rude or have unrealistic expectations. I agreed and could immediately think of dozens of such consultations, often with the Pettit-Lippe family, but others too on our list. Let me describe for you a patient and his typical consultation with me. I don't for a minute expect you to recognise yourself in any way but indulge me for a few minutes and step into my warm brogues.

Mr Earnest Dawdler turns up late but objects that *he* was kept waiting. He complains about how busy and chaotic the waiting room is and how long it took him to get this appointment. This steady trickle of criticism gathers pace and I hear how much better my predecessors were and the lengths they used to go to accommodate him. (I know what they did and didn't do and also what they thought of him though.) He informs me of what people in the Post Office queue think of the surgery. I am advised of the appalling and perilous state of the NHS until (not rising to the bait and in Oscar winning form) I cheerful ask how I may help *today*. There then follows the only silence of the consultation as he carefully removes his cap and outer clothing before helping himself to a seat in a fashion that suggests he may be here for some time. (The analogy of an airport long-stay car park springs to mind but sadly without the same charges applying!). He then commences his oration, which is invariably tangential or a complete jumble of symptoms, rapidly jumping, without warning, from one problem to another and back again. He insists though on getting every irrelevant detail correct, such as whether the dog had been fed or whether it was a Monday or a Tuesday two years ago when he first noticed the swelling. If he does finally move on with his story he will suddenly interrupt himself (which is better than I have so far managing to do!) and correct himself with "no, it was a Wednesday." When I finally do butt in or if he momentarily pauses for breath he will look at me, for the first time, and disapprovingly continue the ramble. My usual strategy in such circumstances, "right, let's try to tie all of this together," falls on suspiciously deaf ears. If I do manage to interpret or even diagnose, this will be quickly dismissed. When he remembers that I am as bad a listener and doctor as he always thought I was he stands up and, taking his aforementioned garments, leaves. If this is with more than a grunt it is not with a "thank you," but rather the awful "thanks anyway," which for me has only ever meant, "..for nothing."

Consultations are of course not for doctors' satisfaction or amusement (but can be!) They are for your benefit, so help us to help you, have a point and stick to it.

TOOTHY PROBLEMS

"I couldn't contact my dentist and I know he's in great demand, Dr Ken, but I'm sure you'll treat my dental abscess," said Ena Mell hopefully. The paucity of dental services in these rural areas has long been a source of frustration to me and a bit of a pain in the canines, so to speak. It's rather annoying to have added to our workload the one area/field/orifice in the whole body that fellow professionals are paid handsomely to deal with. I suspect there would be gnashing of teeth if dentists were called upon to treat chest infections, ingrowing toenails or gynaecological issues if we became a little more elusive.

I am not suggesting your kindly doctor will refuse to deal with true emergencies or avoid all things to do with the mouth, but he will invite you to join the queue at the dental surgery if your problem is clearly a molar or incisor one.

The protuberances from our gums are rather interesting little things though. I once stated that I would not wish to outlive my teeth. Now that I truly am longer in the tooth and have fewer of my original thirty-two meat-tearing implements, I may be forced to reconsider.

It was once commonplace, and almost fashionable, for ladies to have their teeth pulled and pearly white falsers fitted. This may have been after childbirth when deterioration had occurred or simply on reaching adulthood. Of course, if you have precious few teeth left there is little use holding on to them, particularly if the remaining ones don't even meet. When gum finally meets gum the lovely descriptive term "edentulous" may be used. If we are allowed to have favourite words I would include this one in my top ten. By and large, we should hang on to our sixteen upper and sixteen lower adult (or secondary) teeth, as per the original design. Dental or gum disease might be so advanced or accidents unfortunate enough that this may not be possible. One of the saddest and most poignant cases I recall was that of a rather deprived family. The children had an utterly atrocious diet and were quite possibly the fattest weans I have ever seen. Their teeth rotted further with every chocolate bar and sugary drink they consumed. Their mouths harboured nothing but black stumps by the time they reached the age of seven. At this point (or rather due to a lack of points) they could not chew or eat adequately and slimmed back down to an average girth. Whether overweight or not, they were malnourished and this repeating pattern, despite the Health Visitor's best efforts, was nothing short of neglect.

Our wisdom teeth can come through at literally any time in adulthood. I recall one lady in her eighties who was troubled by her dentures gradually becoming less well fitting. It emerged, as did the tooth, that one of these premolars finally was making an appearance and pushing up her lower wallie.

Older folks and others can have a great fear of visiting the dentist and dentophobia is one of the commonest true phobias there is. When Mrs Moody's mother was, after many years of avoiding oral examinations, forced to attend due to intractable pain, her dentist, Mr Phil McAvity, asked her to "hop up" onto the couch. She proceeded to lie with her head at the wrong end and her feet raised up under the arc light. As the astonished dentist turned round to begin his inspection he remarked "My, it is a long time since you were last here!"

Human bites, curiously said to be the dirtiest of animal bites second only to the camel, are seen frequently in surgery. One's little offspring have the socially embarrassing and primitive habit of sinking their ivories into playmates' tender flesh. If teeth penetrate the skin, even an assailant's knuckle on his victim's teeth, antibiotics should be prescribed to avoid serious infection.

Our bite marks, like our fingerprints, are unique. The crime that led to the world's first murder conviction, based on the dental impression of the perpetrator, took place along the road in Biggar.

We cannot all have, nor necessarily want, cosmetically enhanced Hollywood smiles. Our teeth say quite a lot about us though. There is some evidence that the state of them is a reflection of the health of our heart and general wellbeing. Gosh, I'm almost the proverbial toothless lion myself, I'd better get straight back to the gym.

Ena, you certainly need an antibiotic and here's a script for one but I'm no dentist, you know that, just try knocking more loudly on his door.

SKIN DEEP

"Whatever you do Dr Ken, please don't tell mum I've had it done," begged India Incke. Confidentiality and good sense, of course, forbid me from cliping to parents or others when I stumble upon bodily art (tattoos or piercings) during the course of examinations, though I do marvel at the range and the effort people go to.

In my earlier years in practice, tattoos where either to be found on the arms and chests of sailors and navvies or referred to annual military displays, so beloved by tourists. Nowadays it is not unusual to see a butterfly, rose or big cat on a woman's back or to see larger more intricate designs on a chap. Some estimates suggest as many as 15% of people have at least one ink-impregnated, permanent feature about their persons. Most people seem rather proud of their chosen images (at least at the time and assuming indeed they were carefully selected in a state of sobriety!) I rarely pass comment on one's tattoos unless it is the very reason Jack Tarr or Di Green is attending. I have yet to discover a circumferential barbed wire tattoo on the arm of a 90-year-old woman but I daresay the day will come. Emblems expressing undying teenage love or yesteryear's popular culture I reckon are just asking for later regret and indeed these are the commonest requests for removal. Amateur tattoos in fact are easier to remove as the dye tends not to have been injected quite as deeply. My own feeling is that people should pay for their tattoo removal, regardless of purported negative psychological effects, as they almost certainly funded the self-infliction in the first place.

Tattoos have been around for centuries and the word is thought to derive from the Tahitian *Tatau*. Warriors would look fiercer the more ornately inscribed they were. Many South Pacific islanders, including Maori, even today recreate and display these ancient tribal markings. Circumnavigating sailors, before the advent of passports, adopted the practice. Drunken port calls certainly propagated bodily art but the motive (and motifs) was probably to help identification when souls were lost at sea, providing the fish didn't take a particular interest in buxom mermaids and suchlike first.

Many designs are fine works of art and, if enjoyed by the "canvas" his or herself, can be good innocent fun. Others are less innocent and can signal deeper or more sinister elements. I have been practising long enough to remember several concentration camp survivors with numerals tattooed on their inner wrists and appreciate the horrors these simple digits signified. I personally dislike paramilitary or gang logos and find them more than a little offensive. Dark, Gothic stigmata may look rather silly but may signify a deeply troubled or mentally ill young person. The words LOVE and HATE are rarely found imprinted across the knuckles of rocket scientists or Sunday School teachers and almost invariably point to a psychopathic personality.

I once saw a shaven-headed lad whose entire neck, head and face were covered in a continuous close-knit spider's web. Most other pedestrians, naturally, gave him right-of-way but I could not help thinking how sad and pathetic he looked.

I have long been curious about religious designs and insignia. They may of course merely demonstrate another form of sectarianism but I feel, more often, they don't. I also doubt that bishops or moderators of the General Assembly have subjected themselves to an hour in a back-street parlour to get a crucifix or weeping Virgin Mother emblazoned on their bodies, though I suspect such a survey has never been conducted. Instead younger people, who may never set foot inside a church, seem to elect for such religious iconology. Particular themes seem to be influenced by the cult of cool celebrity.

Then there is the pain. I listen attentively when people describe the "sheer agony" of the process and how they "just had" to endure it. The pain may come as a surprise to them, though once started there seems no chickening out. A black panther is admittedly somewhat sexier than his flesh-pink cousin if the recipient changed his mind after the outline had been inscribed. There clearly is machismo at play and I have no doubt bikers, whose bulging chests and arms are continuous tapestries of naked nymphs, skulls and fantasy creatures are showing all admirers and onlookers just how tough they think they are.

Infection of course is the doctor's main concern. AIDS and hepatitis have been spread by shared tattoo needles. In some North American prisons, authorities are so concerned about the spread of serious infections that they have introduced visiting professional tattooists. High street tattoo artists in this country require to be registered and it is imperative that needles are used only once and immediately disposed of safely. I recall one lad who chose to have a red devil as a lifelong companion on his forearm. Unfortunately he had an allergy to the red dye (the commonest colour for such a reaction.) Satan lost his menace, despite being in three-dimensions, as he is not normally portrayed with a pot-belly. Lucifer's fires where finally extinguished by the application of laser.

"Of course your secret's safe with me India."

After she had gone I removed my armband, rolled up my sleeve and took another pensive look at my own "Ken and Mrs Moody, Scotland Forever."

VIEW *IN* THE SURGERY

"Your waiting room could do with a lick of paint, Dr Ken," suggested Jim McPatient as he entered the surgery one day. Initially I bristled a little, noting that the last time I visited Jim at his home I kept my thoughts about the occasional requirement to hoover, tidy up and clean out the budgies' cage to myself. But I couldn't complain, he had a valid point, one that we haven't addressed recently enough.

Is our waiting room, and surgery for that matter, just a little bit tired and curled around the edges?

Normally this column is called *View from the Surgery* but just this week perhaps the above heading is more fitting.

So, that evening, after the last patient had been packed out the door with good advice and prescription in hand, I sat down in the waiting room, literally in the patient's place. I didn't really like what I smelled, saw, heard and felt.

The first thing I noticed was that the air was a little foetid. With so many dozen patients each day, perhaps that's what should be expected. But, as thick as the air was, with a few lungs full of this, even if you arrived in good health, things could quickly change. The only source of ventilation is our surgery front door. Each time a patient enters through it they tend to get blown in by a mild north-easterly, almost as if an invisible hand is pushing them in, should they have any doubt or hesitation about entering. It does however result in substantially lower temperatures for those waiting to be seen.

What I *saw* was a little depressing too. Numerous posters warn of the dangers of smoking, drinking too much, failure to immunize and the fallout from illicit liaisons. I do remember one wag commenting to his fellow patients that all these "Don't posters" are only there to help improve one's quality of life!

Our saving grace perhaps is that we display a few pictures, beautifully crafted by local school children, which enliven the place a little but, although they were done for the coronation of our *present* monarch, this admittedly was a little while ago!

What I *heard* sitting there in the waiting room was questionable too. We have apparently succumbed to what is often described as "elevator music." If the panpipes were ever considered an attractive instrument to listen to they are surely trying the patience of patients, the world over, now.

We found though that music in the waiting room is essential. This is mainly because several patients commented that my strong brogue, especially when speaking with deaf patients, carries beyond the surgery door. There was a perceived threat to deaf patients' confidentiality when I approach a bellow with my third repetition of: "How long have you had piles, sir?" (I do smile when my eighty-decibel voice is still not being understood and I am asked: "Would you like me to turn my hearing aid on doctor?")

Music also, if correctly chosen, has a calming effect. When I arrived, many seasons ago, I chose to have classical music played over the gramophone. One elderly lady praised the "cultured influence" I was evidently bringing to the practice. I was soon however outvoted by our practice staff and we are now back to playing free CDs from Sunday newspapers. This same lady now shakes her head as she enters my room, rather than pass comment, which in fact speaks more for her disappointment than her disliking of popular music.

Lastly, I *felt* the waiting room was just a little bit sad. I could only image the thoughts and anxieties going through patients' minds as they sit waiting for my big face to appear round the door to invite them in. I'm not into Feng Shui (not since I discovered that it isn't a Chinese main course!) but I'll speak to Mrs Mona Lotte our practice manager on Monday to see what we can do to brighten the place up a little.

KEY WORKERS

Miss Pell, our practice secretary, had handed in her notice. Sadly, but typically and typographically, even this letter had three errors and the wrong date, unless February has recently been rounded up to 30 days. We are sorry to see her leave in many ways; she is particularly (and now appropriately!) "out-going" by nature, and the practice morale-boosting nights just wouldn't have been the same without her. She had been given a better offer at the local bingo hall, as a caller. We just hope for her sake that her numeracy skills are superior to her literary ones, or some rather disgruntled "winners" will soon be beating their paths to number four ("knock at the door.")

There is no doubt that doctors rely heavily on their secretarial staff. Without them we would have to depend on our own typing skills. Hevaen fobrid!

Each evening, before leaving surgery, I dictate the letters of the day. Like the tape recorder itself, I rewind back through events that occurred hours earlier. I'll have seen some 40 patients and will refer about ten percent to consultant clinics or other colleagues. I know, that if I don't complete these letters that evening, the details will rapidly depart my grey matter, despite any accompanying scrawled notes I might have made. Occasionally, a particularly long and complex consultation will have led to several referrals and, frankly, I cannot always recall to whom I promised letters. I may have to ring the patient the following day to help reconnect the synapses. Rather than admit to my memory deficiencies I will phone, ostensibly to seek "developments and further clarification," like any compassionate physician or news-hungry reporter should.

I admire the work and dedication of secretaries and typists.

They sit in tiny, cell-like rooms all day long. In our former broom cupboard, the wall-plug apple blossom fragrance is overpowering; but I suspect is there to prevent me from hovering too long. Gone are the days when I dictated to Miss Capps-Locke. She would scribble expertly in shorthand or transcribe onto stenograph. She seemed to know every sentence before I did, and would correct my dubious punctuation and grammar, without comment. Occasionally, I would question her corrections but she would already have bookmarked her Latin, Medical or English dictionaries. I often wonder if she smirked, or even danced in silent celebration, as soon as I left the room.

We hardly ever see our secretarial staff these days. The main reason they emerge, blinking into the light, is to clarify what I said on tape. As these mini cassettes are used over and over again the quality diminishes, or such is my excuse. I would like to think my brogue and dialect is fairly discernible. I accept though, as I pace pensively up and down the bearskin on my consulting room floor (it died of natural causes not tedium!), trying to find the correct adjective, my voice may come and go from range. I was more than happy for Miss Pell to question any particular word used, rather than paraphrase, as there were some real howlers of typos. I recall one missive sent to a gynaecologist. He may still be scratching his head as to why I suggested: "..your terrace may need a sample taken, or to be removed in its entirety." Never claiming to be a landscape gardener, I trust he correctly interpreted my comments to mean that the lady's *uterus* was in need of such attention.

Dictated punctuation marks should not be taken literally either, for "period" in obstetric letters and "colon" used in surgical ones, may cause considerable confusion.

It is not just words that may be transcribed wrongly. Dubious phrases such as: "he is numb from the toes downward," rather than the more plausible "toes upward" occur. I suppose if the patient had been performing a handstand this may have been strictly correct but, if that was his habit, blood rushing from his feet may simply have been the cause of the numbness.

At other times, what we say into the dictating machine may be transcribed accurately but not be exactly as intended. I recall the occasion when I felt Mel-Anne Colley's low moods were beyond (or is that beneath?) my range of expertise and necessitated her seeing a psychiatrist. I later discovered my referral letter stated that "she has been depressed ever since she started attending me five years ago." I don't suppose it really was me who sent her to such depths of despair and I would like to think my contribution was perhaps, even to a slight extent, positive.

I was once asked to prepare a medical report for presentation at court. The traditional oath of honesty is to declare that, what follows is written "on soul and conscience." Quite what the Sheriff must have thought when my efforts were declared to have been written "on soul unconscious," I do not know, but I admit to writing some reports with my mind elsewhere.

I can have no excuses. If I append my signature to a letter, I claim ownership of all that's written above, however ridiculous and error-ridden it may be. It is my responsibility to check all letters and reports. But, as fun as it might be in small doses, I shouldn't really have to tiptoe my way through a minefield of grammatical and typographical incendiaries every day.

THE PERFECT DOCTOR

"My family and I have high standards and are looking to register with the perfect doctor, Dr Moody. Who would you recommend?" So asked our potential new patient, Tyrone Best, without a trace of irony.

What, or who, is the perfect doctor, I wonder? I would suggest that he has an IQ of little short of 200. He never makes a mistake or misdiagnosis but would have the hypothetical humility to admit it if he ever did. The only apologising he ever finds himself doing is on behalf of colleagues for their shortcomings, but he is too gracious to attribute blame and will take criticism on behalf of others, concerned that they may lose face.

We make the assumption that he is indeed male. Unfortunately some people continue to mistake female doctors for nurses. Our doctor has a tremendous working relationship with members of that noble and caring profession and naturally engenders their ongoing considerable respect. It matters not that he is in fact male as he is fully in touch with his own femininity. His empathy and compassion for women and their problems often draws them to him in a way that even his female colleagues cannot emulate.

Children are immediately and invariably put at their ease by his disarming friendliness and ready juvenile manner. His gentle touch can calm the most obstreperous of howling children. His charm and conversational skills can turn the most taciturn of disenchanted youths into pleasant, articulate models of their generation.

He can defuse the tensest of situations and rumour has it the chief constable formally requested him to be the on-call hostage negotiator for the region.

His insight, intuition and diagnostic skills would make Sherlock Holmes appear a bumbling, myopic fool. He does not appear hurried and is never distracted or interrupted during your consultation. His warmth and pleasant smile never waver. He is never negatively influenced by busy surgeries or problematical patients, maintaining a healthy objectivity and interest. His state-of-the-art computer brings results and referral details instantly to hand. He doesn't seem to even glance at it nor break eye contact, as you always have his full and undivided attention. His humour is legendary but always appropriate and never offensive. His razor sharp wit can cut through barriers in ways few other methods could. He is a Solomon. Any disagreements or differences of opinion quickly evaporate, as his argument is so persuasive and logical that you wonder how you could possibly have seen things in any other light. He is only indignant in the most righteous of ways and only when his patients have received less than exemplary service or treatment at the hands of others. He has an issue with our developing two-tier health service but will always get you seen by a specialist with the priority with which your case deserves. (He is of course a specialist himself in all regards but graciously defers to his hospital colleagues and their more publicly recognised skills.) When the situation demands, he will speak with a former fellow cricketing or rowing blue, calling in a favour. That this friend is now only the country's finest hand surgeon and will see you in his rooms tomorrow is more than just fortuitous.

But what does this perfect doctor look like? He is about forty, not too green to suggest inexperience nor too white to arouse suspicion he may be passed it. He may be greying around the temples but this only reinforces how distinguished he looks. His hair always gives the impression it was cut yesterday and he is as expertly shaved as though he stops at a Turkish barber on his way to work each morning. His aftershave hints of days surfing and exotic forests, blended with a rich bouquet of Tuscan lavender. He has a confident, strong and almost stubborn jaw, as all heroes do. His eyes are a piercing blue and you feel he can almost read your very thoughts before you even assemble them. His spectacles seem unnecessary but reiterate he is, in fact, only human. His skin is without blemish and his teeth as straight as Lombardy poplars (without the gaps.) His athletic build and flat stomach lend enormous credibility to the healthy lifestyle advice he freely imparts and recommends. He is smartly dressed in a classic style with a sports jacket and flannels. He declines a sober suit, feeling there are better impressions to make than formality. His tie is always in a Windsor knot, a subtle clue perhaps to those who may not know of his military (possibly secret service) background. This training probably contributes to him being supremely efficient, tidy, fit, punctual and multilingual. His enthusiasm is infectious. He is always dependable, reliable, indefatigable, available and well…able.

His room is welcoming and climate controlled. The tank of tropical fish only adds to the serenity. His beautiful wife and children smile up at him from the ebony framed photograph on his desk. There is the perception of Mozart's Third Horn Concerto or Berlioz' The Shepherds' Farewell but that may be just your imagination. There is a faint aroma of quality Kenyan coffee, possibly received as a gift following his commended voluntary work in that former colonial country. He is a polymath. On his least well-lit wall he has certificates and awards geometrically arranged, as if evidence were needed, of his comprehensive skills and interests. His Olympic medals, like everything else, have no hint of dust on them. His charitable works know no bounds and photos of presentations from world leaders and captains of industry serve to remind that, as much as he has been a gain to medicine, he has been a loss in numerous other fields.

His shelves are neatly arranged with the latest journals and textbooks, modestly concealing his own renowned publications. He is at the cutting edge of research for your condition and several others beside. You rather selfishly worry he will be absent from the practice as he (once again) has been short-listed for the Nobel awards ceremony next month in Oslo. (The substantial prize money naturally is ploughed into practice coffers.) As always, he shuns publicity for fear that it may compromise the care of his patients.

Oh, I'm sorry Mr Best, did you infer it was I being described above? No, it is purely co-incidental that my name appears under the title of this article. Modesty and an ingrained sense of honesty forbid me from claiming ownership of more than one or two of these attributes. So, you'll just have to make do with me. One can only try one's best, Tyrone Best, and I am happy to say that I do.

EMOTIONAL BAGGAGE

On at least one day each week I am the duty doctor for the surgery. This means that from dawn to dusk (at least in the winter, peak season) I see so many patients (cases) that they may as well be on a conveyor belt. I sometimes muse that in these eleven hours of long haul I could have travelled leisurely to the far reaches of the country, or indeed the planet. Instead, I'll have been confined to my own little departure lounge as scores of life's travellers touch base, albeit briefly, with the seat or examination couch. Patients attend for a rapid check-in, check-up and then checkout again; or such is the itinerary. Duty days, though busy, can be satisfying in that problems presented are usually straightforward and of recent onset. Cases can be fairly efficiently handled, packaged and the patient duly dispatched (in a shipment rather than a Shipman sort of way!). Patients are happy with this same-day, no-frills service and quickly and contently fly the scene.

Mondays are the busiest days and, today, I must have seen the equivalent number of patients as might be found on a small passenger plane. Unfortunately, they did not all pass through my room with the speed or enthusiasm of a group of teenage holidaymakers. Some were weary voyagers indeed. There were those who just could not restrict their ailments to manageable numbers, nor resist detailing their terrible lives; full of stresses and woes. As they did the visit before and the one before that! I have great sympathy for those who have chronic illnesses or find themselves in situations beyond their control, and appreciate that some medical and emotional problems are inextricably linked. But I do object to the assumption that I have the time or inclination to listen to how badly the bank or council treated Will Dunn-Bigh when his problem is a gouty toe or sore throat. (Whether the teller or housing officer is subject to details of his throbbing digit or inflamed pharynx is another matter!)

One patient, Eva Wurss, melodramatically enters the room before landing with the grace of a dying hippo on the chair. She will be clutching her head, belly, thigh, back or side depending on what might be the problem necessitating further emergency attention. She never in fact makes routine appointments. But it is her opening gambit that is as predictable as it is improbable. "This is the definitely the worst pain I have ever had, Dr Ken," she remarks. Before I can enquire as to the specifics, she will add: "you have no idea how bad this is." I am fortunate enough not to suffer chronic pain, but is it not a little presumptuous that it is considered truly beyond my comprehension? Almost every day, I deal with patients who endure neuralgia, lumbago, migraine and neuropathy and see and hear how bad these can be. If I did give Eva the benefit of my increasing doubt (that her pain should move so readily and constantly escalate in severity) I would freely admit it is beyond my experience and understanding. I know though she is a deeply unhappy person, and has reason to be, but the emotional baggage she carries requires a veritable team of Sherpas to scale the heights of implausibility and her range of symptoms.

I say I am confined to base for long periods, but I might receive a request for an emergency housecall. It can be a joy to take to the open road, breathe fresh air and even catch the news headlines. But it is rather less joyous if a crowd of disconsolate patients is left behind while it is I who "takes off." One of the most ironical calls was for a chap who took unwell at the end of his holiday in Sydney, Australia. He was little better during his stop-off in the Gulf, or his arrival home in Scotland. The taxi ride to his house was a little longer and more arduous than it otherwise would have been. He lived within two miles of the surgery. His wife was insistent that he could not manage to attend me but had to be seen. In other words, he covered 10, 000 miles but not the final two, or 99.98% of the way, to see his doctor. Perhaps with a little more endurance he would have made it. Travel sickness is a terrible thing.

Another type of patient is one who indeed has an acute problem but is so wrapped up in other more established issues that she forgets why she attended at all. Like a good baggage handler, I bump and nudge the conversation back to where it started or seemed originally to be going but, like a luggage carousel, it just goes round and around. And so it was today with Val Ise; her case is never brief. Consultations are not limited to single or simple issues and her boyfriend's questionable devotion and intentions should be left for another day.

People should have a baggage allowance at these emergency surgeries. Restrictions for the sake and sanity of others are necessary. "Emotional hand luggage only" might be a sign I place on my door.

BRIEF ENCOUNTERS

"My mother prepared me for this day, Dr Ken. She advised me to change my underwear daily in case I was ever hit by a bus, for I would not know who might be examining me." This cliché, of probable Edwardian origin, demonstrating greater concern for appearance and sensitivities over more weighty matters, has always mildly amused me. Old Nick Kerr indeed stumbled alighting from the Number 13 service but fortunately had not taken a direct hit by ten tonnes of steel, or I suspect our discussion would not have been taking place at all. After helping him with his waistcoat, string vest and various buttons, flies and ties, I ensured he had no abdominal or pelvic injuries and made good his various cuts and abrasions.

As doctors we are frequently exposed (so to speak!) to the cotton, silk or lace people choose for the buffering layer between their flesh and outer garments. The variety is truly astounding. The generation gap, in this context, is perhaps at its most apparent. Whether this is due to persisting wartime fashions; a lack of concern for the wish to appear attractive or simple bodily comfort is hard to say. Not many young women these days wear the marvellously practical foundation garment and even I would probably baulk at a septuagenarian should he or she be wearing nought but a thong.

If the elastic and credibility could take the strain, one could almost make a list of undergarments from A to Z. At the top of the pile would sit a neatly pressed A-shirt (sleeveless vest,) atop a bodice, corset and drawers, passing right down to the vest, whalebone corset, X-your-heart brassiere and finally, Y-fronts. Like many well-worn items the end has become rather too frayed to determine the figure or letter Z. (Like the folding bed, should such a garment ever be invented, I imagine it would be particularly well levered and sprung!)

Most items are in the factory issue, white. The reality though is that one's smalls have often at some time or another found themselves in a non-colourfast wash. The result is innumerable shades of grey, perhaps just as useful but not likely to fly off department store shelves nor make the pages of designer catalogues.

Underwear is really only of any particular interest in the surgery when the removal of it takes considerable time to achieve. Elderly ladies, regardless of the season, often have so many layers that to perform any satisfactory examination the services of nursing staff are required. Such hooks and straps are vaguely reminiscent of the (probably fictitious) mediaeval chastity belt and, similarly, the would-be assailant/examiner is likely to start losing interest after the first quarter of an hour.

Voluminous petticoats and underskirts beloved by débutantes and their admirers are largely only seen on the stage these days.

Amelia Jenks Bloomer (1818-1894) with her eponymous famous undergarments probably advanced the cause and freedom of women the world over more than any women's libber did. Her detractors accused her of great immodesty, a far cry from what would gain the same derision these days. I confess to finding several inches of crumpled cotton boxers, exposed above sagging jeans, as being a little less than smart and think the only liberating that might occur is one's self, from all modesty.

Some people indeed choose to wear no underwear, or "go commando" as the saying goes. The roughness of denim or wool on skin would be too uncomfortable and unhygienic for most, but as long as the dangers of zip fasteners are appreciated it the individual's prerogative. Here in Scotland, of course, a so-called true native is believed to be *sans* drawers under the kilt. Having attended many weddings in England, I rather tire of this frequent enquiry (by tipsy overly familiar revellers.) I now prefer the relative safety and dignity of tartan trews; lest I be tempted to unceremoniously settle the question for good, though my defence union and others may not look too favourably on the spectacle!

I digress, Nick. I'm happy to say, although you came off second best to the omnibus, you'll live to tell the tale and your Saltire briefs are quite the most handsome pair I've seen this side of Edinburgh.

GETTING TO THE BONES OF IT

"Can you do anything to stop my bones thinning further, Dr Ken?" asked Lottie Feathers.

Patients, perhaps more than ever before, are "bone aware" and keen to avoid the problems associated with osteoporosis or even normal bone thinning that comes with age.

Humans have two-hundred and six of them, from the mighty femur (or thigh bone) to the ultra delicate inner-ear ossicles, which people always seem able to name: the hammer, anvil and stirrup (conjuring, for me, images of an equestrian country pub).

Children's bones are much more flexible, to absorb the impact of numerous spills and tumbles, and only as they grow do they become more rigid. Kids may suffer "greenstick" fractures where they get a splintering on one side of the bone without suffering a clean break, rather like a damp twig. Of course, if the force is sufficient the bone will simply snap. The term "compound fracture" means that a spike of bone has become exposed by piercing through the skin (liable to induce fainting in unseasoned onlookers!) and is generally more serious, with infection being a particular concern.

From the age of 35 or so our bones lose at least 1% of their mass each year. The change of life for women certainly accelerates bone thinning but men are affected too, perhaps as testosterone levels fall. It is estimated that half of all women and a fifth of all men over the age of 50 suffer fractures from, often relatively minor, injuries due to this. Illness, immobility, smoking, being very underweight and certain medicines, especially steroids, can cause osteoporosis.

If we suspect someone has osteoporosis from a combination of the above or "mother had a dowager's hump" (whether or not she was indeed a dowager duchess) a simple DEXA (or bone density) scan can tell us what the actual position or risk is.

It is not inevitable though that breakages occur as we get older. One reader told me she was tickled to learn that at the grand age of ninety her bones, as assessed by a DEXA scan, were described as being "those of a fifty year old." Rather than existing as a jellyfish for her first four decades, I suspect she just enjoyed good health, lived well and chose her parents carefully.

Certain medicines, sometimes taken as little as once monthly, can drastically reduce the rate bone is lost and can even strengthen it to a degree.

It is interesting how bones have entered the language. I have been called a sawbones on occasion. As much as I enjoyed Orthopaedics, a rural GP is unlikely to be called upon to perform limb amputations, though in a desperate situation it may be required. I would sooner be called a sawbones than bone-idle and would consider the latter to be a bit close to the bone. Aggrieved patients may feel they have a bone to pick with me if I arrived at an erroneous diagnosis based only on a feeling in my bones rather than blood tests or other objective means. They may make no bones about calling me a bonehead and this may become a bone of contention. I would probably take the attitude that "sticks and stones…", but would feel compelled to dust off my textbooks and bone up again. These tomes (not tombs, as in a boneyard) should be in the basement, which I hope is bone-dry. In there I should also find a skeleton from my student days (previously removed from the closet) and my graduation certificate confirming I'm a *bona fide* doctor!

So, yes Miss Feathers, this prescription should prevent your bones from becoming as thin as your mum's did. You must remember though to keep active and eat well.

Bon(e) Chance!

GUARANTEES? I'M NOT SO SURE

"Can you guarantee that it's gallstones causing my pain, Dr Ken?" asked Abbie-Sue Lute in surgery one afternoon.

Patients often seek assurances that problems will or won't happen but, quite frankly, life and the weather being as they are, guarantees cannot be given. The tablets we prescribe may make you sick(er), the blood pressure medication may not prevent your second heart attack and, despite my strong belief to the contrary, the mole on your back may in fact be turning bad. (I do not of course mean that the velvety black burrowing animal of the *Talpide* family might be embarking on a life of crime!)

As much of a shock as it may be to some readers, doctors are less than perfect. There, I've said it, so now you know. Read on, but only when you've composed yourself. Medics are flawed human beings, like the rest of the population. Some are even more flawed. Amongst the greatest skills physicians and surgeons possess are: knowing what they know; knowing what they don't know and sensing when they may be wrong. Imperfection and unpredictability, such as they are, mean that doctors cannot and should not give absolute assurances. There are no certainties in life, other than death and taxes. The Grim Reaper will eventually catch up with us all, as will the taxman. Occasionally it will be in that particular order but I'll save my opinions about inheritance tax for another day.

The problem is, patients often attend because they want to hear that their fracture will heal completely or that they will indeed see their ninetieth birthday. Patients don't want their suicidal depression to recur or inflammatory bowel disease to interfere with chosen careers. Nor do we, but if I confidently declared to everyone exactly what they wanted to hear I would be the most marvellously popular and lauded doctor in the county, but not for long. Like a house of cards, my reputation would come tumbling down and rightly so. Charlatans have tried this tactic, made their fortunes, and slithered out of sight as fast as it takes to say "snake oil."

I read recently of a so-called celebrity who is not slow in giving his opinion about anything he fancies. Unfortunately, just by being a public figure, his comments are given airtime and credence by many. His latest assertion is that global warming simply isn't occurring and is some sort of "conspiracy." He states that, until all scientists are in full agreement over the "theory" of climate change, he will continue to live and consume excessively in the belief that whatever man does will have no influence on our planet. One irritated newspaper correspondent asked, that if a single scientist informed this celeb that gravity does not exist would he thenceforth refuse to believe in that particular force, as there would no longer be a consensus opinion?

Mr Celebrity was looking for absolutes and, just as in medicine, they don't exist.

Most patients, I suspect, understand that we cannot give guarantees. When I say in surgery that "I am really not sure," I think my honesty is generally appreciated, even if it may come as a disappointment. But if I spoke in a "small print" sort of way I might say: "I naturally cannot be certain but, with my years of training and decades of experience, it is my considered and impartial opinion that your baldness is indeed permanent and I'm pretty sure that if you don't lose eight stone you won't live to see your children grow up."

At the beginning I compared the lack of absolutes in life and medicine with the weather. I notice that forecasters increasingly use percentages; "there is a sixty percent chance of rain and a twenty-six percent chance of fog." I admit to being a bit unconvinced by this format, but take fifty percent to be some sort of "watershed." If over fifty, I'll venture out with my brolly and if under this mark, I'll leave it on the hat-stand.

I may tell Abbie-Sue Lute she has a seventy percent chance of having gallstones but a scan will give us a better idea and we can decide on surgery in the light of that.

By all means ask your doctor for his opinion, but he may not tell you what you want to hear. But he will decline to give you a cast-iron, or any other softer metal, guarantee; and I'm sure of that.

IT'S ALL GREEK TO ME

"… and I said to him, what's that in English, doctor?" I had referred Jean McPatient to a consultant at the City Hospital for specialist review. She had naturally been anxious about going and was not put at her ease once there. She was suggesting that the consultant had spoken gobbledegook or, only marginally better than that, medical jargon. As doctors we sometimes forget that patients have not been to medical school nor necessarily studied the Classics. Even today, many of the medical words and terms doctors use are derived from Latin and Greek but that should not mean that we fail to translate and explain where appropriate. I wondered what it was he said that had caused such confusion but reading the hospital letter I could see the problem. "The aetiology is uncertain but I presume her's are coryzal symptoms causing sternutation and anosmia but accept that it could be a Glioblastoma Multiforme with olfactory nerve compression. Axial scanning is pending." Even I had a little cross-referencing to do before deducing that she probably has a common cold but could have a brain tumour and further tests need to be done.

That may have been easy for him to say (!) but a little heavy for poor Jean. We should speak to patients in ways, and in words, that they themselves use and are familiar with. If my washing machine breaks down, I want my plumber to tell me what's wrong with it in a way a non-techno can understand and whether he can fix it. I think some doctors fear being described as patronising or fear that their own intellect may be questioned (heaven forbid!) so don't speak simply and plainly. I also think some doctors are quite unable to speak appropriately to patients, either due to a lack of training in this area or lack of insight into their own communication problems. Regardless of how skilled and clever a physician or surgeon may be, if he or she cannot make eye contact, break bad news or speak in words of less than eight syllables then they should be employed elsewhere. There are plenty microscopes to be peered through and test tubes to be shaken.

General practitioners nowadays have "consultation skills" taught during our training. Video recording is a big part of this. There is little that is more informative (or cringing) than watching one's self conduct consultations. This is only ever done with each patient's full consent, but be prepared for your doctor to ask you. I recall one middle-aged lady who agreed (rather eagerly) to let the camera roll during her consultation. She had come to tell me how much her joints had improved since the last prescription. She proceeded however to demonstrate (turning to the camera) by performing pirouettes and demi-pliés (or "posh squats" as she explained for her audience's benefit!)

Perhaps all doctors should be given such video training. Many would get a shock to see themselves but would learn from constructive criticism in the process. They would also discover that patients, importantly, are individuals and if they got the privilege of a performance such as I did, would discover many have talents and abilities themselves. It could even be fun.

BLOWING HOT AND COLD

"It freezing in here, Dr Ken. Is your heating not working again?" asked Thelma Statt as she entered my room. It amuses me that patients are often quick to comment on the ambient temperature of the surgery, whether high or low, during their ten-minute appointments. It may suggest that the problem Thelma is about to mention cannot be too serious if her immediate concern is for her surroundings, or it may indeed be the very reason she's here. I once read about fast food restaurants that design their seats so that diners start to become uncomfortable around the same time as they finish their food. Perhaps subconsciously, I keep my room a little too cool for comfort to prevent patients listing more than half-a-dozen problems at one "sitting." The more innocent alternative though, and she's right, is that the radiator's kaput.

I feel that as long as the temperature is not truly Baltic or Saharan, but set at an approximate temperate level, Health & Safety cannot have too much to complain about. I feel a greater priority is to ensure the air is of reasonable quality and if having a window ajar lowers the temperature a little, then too bad. If Alfie Niff pulled his socks off earlier to show me a superb example of Athlete's foot I feel it is only fair that subsequent patients don't have to share the experience with me.

But the British do have rather an obsession with temperatures and the weather in general, don't we? It can be an icebreaker, so to speak, to comment (read, complain) about how undesirable the weather is or how inaccurate the forecasters seem to be.

Apart from comments like Thelma's, temperature is often discussed in general practice. Body temperature is 37 degrees Celsius

(98.6 Fahrenheit.) Patients still tend to use the two scales equally, but fevers described as being "over 100" sound more impressive than "over 40," although the latter would give me more cause for concern.

The correct answer to the common question: "Has the patient got a temperature?" is of course always yes. But leaving aside pedantry, it is common parlance to ask this when we really mean *raised* temperature. Body temperature of course falls after death and forensic pathologists, as every armchair detective knows, can determine reasonably accurately the time of death using body and environmental temperatures.

Our own temperatures vary up to 1F (0.6C) throughout the day and it is thought that older people maintain slightly lower normal temperatures. Young children generally have more variable temperatures than adults. The "core" temperature is most accurately taken where the French tend to administer most of their medicines, and this should not vary with the length of time one occupies a restaurant, or any other type of, seat.

The hypothalamus, near the middle of the brain, is the body's thermostat. The commonest cause of raised temperature is of course fever, from infection. Theories abound as to why our temperatures rise and it is thought the body turns the heat up to try to reach a level at which the invading bacteria or viruses will not survive.

Other conditions such as an overactive thyroid, certain blood disorders and tumours can turn up the dial on the stat as well. Some women rely on the increase in temperature with ovulation midmonth as a form of natural contraception.

In my experience, women complain of the cold more often then men. In truth, women have a greater percentage of body weight as fat (chiefly in the form of the hips and breasts, whatever the form!) You would possibly expect this natural insulation to reduce complaints of cold but perhaps women complain more....(editorial note, stopping digging Doc!) One explanation may be that women do suffer a condition called Raynaud's disease far more often. This is where the fingers and toes can become extremely painful even with only moderate cold, especially water. The blood vessels go into spasm, depriving the extremities of sufficient blood. The digits tend to turn white, then blue followed sometimes by red.

Then there are the ways people dress. Younger folk tend to under-dress for the conditions; whether in excuses for jackets, short skirts, bare-midriffs or torn jeans. I am reliably informed these go under the name of "fashion." What would I know? Most of my clothes came from my father and I am not sure they were new on him either. Other middle-aged people may be said sometimes to over-dress, shunning the above fashions for sensible undergarments and layers abundant. A cloth cap, particularly atop a balding pate, is a wise thing to don considering most of our body heat is lost through our heads, and I am not talking through a hole in my hat this time.

One of the greatest tragedies in our society is when older people are, or think they are, unable to adequately heat their homes during winter months. The solution may not be just to give more money (though it will help in many cases) but to ensure greater insulation and efficiency with modern safe appliances.

"I'm sorry Thelma if my room is a little less warm than you would like it today. Perhaps you should just keep your coat on and sit right down in this lovely chair that I've just had delivered from Ken's Lucky Fried McDanger Burgers."

YOUR OWN GP IS NOT ALWAYS THERE FOR YOU

"I was surprised not to speak to you when I called last night, Dr Ken?" commented Miss Patience Virtue in surgery one morning. Patience had felt unwell the previous night and had rung the surgery for advice. Her called had been relayed to the out-of-hours service and dealt with appropriately.

General practitioners have existed for centuries (as a group and not individuals, although my partner Dr Bodie Aiken may be the exception to this rule!) Our role in the community, and at an individual level, has remained much the same, although contractual and other issues have entered the equation of late. When I joined our practice, I worked six days and two nights each week. I was serving my apprenticeship but was part of a team and we all worked equally hard. We literally provided a round-the-clock and round-the-calendar service to our local, but widespread, community. It was a service where, regardless of the time and circumstances, you could telephone and within half an hour, you would see your smiling, friendly doctor (often having thrown his jacket and trews over his night attire) standing there at your bedside whether rain, snow, hell or high-water. He was as dependable as the seasons and the grandfather clock in the hall. He was seemingly tireless and undoubtedly trustworthy, knowledgeable, wise, compassionate and most of all…available.

But all this came to an end in recent years. After teatime, when night has fallen and supper has been supped, if you call the surgery, it is not your doctor or his trusty, but slightly formidable, wife at the other end of the phone. Instead it is Faye Afar who answers. She may be in Clydebank as she claims but you have a nagging suspicion that you have been put through to somewhere in southern India. Either way, you are not speaking with someone who knows you and your family, nor someone who you last bumped into whilst doing the conga at the *Jolly Beggar* last New Year. How could Drs Aiken and Moody, after all these years have let us down? How could they have tended to our needs and foibles for generations and now hand (us) over to a "call centre?" Where has their care and compassion gone? Have they sold themselves down the Tweed?

These are questions we have been asked since we handed over the out-of hours responsibility to another agency. It is true, we are now "available" little over 30% of the entire week. What was previously 168 hours a week is now "only" 50 hours. We are in surgery 8am until 6pm, Monday to Friday, but this is "not (good) enough" for some.

General practice has changed, but only (and I believe through the need to survive) in line with the changes in society. As the "supermarket culture" prevails consumers expect to obtain anything, any time, they wish. As a small but proud "corner shop" we could not compete.

Demands (for they were rarely requests!) had become unsustainable. Years ago, if we were summoned in the middle of the night, by Jove, it was for good reason. More recently it was because Ethan Ole had fallen again, sustaining injuries while inebriated, or Mr Vurka Holick, the Polish merchant banker, had retuned from all-day meetings with a bit of indigestion. It became the norm to be called late in the evening with sniffles that had "lasted all day" or from people "unable to sleep" (join the club!) It was increasingly difficult to be bright-eyed and impossible to be bushy-tailed for surgery the following morning under these circumstances. We had tried barking down the phone at people in the middle of the night when calls were unreasonable but found it, not only made us unpopular but, was sapping us of energy, enthusiasm and compassion for our patients, and they deserved better.

It is not true to say "a GP is not available now when you need one." It may not be your usual one who you speak to at 2am but it is a fresh, alert (equally skilled and trained) one who is ready to deal with your urgent query.

It is an urgent query, that can't wait until the morning, isn't it?

MAKING LIFE-CHANGING DECISIONS

"So, do you think I should leave my husband, Dr Moody?" Gosh, it was not an unknown question Mrs Di Lemar was asking me, but one with which I am always taken aback.

I should perhaps count it an honour that patients ask me about, or involve me in, the most difficult and significant decisions *they* are ever likely to make. Whether I have known the patient for years or am even meeting her/him for the first time, I mention that I may be able to help but stress it is ultimately their decision to make.

I once had a woman sitting across the desk from me, torn between staying with her husband and children and leaving them for her boyfriend, with whom she was still in the throes of "unimaginable passion" (I could *only* imagine!) Her story, which any Hollywood director would have seized, culminated in her question to me: "so, can you help me deal with the guilt I am feeling?" Perhaps I should have admired this pang of conscience or even morality (a notion practically unheard of out of the confessional these days, and hardly ever in the courtroom!) but I confess that I was staggered by this unabashed attempt at shrugging off responsibility and doubts she may have had.

I am no moralist and am not paid to be one either. It is not my place to tell patients the "right" or the "wrong" thing to do. I may have some reservations about referring patients for abortions for purely social reasons or about partners "playing away from home," but I will not metaphorically wag the right index at them. I suspect some people in this modern society of ours are indeed looking (to me) for such guidance but my job is to identify and treat or to prevent illness, no more, no less.

Many such "heavy" questions indeed concern relationships, but there are others too. "Should I study away from home?", "Should I take this demanding job?" or the more everyday: "When should I return to work?." There may be relevant medical factors involved, such as previous or ongoing psychological, psychiatric or physical illnesses, and I would be happy to venture an opinion in such cases. But when people look for excuses, or have some warped concept of being granted official sanction to continue their dalliances or hurtful behaviour, they can go and look for it elsewhere.

I am no marriage guidance counsellor and neither pretend to be nor have ever been one. Relationship counsellors may be inundated but it is to them that I will direct couples, and only if they both want the relationship to work. She may not have married her prince but he cannot be frog-marched along to counselling (and looks don't come into it!).

If you choose your doctor, as the professional that he is, to help you make a big decision be aware that only you can ultimately make it. As a GP I can advise, from a medical point of view, bringing in experience and even (some Moody) wisdom. Be prepared though for your doctor (if he thinks your requests are unreasonable or inappropriate) to show you the door, or at least the door of another more suitable colleague or agency.

The soundest advice I believe I can give is this: weigh up all your options carefully; involve others if they are discreet and can give you a balanced, impartial view; don't make a decision in the heat of the moment and whatever you decide ensure it is done for the right reasons.

COMPLAINTS, GRIPES AND MOANS

"D'you no think we're getting more complaints these days, Ken?" Dr. Bodie Aiken asked me the other day. I'm never sure if he is being friendly finishing every question with my name or just being the Fifer that he is, but he probably has a point. We have been getting more complaints over recent years than ever before. It set me wondering why this should be. Have we made any blunders or have we had, as the media paradoxically says "near misses"? Or are our standards just slipping? We are still given the odd pheasant and duck at Christmas, so we must be doing something right.

I set about re-reading these written complaints to see if there was a common theme to them. Some were valid and steps had been taken, some were misunderstandings that were fairly easily resolved but some were just plain silly or even malicious.

Studies, nationally, have repeatedly shown that communication, or lack thereof, is the commonest gripe amongst patients. "Doctor said he'd ring me with my results, but he's obviously forgotten." It emerged though that doctor had tried three times that week and got an engaged tone each time. A letter had therefore been sent but the patient hadn't notified us of a change of address. One patient complained that his diabetic test strips were the wrong type but we could show him that his request was for what had been given. (If he had egg on his face it was hopefully poached and not fried for his sake!) I am delighted to say that doctors' illegible handwriting is receding into history as 99% of prescriptions are now printed (though the wrong buttons can be pressed!)

A more serious complaint is when patients with urgent problems cannot get through to speak to a doctor. The lines may be engaged with other callers (hopefully not complaining) or with us phoning out. True emergencies do of course need the caller to dial 999 or 112 but we appreciate many things need quick attention and whenever possible we try to be available to provide it.

I have no doubt that we are becoming more of a consumer society. Everything has to be now and we have the "right" to anything, any time we please. Unfortunately this cannot be infinitely accommodated within the NHS. Society is sadly losing sight of its corresponding responsibilities. If people want private medicine they are welcome to go and pay for it elsewhere.

Yes, Dr Aiken, there are more complaints these days but, chin up, we're still doing a pretty good job out here.

LOOSE TONGUES

"I've got this wretched ulcer and it just doesn't seem to heal," moaned Gus Sypp in surgery one morning. He proceeded to project between his upper and lower incisors a large pink lingua, which indeed had a small crater, showing no signs of disappearing.

Gus tried to elaborate on the history but was not making himself particularly clear. I suggested he return his tongue to its rightful resting place, behind his teeth. I too had seen enough, had my suspicions, and would promptly arrange for a biopsy.

Unfortunately, Gus was wont to sit with his pipe in his mouth, only removing it to share what he knew, or thought he knew, of others. Friends, neighbours or acquaintances; none were spared. He passed on information on who was stepping out with whom. He knew those who had come into money and those falling on hard times. He spread rumour and conjecture, fable and (occasionally) fact. No secret was safe. No doubt about it, he was an inveterate gossip.

The tongue, as an organ, is sometimes described as being the strongest muscle in the body. Whether it does indeed have the greatest density of muscle fibres, I do not know, but its influence is certainly greater than any other muscle. Kind words can help others through difficult times but harsh, chastising ones may scar individuals for evermore.

The tongue comes into speech rather a lot. Well, of course it does you say, it is essential, as the ancient pyramid builders knew when theirs were removed to prevent spreading the secrets of construction. What I really meant was, reference to it in speech is common. What are they called? I can't think of the word but it is on the tip of my tongue, oh yes, multilinguists. They have a gift for speaking in many tongues, as well as their mother tongue. I am sometimes subject to tongue-lashings at home and at work, but avoid escalation by often biting the said fleshy bit (mine not theirs!) Though never tongue-tied, I am informed by readers that this column is largely tongue-in-cheek, though such accusations of mere levity leave me momentarily speechless!

But it is the loose tongue that comes to my attention in surgery more than any other glossal complaint. In truth, it is particularly well anchored to the back of the throat. (A more traditional butcher may display an entire ox tongue, root and all, in his window but few of us still purchase this for the family's sandwiches.) Gossip, though, is like a cancer. It can be the most malicious and malignant, rapidly spreading condition in communities. I cannot recall any medical school lectures being dedicated to the subject, but advice to recognize the signs and effects of it should be fundamental in the training of country doctors. I daresay, in cities the loose tongue may be a little less potent but no-one is really immune to its virulence. Patients visit me, devastated and depressed by the effects of circulating rumours. Wartime posters proclaimed: "Careless talk costs lives," but the same could perhaps be said in these more peaceable times too. I think it is within some people's natures to wish to be party to knowledge and have the dubious credit of informing as many others as possible. They see it as their duty to relay to neighbours, or anyone within earshot or email, what they heard or think they heard. When challenged to the accuracy of their "news," the cliched "no smoke without fire," comment invariably chimes out. If nothing else, it shows that the gossipmonger is fanning the embers and the resulting flames can be deadly. It may be of course that what is spreading like wildfire around the community is accurate or partly correct, but what business is it of anyone else's anyway? I once suggested to Rue Moor that she minded her own business when she glanced melodramatically over her shoulder before launching into a tale about another patient sitting innocently in the waiting room. She upped and left, taking her supposed indignation with her.

Gus's biopsy came back, the results were not good. The hot pipe tip, pressed to the side of his tongue over the years, had led to carcinoma. He would need surgery and radiotherapy. Word got to me that there were those who felt Gus got what he deserved. For the first time, Gus was the subject of gossip. I was not interested enough to enquire whether this was with reference to his smoking or the other infamous use of his tongue, but there was indeed a certain cruel irony. Gus would never gossip again, sadly he may never talk again either.

A GOLDEN AGE? IT SHOULD BE

"We'll all get old one day Dr Ken," said Bert McPatient, slowly pulling his braces back up over his shoulders. I don't often pick people up on what they say but I do find this old cliché particularly grinding. We may have an increasingly elderly population, with all the associated health problems and economic issues, but people still die tragically young from illness, accident and by their own hand. It should be a luxury to live into old age and to enjoy one's twilight years but those who do achieve this sadly often suffer illness, are frustrated by debility or, perhaps worst of all, are ignored and disparaged by others. It is said that the mark of a civilized society is how it treats its dependent members and this certainly includes the elderly. We read about the pensions crisis and how we increasingly cannot provide for ourselves, never mind others, when we might live for forty years after receiving the carriage clock and lump sum. The Old are increasingly seen as a burden and a drain having "served their purpose." Yet another cliché is that "we should all get a pill at the age of seventy." Strangely these words never seem to pass the lips of septuagenarians who are enjoying good health.

I like visiting our local care home, especially when I have time to listen to the tales old people tell. They are our remaining link with the past. Some may have chatted with King George V, shaken hands with legendary presidents or been cogs in the wheels of the British Empire. Even the first-hand accounts of life at home during wartime and the spirit of survival and comradeship can be truly humbling. Our own aging grandparents and parents are often forgotten about in our haste and business of everyday life. We find it a chore to visit even at Christmas and birthdays and, when there, often make excuses to leave early.

Old age should be admired, desired and respected. It is not inevitably accompanied by pain, ill health, suffering and dementia, though these conditions do become more common. Medical care is not, and should not be, rationed on the basis of age alone. But there does come a time where active treatment is not always in someone's best interests and nature is best left to take its course.

Old age should be a time of reflection on a life well lived. It should be a time for taking pleasure in the achievements and developments of younger family and friends. It should also be a time for having fun, whether that is playing bridge, cycling or skydiving (well, within reason!).

Finally, I've yet to offend anyone with my solemn diagnosis that the patient may suffering from "TMB." The atmosphere is lightened when I explain that this is Too Many Birthdays.

IT'S ALL IN THE SMALL PRINT
YOU KNOW

"Yon medicine leaflets are the bane of my life Ken," moaned Dr Bodie Aiken to me over coffee. He was referring to the patient information leaflets (or the acronymous PILs) found in the packaging of all prescribed medicines. It is of course important to warn patients about possible side effects or interactions with other medicines, but these leaflets often run to several thousand words and are in a multitude of languages. Oddly enough, as pharmacies constantly source the cheapest European manufacturer of medicines, these languages don't always include English! This also means the packaging and appearance of a tablet/capsule can vary with each issue, causing considerable confusion–but that is perhaps a moan for another day! These PILs remind me of the small print with which mortgage lenders finish their adverts: "Your home is at risk if you do not keep up repayments..." Retail companies, whose product offers are too good to be true, will append volumes of small print stating, in effect, that once the dotted line is signed you will be taken to the cleaners. (Appropriate perhaps for deals at the Laundromat but not for a life assurance policy!) My dictionary says of small print that it is "considered to be a trap for the unwary." Any letters or leaflets we provide for patients have to be printed in font size 12 but there is no such restriction on PILs, which are commonly written in font size 8 or less. Ironic really when you consider that older people (who may have impaired vision) are the most likely to suffer ill effects from medicines.

Side effects are generally listed in decreasing order of occurrence. Nausea, vomiting and rash usually top the list but interestingly impotence, well down the list, is enough for many chaps to flush their tablets down the toilet. (Amusingly, the most effective anti-smoking message ever on cigarette packets was the blunt "smoking causes impotence"!)

But what Dr Bodie Aiken was really complaining about is the near daily quizzing we get. "You didn't tell me I might get a mild headache (with this life saving medicine)" or "it says that when taking this, the other medicine for my fungal toenails may be 5% less effective." Dr Aiken does not pretend that we never make mistakes and would agree that a patient's inquisitiveness could prevent a doctor's or pharmacist's blunder occurring. Our computers warn us of possible interactions or problems and our ever-reliable pharmacist and herbalist Mrs Lo Ti On is always free to call us with concerns. It does however become rather tiresome when patients call, often interrupting surgeries, because doubts (essentially about our abilities as prescribers and doctors) are raised by comments from pharmaceutical companies in these PILs. They are clearly fearful that they may be accused of not warning patients of risks, regardless of how minuscule they may be.

These leaflets are necessary but should be appropriately and responsibly written. It seems though that they are written more as disclaimers with the lawyers in mind rather than patients.

ANSWERS TO QUESTIONS

"But if it is not that, what is the very worst it could be, doctor?" This is what I call the "worst case scenario" (or Armageddon) question and it is quite often fired at me across the consulting room desk. I used to be caught off guard with it but have become more diplomatic or jokey in my reply: "Let's just work on what we know" or "you might not get much beyond 100 now!" The true and logical answer to any such question is ultimately "death" of course, but is perhaps not particularly helpful nor what the patient is prepared for! A spot could, however unlikely, be cancerous and headaches and coughs could also signify underlying serious disease. Our job is, through our experience and knowledge, to keep things in context and obtain tests or further opinions if we have any doubts or questions of our own.

Some doctors are brutally honest in all regards and might tell the patient: "it could be just swollen glands or it could be cancer." This may be factually correct but is pretty insensitive. I don't feel it is good medicine to "think aloud" like this. Of course we can also be criticised for not having "discussed all possibilities," but it is sometimes quite inappropriate to do so.

Sometimes we just can't win, nor should we try. Such frank doctors may alternatively say to a patient when asked for a diagnosis: "sorry, I haven't a clue what's wrong with you ma'am" (I daresay the vagaries of general practice wouldn't attract such doctors to our ranks though). This probably is not a very reassuring comment from a patient's point of view but, in truth, we cannot diagnose everything in everyone all of the time (especially at ten minute intervals!) If we could we wouldn't need to refer patients to specialists, take blood tests or send people for scans and X-rays. People however like their surgeon to make firm decisions and to stick to their convictions. "Right, we'll whip out the offending organ and have you back on your feet in no time." GPs can rarely be as dogmatic as this (perhaps our tools are just blunter!) and we can find ourselves trying "some of this" followed by "some of that," for instance in the treatment of high blood pressure. The reality is that people react remarkably differently and unpredictably to medicines and constant assurances or predictions would be little more than "hit or miss." This would make us little more than astrologers.

So, you can ask your doctor what the worst could be, but be prepared for an answer you might not like.

WEE BEASTIES

Anita O'Hare and her mum came to see me in surgery complaining about the "wee beasties" inhabiting and infesting Anita's hair and scalp. For as long as I had known her, Anita always had the most lovely waist-length golden locks, brushed one-hundred times each evening. I had sympathy with her, as the tears rolled down her cheeks and the blood oozed from her scalp. Closer, gloved inspection unfortunately revealed that the wee lass did indeed have dozens of *Pediculus capitis* at various stages of development. From a zoological and arthropodal point of view, hers would have been a most fascinating case study.

Head lice or "nits" is a fairly common complaint in general practice. It is most often seen in primary school children, those with longer hair and in those from larger families. I don't know whether, as legend has it, the beasties prefer cleaner hair but certainly no kid is immune. Some researchers (or nit nurses seeking to make a name for themselves!) have calculated that about 5% of all young school kids are plagued by these insects. Pharmacists are best placed to advise parents about the current recommended insecticide and it tends to be only the more resistant cases that come our way. Usually it is just the eggs that we see attached to the hair shafts but if we are "lucky" we may see the mature winged bugs themselves, right at home in a thick mop of hair. Adult female nits live for up to a month and lay about five eggs each day. These eggs take a week to hatch and young nits mature in only one further week, before themselves reproducing. I tend not to detail these impressive breeding habits and statistics to young patients nor mention that they are the subject of a microscopic feeding frenzy as the parasites thrive by sucking blood from their tender and juicy scalps. Parents are often the most upset, feeling I might accuse them of neglect or allowing hygiene levels to be compromised. I may once have suggested to a particularly upset mother to "keep your hair on," but memory does not serve me well and I probably suggested the opposite to her daughter, as being shorn of one's braids is often the best initial advice that can be given. Long hair is the preferred breeding ground and girls sharing secrets, whispering shyly in each others' ears is the perfect condition for the bugs to play leapfrog and seek pastures, tresses and locks anew.

It is not only parents who panic when Anita or her classmates are confirmed to be infested. The school sees itself as dutybound to formally notify parents that *Pediculus*, like aliens, have landed. It is inappropriate to demand school exclusion until being fully rid of them as the condition is really not that serious and this may only added to the stigma that often results.

The helpful pharmacist will have recommended the treatment-of-the-month and most cases are resolved by two applications, one week apart. I often hear that parents diligently wash sheets, pillowcases and clothes every day for weeks but, as the beasties only survive for half an hour when isolated, such cleanliness and sterilising may be good for the soul but does little to rid Anita and her pals of the nuisance.

Combs are often helpful. Metal fine-toothed ones are best and some now have small electrical charges running through them, designed to electrocute the offenders. I think there is a certain satisfaction gained in frying the blighters, as if poisoning weren't enough!

Whether it is just an observation, resistance to the more traditional insecticide treatments seems to be becoming more of a problem. If so, and because treatments until now have been toxic and non-organic, I am sometimes asked if there are greener and more environmentally (and even child!) friendly- but definitely not nit-friendly- lotions available. There is a new and different product called Dimeticone (Hedrin) now available but whether this is truly superior or will not just become another "acquired taste" to the parasites remains to be seen.

So, I duly signed the script and suggested Anita and her mum march round to the chemist as quickly as the armies were on manoeuvres around her scalp. As ever in these cases though, whether it is just auto-suggestion or psychological, I found myself scratching for the rest of the day.

BACK T'MILL

Returning to work from holiday is never an easy experience. All GPs, and all workers for that matter, look forward to their vacations. I would be surprised and concerned if an employee pleaded with his line manager to deny him paid-leave and allocate extra duties. He may request some overtime to finance the anticipated trip, but to work 52 weeks in a year is positively unhealthy and impossible to sustain.

Between you, me and the surgery door, in the run up to a period of leave I get a little stale. Not mothball stale, though Mrs Mona Lotte our practice manager may pass comment on my aging tweed sports jacket! Of course, I always try to give each patient and each case my undivided attention but, in truth, my mind can wander and I'm probably not as sharp as I might be. In addition, I try to clear my desk and have the paperwork up-to-date. I can be rather guilty of letting complex and involved reports drift to the bottom of the in-tray but preparing for a scheduled break means it is only fair to all that they are completed. Besides, I do not wish to return to these copious forms after my travels when my memory of the details is fading faster than my tan.

I say "travels" but we have not in fact left these shores for many years. Mrs Moody and I feel our days of globetrotting are most likely over, particularly when there are still corners of this great nation as yet unexplored. I also have a problem with budget airlines and burgeoning passenger numbers, mindful that the attendant carbon emissions are accelerating the demise of our planet.

We always take a cottage either on the Scottish or English East coast. The lure of the sea and fresh fish every evening perhaps, but links golf is what really appeals. The game was never meant to be played inland! I purposely never take medical reading material that week and being anonymous in a community has its definite advantages when it comes to relaxation. I like to return to spend the second week pottering around the garden, doing the annual hedge-cut and painting the flaky bits of the house. I am far from being anonymous of course in this community and even popping down to the ironmonger's likely means I'll be asked to look at a rash, a growth or to give an opinion about a high temperature. Comments about my shabby attire are inevitable and, if nothing else, serve to remind that I am not always working. I usually pop into the surgery after twilight at least once to open letters, catch up with the progress and regress of patients and prepare myself, softening the blow, for my return to the "mill."

Monday morning duly comes round and the dry-cleaned jacket is donned again. Both it and I look a little less crumpled and smell slightly fresher. My usual and faithful patients have saved their new and old ailments for my return. The first few days are booked predominantly with those who tell me they have waited weeks to see me. Some, seemingly need informed or reminded that this is not really a reflection on general waiting times and if they insist on seeing no other they must understand I am entitled to holidays. It is quite pleasing to be held in this regard but, in truth, most conditions could just as efficiently have been dealt with by colleagues. I do accept that some more chronic and complex cases may be best known and dealt with by me, but there really is no need for common colds to be stored and nurtured for my return, if they need medical attention at all! What I do not appreciate is for patients to inform me of how the treatment they received in my absence was perceived as being inferior. I am not infallible, will not be here for ever and am only, at best, as good as my colleagues.

I never know whether to feel relieved, to hear on my return, that things have been quiet, particularly when the first day back is dreadfully busy. Perhaps we feel more refreshed to have been absent during a hectic spell though I do have pangs of guilt if colleagues have been beleaguered with the volume of work. They, of course, will be looking forward to, and be deserving of, their own vacations.

Life in the surgery, like the waterwheel, keeps turning. The flow of patients may reduce to a mere trickle or be the more usual torrent, but it never stops. I am content to know that my presence is not essential to its working. I love every moment being away from the surgery (for the right reasons you understand!) and the return to work never looms ominously for me.

With the diverse and talented healthcare team to which I now belong, I really am a fairly small cog within the machinery.

LOSING ONE'S MARBLES

Vincent & Dot Taige sat before me in surgery one afternoon, or at least Dot did, for no amount of persuasion could convince Vin to sit down. "Vin" was his chosen name but sadly he did not answer to even that now. Besides this restlessness, Dot was increasingly concerned that her 68-year old husband was failing to keep up with conversations, could not distinguish night from day and was unsafe leaving the house unaccompanied. At first it had not been obvious, and she had given him the benefit of considerable doubt, but there was just no escaping the fact that Vin was, in his wife's own words, "losing his marbles."

Poor Vin needed prompting for hitherto taken-for-granted tasks such as dressing, eating and even lighter jobs around the garden. Continence had been a variable problem but the final straw had been when Vin visited the lavatory and forgot, or had not appreciated, the need to first pull down his undergarments.

We start life with 100 billion brain cells, or neurones. These progressively diminish in number as the years go by, but also with various other factors, such as head injuries. It is not simply the number of surviving cells that determines whether one develops dementia, but the complexity of their interconnections. Astonishingly, each brain cell is thought to connect with up to 10,000 others.

I was sorry it took ages for the Taiges to visit me. They hardly attended surgery year to year and, as a couple, kept in fairly good physical health. They were also rather proud and private individuals. As in all cases of suspected dementia, it is imperative that I exclude other conditions as causes for a gradual change and decline in one's abilities. Occasionally, an underactive thyroid or liver, kidney and lung disease will cause a confusional or dementia- like state. Tumours or bleeds within the brain (particularly the traumatic subdural type, even months after a relatively innocuous blow to the head) can present in this way. The alert physician should not overlook the possibility of severe depression, either, in an elderly person, as being a cause of social withdrawal, change in personality or even the inability to speak. After a general examination and blood tests, a brain scan may be greatly useful in arriving at a diagnosis. Several of the above conditions are readily treatable (and a joy to witness if any improvement or resolution occurs!) It would be correct to assume that generally the sooner a condition is detected, the more likely treatment is to be effective, and vice versa. Often a CT brain scan shows cerebral atrophy, which is a general shrinkage of the brain with time. Like the wrinkling of the skin, the brain, which is normally 80% water, seems to dry out somewhat. Such physical shrinkage itself does not directly cause dementia, but in severer cases would be associated with loss of mental functioning.

I am fully in favour of keeping the brain active and challenged on a daily basis. For me it is crosswords. There is ample evidence that this helps preserve many functions and slows deterioration. It can be too easy for people, whether working or not, to find themselves in such routines that life can be led in near "autopilot." Problem-solving is just one means of mental exercise. Taking up a new hobby, such as learning to play a musical instrument, may not necessarily be welcomed by the neighbours, but importantly stimulates the grey matter. Life and Medicine do not provide guarantees and even such mental gymnastics will not prevent dementing illnesses occurring. The brain is the most complex of organs and I knew a patient with an advanced dementia who continued to play the piano beautifully despite being unable to button his own shirt. In another case, a lady could complete cryptic crosswords with ease, despite being unable to hold the simplest of conversations.

When Alzheimer's disease is diagnosed there are certain medicines, now available, which may slow or even halt progression. The initiation of these, rather expensive, "cognitive enhancer" drugs tends to be left to the discretion of Psychogeriatricians. These specialists, in mental health in the elderly, sometimes give patients a trial of medication but suggest stopping if no improvement is observed after several months. This particular scenario is often difficult for relatives as they may feel Mum is being discriminated against on the basis of her age, or it is a case of rationing, but this far from the case.

It became clear to all concerned that Vin Taige was too much work for his wife. As hard as she tried, and with the help of round-the-clock carers, he remained a liability.

His dementia was of a more straightforward type, if that is not a paradox in itself. He suffered from vascular dementia. As the blood supply to various parts of his brain was being compromised; like a large house, his brain was having doors slammed shut and locked for the last time. His illness was progressive and when it is so, life expectancy is usually somewhat shortened. The brain can only take so much damage. Dot visited him faithfully every day while he was there, but he died in a local care facility some six months later.

DOMESTIC SQUABBLES

The last patient of the evening had just left and I could hear a gathering storm outside my room. "Right, is he in here? He's got to be told after this." From behind the door I could hear, "He's in for a piece of my mind, he is. How dare he?" More curious then cautious, more weary than wary, I bellowed: "Come," as I usually do when secretaries and others hesitate on the creaky threshold before entering.

Without knocking, in strode a short, red-faced woman whom I had never met. She carried with her a laden sack, one I recognized as having been acquired by me from a local brewery. She was closely followed by our, fiercer than usual, surgery cleaner, Mrs A Jacks. "What is the meaning of this?" barked the vanguard. "Yes, what is the meaning of this?" came the echo from the rear. I carefully laid down my fountain pen and deliberately removed my half-moon specs, as I am wont to do when I sense confrontation. Aware that my contacts with the constabulary have been largely professional and social, I was confident that even if these aggressors in overalls were undercover cops, my conscience was clear. My misdemeanors, it emerged, were not of a truly criminal nature but related to my misuse of the surgery bins. Yes, I had been taking it upon myself to dispose of a little excess refuse from chez Moody. We had done some entertaining and clearing of the garage over recent weeks and I had popped a bag or two in the industrial-sized bin, stationed at the rear of the surgery. As it is emptied twice weekly, I felt one or two extra sacks would make little difference. I didn't broadcast the fact I had done this, thinking it trivial, but I had been seen. The domestic supervisor had apparently travelled a great distance to confront me about this. The Health Board and "The Union" had been notified and now there was photographic evidence of the offending items: a sack of lath and plaster, a stained floral lampshade and a torn Chinese dragon kite. This evidence would be reviewed by an even higher authority in the domestic world (the mind boggled!) and I would have to await the outcome. I dared not query the sanctions they might inflict upon me, but did wonder if in a bygone age: would my predecessors have had to deal with such an impromptu domestic ordeal and trial?

Having heard this irrefutable catalogue of "crimes" and with as much interest and energy as I could muster after a surgery dealing with bereaved and suffering patients, I put forward the case as I saw it. The issue of waste disposal has long been a concern of mine, here in the surgery. For this reason I provide crates where we place our recyclable material. The pharmaceutical advertising leaflets and hastily-read journals are piled high, and each Friday evening, when departing, I remove this pulp to our own recycling bin. It was my contention that this rather minor, but worthy, effort made enough space for my occasional reciprocal disposal of household garbage. The red-faced pair knew of no such provision for this in their rule book and training manual. (Perhaps the same rules that forbid the washing of coffee cups, even the lipsticked ones Mrs Jacks leaves behind!)

Increasingly irritated that my dinner would be getting cold, I decided to speak my mind about our complaining cleaner. On her arrival each afternoon, at four o'clock or so and after the first of many cigarettes, on goes the vacuum cleaner. I did not know that the industrial carpet in the corridor needed an hour of suction every afternoon (perhaps it started life as a shag-pile carpet!) With deafer patients I have asked Mrs Jacks to vacuum elsewhere but she too signs that she cannot hear me, raises her penciled eyebrows, and carries on regardless. The stale tobacco aroma each morning reminds me only that the cleaner has entered my room, as nothing else indicates her presence. On several occasions, I have returned to surgery in the late evening to find windows left open or lights on and am aware, ensuring a secured surgery is within her contracted responsibility. There, as theirs was a rather personal attack on me, I had mentioned a few niggles of my own which I felt rather outweighed the transgressions, of which I was being accused. This posse's ambushed meeting with me terminated with the warning that I had better not repeat my offending behaviour.

Mrs Jacks and I did not speak for the next few days. I considered forbidding her entry to my room but realized, by not having my basin even cursorily wiped, I stood to lose out. I was not impressed by her failing to politely point out any difficulties I was inadvertently causing or by her letting off the leash the domestic equivalent of a Doberman Pincher.

I was not very proud though of my rather candidly expressed grievances and irritations with our cleaner. Of course, I do not approve of her bringing unmistakable cigarette odour into my room, prompting comments from patients. I should have spoken with her long before, even if it necessitated me switching off the vacuum cleaner at the mains to gain her attention.

Anyway, I shall polish up my skills of persuasion and negotiation and hire a skip when necessary. Mrs Jacks seemed also to be duly chastised and I have to say, smartened up her smartening up of the surgery.

I do the doctoring, she does the cleaning but we have both wiped the slate clean.

THE SADDEST STORY

Moira was a beautiful baby. Her parents had tried for a few years before she was born, and the pregnancy had not been without its problems either. Her baptism twenty summers ago had been on a glorious June day. I remember the champagne quenched our thirst deliciously when we returned to the house for the celebratory lunch. As she grew, Moira had a lovely cheeky grin and was a most endearing child. She forgave me for administering each of the childhood and pre-school immunizations. Off to school she went; rosettes and medals at gymkhana and swimming and sports champion in her final year of primary school. By early secondary school she was excelling, particularly in athletics and hockey, and had trials for the international squads. Her parents' proudest moment was when she broke the junior 400 metres track record.

On her sixteenth birthday she was allowed to go out with some other girls. The well-planned parties with games, dolls and jelly and ice cream were over. She had promised to be home by ten. By midnight, and with her mobile apparently switched off, Mrs and Mrs Finn started to worry. Several hours later it came almost as a relief when the hospital phoned. Moira had consumed copious amounts of vodka and was having her stomach pumped. It emerged the laboratory had never seen such an elevated serum ethanol reading in one of her years but this time her record-setting was not a source of pleasure or pride.

She was rather grey and sheepish on her discharge the following day. Her parents came to me for advice on how they should best handle the situation. I suggested they should regard it as a foolish mistake and a hard lesson learned. They were dreadfully upset but, after sitting down with her, accepted the assurances that she was truly sorry and would not find herself in the same state again. She did seem to appreciate that they only acted out of love and concern.

A month or two later, she attended me for emergency contraception. She said she hoped it would not be me in surgery and almost left the building when she realized I was on duty that day. She was at both a vulnerable time of the month and time in her life. I try not to be too fogyish or paternalistic in such circumstances. Of course I wouldn't tell her parents, I reassured her. I would not and could not. I probably was an avuncular figure, of sorts. Disease, unwanted pregnancy, missing the best years of young life were areas I discussed with her that day but Moira clearly just wanted to be out of the surgery, as quickly as possible.

It emerged she had hooked up with some wretch several years older. He had been in and out of jail for drug and other offences and was undoubtedly exploiting her innocence and good nature. Her parents learned of her alliance when she announced she was moving in with him. "He just had a bad start in life," she would argue and evidently needed her help to change.

I hardly recognized her on the next occasion we met. She was seriously underweight and her skin had lost its freshness. She was unkempt and her hair uncared for. Not only was there no sparkle in her now sunken eyes but they had a rather haunted look about them. She was on a methadone programme but her counsellor was certain she was still using. Her voice was flat and her speech dull. If she even remembered who I was, or cared, she didn't say. Her purpose that day was no more than to get her latest prescription, and if she could wangle any increase in the amount, so much the better. Her parents had aged markedly in these few months. They would never stop loving her but hope was ebbing. She showed no signs of even wanting to escape the malign influence of her partner or the life she was leading. Nobody could reach her.

She was found in that squalid bedsit with the needle still in her arm. Doctors do not often weep but I did the day Moira died.

A GOOD EAR

It is pleasing to be commended by someone, unless it is the opening gambit to being asked for a favour! "Thanks for listening, Dr Ken. You're a good ear," declared Harry Lugg in surgery one day. I thought I had done little more than just hear him out and offer some common sense advice, but it had obviously meant something to him.

I am in fact the proud possessor of *two* shell-like auricles, or *pinnae* as they are properly called. If they can indeed be accurately compared to shells, my protuberant appendages might be likened to giant conchs, as no-one would suggest they are undersized. They certainly support the theory that ears continue to grow throughout life. Being also on the hirsute side, the tufts of sprouting thick hair need constant trimming. My razor and scissors are required more often and widely and become rapidly blunted these days. But it was not of course to the actual anatomy or need for follicular self-topiary that Harry referred.

The very basics of Medicine and the art of healing are about taking a good history. This means that regardless of how chatty, erudite, incisive or skilled a diagnostician a doctor may be, he just has to button it and let the patient spout forth. Initially at least. It may of course emerge, that conversely, the patient is taciturn, inarticulate, vague and inconsistent, but he will drop clues along the way as to what is the problem. The physician, if a good ear, will not constantly interrupt, express doubt or contradict his patient. He may seek clarification or gently nudge the rambling narrative back on track but importantly, he will listen.

I don't suppose, though, mine would be considered a difficult job if I simply sat back and let a patient tell her story from start to, uninterrupted, finish. As truth is stranger than fiction, I might be rather entertained to hear, in soap opera fashion, weekly installments of quarrels, reconciliations and love lost and found. The trouble is, of course, that most patients through necessity are allocated only ten minute slots. We simply do not have the time to let people speak so liberally and so often. Even if I did, it would be a fairly poor way to practise medicine and of no favour to other patients. Even counsellors during their hour-long appointments will not allow clients to simply rabbit on.

Mrs Moody has never suggested that I am a good ear. I do *have* a good and a bad ear, having strayed rather too close to an incendiary device during National Service. As my betrothed details our social itinerary for the forthcoming month, the extent of my interest often amounts to no more than a grunt from behind the newspaper. I used to challenge her when she claimed she had previously informed me of an engagement. Now I graciously accept that she probably did. What does get my attention is a good programme on Radio Scotland. I will literally tune in to the exclusion of all other distractions. Call me old fashioned if you will but I remain more of a listener than a viewer.

With most complaints that are levelled at doctors, the common factor is said to be a lack of communication. If doctors only took the time to listen to what their patients say misunderstanding and error might be avoided. Of all the complaints I have received over the years (justified or otherwise!) I am happy to say not one has been an accusation that I just haven't listened. Some were brought about by the fact the patient or family obviously hadn't heard what I said, or what was said had not been to their liking. I admit that I can be a little frank at times and have issued apologies for not being sufficiently politic, diplomatic or circumspect.

So Harry, if by raising an eyebrow and intermittently directing my fleshy radar disc in your direction helped you through a difficult time, I'm only too happy to have obliged.

ON DUTY

OUT AND ABOUT

THE SCHOOL DOCTOR

"The kids have been talking about you coming for weeks now, Dr Ken. Glad you finally made it," teased Dom Inee, the infant teacher, gently. I had put it off for as long as even a busy doctor decently can, but relented by agreeing to talk to the junior class about "being a doctor."

I consider myself somewhat of a seasoned raconteur when it comes to after-dinner speaking and suchlike, but confess to having had rather broken sleep the night before and a slightly beaded brow at the time. Utterly ridiculous I know, perhaps because both this audience and I lacked the usual prandial lubrication or was it just the sheer unpredictability of the whole scenario? How should I approach it? A dry speech about sticking in at school, graduating from university and moving onto the wards would have had even the politest audience in deepest slumber or sneaking out the fire exits. No, there could be no "delivery" as such, children and most others enjoy and learn best by interaction and anecdote.

I introduced myself to these twenty Lilliputians. Theatrically tripping over a misplaced school bag in a style Chaplin himself would have been proud, I asked what might have happened to my poor leg. Several little hands shot up volunteering personal or second hand experience of such folly and mishap. The conversation, for that is what it quickly became, sprang from there. Spots, stookies, slings and sick were most children's concepts of illness and ill health, and who was I to interfere with such imagery (and alliteration)? I have never actually treated anyone covered entirely, like an Egyptian mummy, in bandages but several kids described their idea of a "hospital patient" as such.

I had prepared, like a conjurer, my medical bag. For years I've used a camera bag my motive being that, in the less salubrious areas I used to visit, I was less likely to be mugged for my lenses as a "photographer" than for my drugs as an attending physician. In it there are numerous compartments that tightly encase instruments and other medical tools and pills. The lolly-stick tongue depressors were gleefully employed by the urchins to induce gagging in each other and gazes of wondrous concentration resulted from listening with the "tubes and bell" to each other's rapid little hearts. My pen torch proved of interest when shone directly into wide eyes. Bright light, we discovered, causes the pupils to shrink (the ophthalmic variety that is, or parents would have had plenty cause for complaint!) Pharmaceutically labelled pens (logos carefully selected to avoid awkward explanations) found their way into a score of grasping hands.

The greatest expression of surprise though was when, from the deepest recess of my bag, chocolate was discovered (I believe the dentist was scheduled to speak to them the following week, so my name will be mud!) Arguably though, it's an essential remedy for treating hypoglycaemic patients or doctors running late for lunch.

Children of course are a substantial part of GPs' workloads. However, they are never invited to complete patient satisfaction surveys, so it is of value and amusing to hear what the nippers actually say about us. "I think my doctor is a kind old man and he makes me laugh"; "Dr Ken smells a bit like auntie's mothballs" and "I like my doctor because he makes me and my family stay well." Perhaps not what researchers conceive as particularly constructive comments or actual point scorers, but certainly give one food for thought (and reason to review one's wardrobe!) Unlike adults, children have no hidden agendae or preconceived ideas, other than their own. They are honest and open, telling you what they really think and feel.

It was far better fun than I imagined it would be. Perhaps I can now add Children's Entertainer to my list of credentials. I wonder who's doing Santa this Christmas.

OUT ON A VISIT

A home visit was requested one morning for a man in his twenties. The receptionist logged it with the message "unwell, cannot look at light, dehydrated, cannot get out of bed." I had never met him but he was registered with me, so as soon as my surgery had finished, I got his file and checked his computer records. I reached his semi-detached council house, where he lived with his mother, within an hour of the request being made. There was no answer at the door so I rang from my mobile, only to hear it ring out in the house. All of the upstairs curtains were drawn and a car was in the driveway. Visiting the surrounding houses, the neighbours described them as "private people" and said they had seen him the previous evening and that his mother was a domestic cleaner.

After half an hour of enquires, by which time I felt more like a detective than a doctor, I telephoned the police. The burly policeman who appeared stated a passing knowledge of my patient. Between us we phoned various people and places suggested to us in an effort to contact the mother, but failed to find her. I explained that I was sufficiently concerned that my patient was unconscious or dead and felt that I had to gain entry. The rear door proved stronger than it looked. The overweight sergeant was probably ruing his lack of fitness, as by now he was as red as the door, his hat was askew and he had a respiratory rate giving me yet more cause for concern. A neighbour helpfully provided a crow bar, which until then I had never considered a useful tool for an on-call doctor.

Stepping gingerly over broken glass we discovered the house was empty and untidy which, with the door swinging on a single hinge, made it seem as if it had been burgled. Seething at this presumed misuse of medical services by the patient and his family. I left the policeman to keep guard and find a good joiner.

I returned to the surgery and, to my horror, discovered that the given address was elsewhere. It emerged that the patient had stayed overnight with a girlfriend. As I had duties elsewhere by this time, a colleague visited him, only to diagnose a self-limiting 'flu-like illness.

I spoke with his mother the following day to apologise about her door and explained that what I did was in her son's best interests, given the information I had at the time.

The door was duly repaired at the local council's expense, despite my offer to them to contribute.

In the past, if a patient is out I leave a note requesting that they contact me as soon as possible. On these rare occasions it is usually because the patient has simply forgotten. Alternatively, the patient may have gone straight to hospital, but I had excluded this by checking with ambulance control.

My defence union had not heard of a similar situation but were aware of the converse, where a doctor had failed to see a patient only for him to be later found dead.

With our system as it was, such scenarios could arise. The computer and paper records have the permanent given address but if the patient is said to be elsewhere this may be overlooked in the rush of retrieving notes for myriad visits.

People, especially young adults, may have "informal" sleeping or living arrangements or, at times of illness, stay elsewhere and we don't always have time to phone ahead to establish the facts.

Our receptionists now, when a visit is requested, note the telephone number and current address. Any discrepancies with our records are checked. Any changes, whether temporary or permanent, are highlighted in the visits book.

When there is a possibility of a patient having meningitis or sounds very unwell the duty doctor is informed as soon as possible.

I believe I acted appropriately in these unusual circumstances.

I telephoned the surgery confirming I had the right patient on the right day but unfortunately didn't confirm the address. I thought I had "covered all bases" in the search for my patient, but perhaps not the most obvious.

My partners encouraged me to see the funny side of it. I suspect it is still talked about in the local pub.

DRIVEN TO DISTRACTION

"Was that you I cut up on the back road last week, Dr Ken?" enquired Sadie Gonzales, when she attended recently for a blood test. My opinion of Sadie plummeted faster than does the speedometer needle when a car hits a brick wall. She had overtaken dangerously on a dull, wet evening forcing me to brake sharply. She pulled in just in time to avoid being hit by a tractor coming the other way. I'm a benign, mild mannered sort of chap as you know, but inconsiderate and mindless driving raises my hackles in a way few other things do. People can play Russian roulette with their own lives if they wish but how dare they do so with others'.

Once or twice each week I have to dash off to an assumed or actual medical emergency. I'm no Stirling Moss but can shift when I have to. I'm left rather bemused though, when I'm travelling quickly. Delivery vans, mail vans (post-haste?) or folk going to work (often blethering distractedly on their mobiles) still manage to pass me. I would be prepared to argue (M'lud!) that the need for customers to receive their internet shopping, letters, carpets or groceries is a little less important than the need for a doctor to reach his ailing patient.

I've known some doctors, though, to misuse their positions. One ill-advised colleague, running late for a football match, drove up the hard shoulder undertaking queuing traffic. Noticing a police car, he proceeded to wave his stethoscope. The traffic cop in reply, with an admirable sense of comic timing, duly waved his handcuffs. He found it difficult to argue that, even as a doctor, he was legitimately rushing to attend an injured player when the match hadn't yet started!

Many people take enormous pride in their automobiles. It is often the most expensive purchase after one's house. They may bedeck their vehicles with go-faster stripes, pedestrian-unfriendly paraphernalia like bull-bars or fit exhaust pipes into which small dogs could inadvertently wander. I admit to enjoy watching professional motorsport, but have never been one to avidly read the motoring supplements of the weekend newspapers or been moved by the adrenaline, engine grease and testosterone of supercharged and supposedly sexy motors. Private registrations are perhaps part of this image but I have to come clean here and confess that I too have one. The plate was salvaged from a 1969 Ford Zephyr several years ago. It has my initials, KBM, followed by three numbers. When Kelso Binary Machines, with the advent of calculators, went into receivership I was there, like a vulture, at the auction. Having no obvious practical uses, a private registration does have its disadvantages. One of our receptionists once attempted to fob off a particularly hypochondriacal and trying patient by saying that Dr Moody was not actually in the surgery. "That's strange," my patient snorted, "there's a car with his initials on it, parked outside!"

People seem to lose sight of just how dangerous our roads are. In all the years I've worked here we've lost at least one patient annually on local roads. I suppose this tallies, when you consider one percent of the population is going to meet their fate this way or that, globally, one million people perish on the roads each year. I read recently that the insurance industry in the UK calculates that the average person has a road accident every six years. Little comfort to those who have driven for decades trouble-free as boy (write-off-a-month) racer may be coming your way, literally.

Normally this column is composed of a few dry and dare I say witty observations but allow me to pull over, remove my goggles and driving gloves and express my, admittedly forthright, views.

It is a recipe for disaster to have any two vehicles travelling towards each other when the slightest error could (and does) result in carnage. Expensive as it would be, I believe all roads should be unidirectional, or at least have an impenetrable barrier between the two carriageways. As speed is a factor in most road deaths, I believe velocity should be constantly monitored. Rather than obvious, occasional cameras I would have every road stripe or cat's eye containing a sensor. On every residential road I would have numerous well-marked humps, as all other speed deterrents seem to be ignored by some drivers. Convictions for serious driving offences should lead to lifetime bans and flouting of these bans to imprisonment. Drivers on reaching the age of seventy at present are asked simply to declare to the DVLA whether they suffer any medical conditions that may impair their ability to drive. I believe this should be far more objective and independent medical assessment of health, reaction times and spatial awareness conducted. This is *not* the same as asking a septuagenarian driver to resit his driving test.

All strong stuff I know and I anticipate a fuller mailbox than usual this week in response.

"So, Sadie Gonzales, I'm not impressed by your poor and dangerous driving. Roll up your sleeve please. I'll just pop this needle in your vein, but for the sake of other road users I should really be sticking it in your tyres."

VISITING PATIENTS

"I've heard you no longer visit patients at home, Dr Ken," stated Isadora Jarr quite erroneously. The nature of general practice has changed considerably in recent years and indeed the way it is practised but this does not, and I doubt ever will, include the "abolition" of home visits (house calls). Work has become more intense and generally busier and as a consequence we had to take a hard look at what qualifies for a house call and what can be dealt with by other means. Visits to patients at home naturally take longer than consultations in surgery, and if fewer people get seen overall can we possibly justify this?

There is no doubt that, although we saw fewer patients in a working week, Dr Bodie Aiken and I used to visit far more patients than we do now. In days when life, and even the Tweed, seemed to flow just that little bit more slowly we could find ourselves calling on a dozen or more patients each day. It is perhaps about a third of that now. There was a certain pleasure and sociability about these visits and my tea consumption could be counted in gallons and capacity for shortbread knew almost no bounds. To the envy of any ambitious estate agent, I could claim to have been in almost every house in the practice, before the new–builds went up.

Seeing people in their own environment can be useful. Various "clues" can support or prompt diagnoses such as: numerous lemonade bottles and undiagnosed diabetes; twittering budgies and lung diseases or abject squalor and developing dementia. There was also a certain luxury to be able to concentrate on one patient at a time before the advent of the ubiquitous and intrusive mobile phone. I recall, when working at another practice, visiting an elderly couple one Friday morning. After dealing with their ailments they invited me to take a seat on the couch and, as the late Dr Slouch used to do, have an hour's sleep. "He worked so hard during the week," they explained, "We were always so grateful for his visits and happy for him to get some rest." I often wonder if he had four other households, equally grateful for his weekly visits!

In retrospect, many of the numerous house calls we did were really not necessary. If a doctor *needs* to visit it should be when the patient is too unwell or simply unable to leave the house. It was, and is, irritating to drive miles to a house to find a note taped to the front door, "At the hairdresser's, back in an hour." (I am not suggesting that better planning would have meant a rendezvous at the salon but rather that this lady's priorities and thoughts of appropriate use of the medical services were as curled as her locks are now.)

We never have a problem visiting the likes of old Miss Niamh Ver Owt. She is housebound and although she manages to get around her sheltered house, could not safely cross the threshold without the near certainty of falling and fracturing the other hip. Of course, anyone at any time can become too unwell to leave the house and we will make every effort to visit. We also try to call on people recently discharged from hospital after major surgery or serious illness. Terminally ill patients appreciate, and often need, regular visits and District and McMillan nurses have an invaluable role here too.

In order to apportion our time and work as effectively as we can, we like to speak to patients or carers when they request a visit. Some issues can clearly be dealt with appropriately over the phone and sometimes the reason for a request is rather spurious (such as the wish not to miss the TV repair man!) Even in the emergency situation a brief description, rather than the abrupt message, "Tell the doctor to visit," can make all the difference to when and how we respond.

So, although doctors in most European countries don't do visits at all, we still do here. It may not be on demand or as sociably and as often as before, but we do still visit, Mrs Jarr.

UPSTAIRS, DOWNSTAIRS

"Excuse the mess, Dr Ken," apologised Kay Oss as I stepped gingerly over a pile of laundry and slalomed around warring cats and children. GPs do not visit patients at home quite as often (or as liberally) as we once did and have become used to the relative sterility, convenience and safety of the surgery, It is often assumed, perhaps correctly, that doctors don't like venturing out. Don't breathe a word of this to my partner Dr Bodie Aiken, as it goes against all current medical thinking, but I really do rather enjoy house calls. Seeing patients in their own environments can be enlightening and reconnects me to the realities of life. This may be witnessing teenagers' angst with their Gothic wall decorations and music or understanding the plight of elderly folk shivering in a frigid room having run out of coins for the meter.

I enjoy travelling to people's homes. In finer weather I've been known to ride my 1928 Roadmaster bicycle to some of our more local patients, but during the other eleven months of the year the jalopy has to do. I enjoy classical music, so leaving behind the pressures of the surgery and humming along to Haydn or giving a rendition of Don Giovanni, that is more karaoke than Carreras, can be a tremendously therapeutic thing (but not for those who stumble within earshot, I daresay!)

Mrs Moody subscribes to monthly magazines such as *Impossibly Perfect Celebrity Homes* and *Country Homes in the City*. I usually scoff at such "commercial shallow nonsense" (I don't pretend to be easy to live with) but in idle and unguarded moments have been discovered leafing through them too. My usual spluttered excuse is that I am ensuring they are suitable for the surgery waiting room.

Some residences I visit are reminiscent of these images but many are, well, not. It would be unfair to pass judgement on the tidiness or otherwise of homes when the occupant is ill but certain clues can be garnered about how people live. Never being one to inspect a moistened index finger drawn over a dusty surface, but dirty riding stirrups in the dishwasher and warm damp sticky sofas don't require a forensic mind to ascertain that a less than magazine lifestyle is practised therein.

Most people do live proudly and keep their homes in a presentable fashion. In these more rural parts I admire the antique furniture and instruments people have on display, my particular favourites being longcase clocks and barometers. Often these were made locally a century and a half, or longer, ago. The craftsmanship and talent that existed in these rural communities have now largely been lost. People are always happy to discuss the provenance of such heirlooms, though I ensure I only enquire once the "medical business" is done.

Retirement carriage clocks (remind me to accept mine graciously, Mrs Moody), souvenirs from yesteryear's Greek Island holiday and greetings cards commonly decorate mantelpieces. Early colour family wedding photos or sepia prints of previous generations' celebrations are often fixed to the wall. Children's early school pictures or later ones of graduations will be proudly discussed if commented upon.

But the television with all its viewing paraphernalia is the focus of most modern living rooms. The altar at which we worship. Perhaps fearing less than the maximum value for the license fee, it seems to be invariable left on. I recall once sounding a sick little girl's chest and found that her faint breath and heart sounds were easily drowned out by the dog and the daytime TV quiz show. Without removing my stethoscope I gestured to father saying, "do you mind…?" "Sorry doc", he replied but, misunderstanding me, simply changed channels.

The patient may be too sick to even make it down to the living room. A few bounds up, past the stairlift or yet more washing, finds me on the landing. From there I have to deduce behind which of the five doors my patient ails.

Bedrooms are usually little more than an over-proportioned double bed and an angular wardrobe jammed against a wall. Occasionally an exercise bike or clotheshorse is wedged in somehow. The patient is *always* on the further away side of the bed and examinations have to be conducted with me kneeling across the vacant half. Only once has a wooden mattress support snapped under my great muckle knee (better that than my back I suppose!)

Crikey, wait a minute, it's Friday today. Mrs Mhairi Gould our cleaner will be at our house, this morning. Last night I threw my long johns only vaguely in the direction of the laundry basket. Here am I describing other folks' houses and my own is a tip. I'd better phone Mrs Moody right now. We can't have Mhairi describing to the whole town the squalor in which the doctor lives.

THE BLUE LIGHT

Contrary to what TV dramas would have us believe, much of general practice is actually fairly humdrum. Days go by without anything of particular novelty or interest occurring. I, of course, give each case my undivided attention and treat it on its own merits. Or, at least I try. But as seasoned and curmudgeonly as you know me to be, you'd be a little suspicious of my sincerity (and sanity) were I to dance excitedly around the surgery whenever a fungal toenail or warty finger is pointed in my direction. I would actually say that, if this were the entire range of pathology I encounter in the four-decade career in which I sail, I would have abandoned the good ship *Medicine* long ago.

No, it the excitement of the emergency situation that pumps the adrenaline, quickens the pulse and dries the throat. It serves to remind us what we were trained to do, and few doctors shy away from the challenges it brings. By its very nature the emergency is unexpected, unpredictable and, well, pretty unbeatable to tell you the truth.

From a purely practical point of view though, emergencies can be wretched nuisances. Surgeries unavoidably run late and there is a danger of less serious, or even other urgent, cases failing to receive the attention they deserve.

Living rurally as we do, we are rather removed from the main hospitals. As governments consolidate and modernize (read "cutback") care and resources, we sometimes find ourselves being, and feeling, even more isolated. It is in Critical and Emergency care that proximity to treatment matters most.

Not being a politician or even that way inclined (I could never shed the corduroy and tweed!) I don't have much influence over such services. I therefore feel that the onus is on me to attend injuries, collapses and other medical emergencies when they occur in this domain. Local and medical knowledge of our patients, and even the familiar geography, can make a vital difference.

We have a good relationship with the attending paramedics and ambulance crews. Although they are still based locally, gone are the days when a quick call to the unit, or even Lance St John lunching at home, was sufficient. Our calls are now relayed to a distant centre and I have the apparent pleasure of speaking to a different operator each time. Once she has asked me to spell my name (how much more phonetic could it be?) and the surgery's full postal address, only then can I pass on the needs of my ailing patient. I am then asked "what priority of response is being requested, doctor?" Such levels of priority are arbitrarily: blue light; within the hour or within four hours. I know of colleagues (elsewhere of course) who exaggerate a little to "upgrade" the situation. This may seem to be to a patient's advantage but I have a little difficulty with this. Only last week, I was criticised by a family over my stance. An older man, weighing little less than a small family car, crashed over. Hugh Morris's upper arm was almost certainly broken and neither he nor I could get him to his feet again. I asked for an ambulance to arrive within the hour, as I would have felt uncomfortable requesting a "blue light" response. I am not going to subject other road users to risk by initiating an ambulance that will travel at break-neck speed, jumping red lights to whisk Hugh to the infirmary. I hoped that it might arrive within twenty minutes but it took the full sixty to draw up outside the house. The family could not share my interpretation of priority or see the broader picture, but there you are.

As rural doctors, we need to carry with us quite a collection of emergency equipment, as we're often first on the scene. In the boot of my car there are various cases of medicines and bandages, but by far the most important and useful item is my *Sandpiper* bag. This is a comprehensive kit bag that was designed and equipped by doctors who work regularly in roadside/bedside/countryside emergency care. These bags are gifted to appropriately trained medics by the *Sandpiper Trust*. This marvellous organisation was created by a family in central Scotland after the tragic loss of their 14-year-old son, by drowning. To date over 500 bags have been distributed throughout Scotland, each at great expense. It is the Trust's hope that lives will be saved through the ready availability of this emergency equipment. I agree with them that this is the greatest legacy there could be to the memory of young Sandy Dickson.

The week after I received my bag, I attended a biker who failed to negotiate a corner, striking a telegraph pole. His shoulder was shattered and a damaged lung rapidly filled with blood. I quickly placed him in a cervical collar, drained his lung and got him promptly off to hospital. I am sure I did not save his life but felt so much more confident at the availability of the bag and its contents and also at the expert tuition, fresh in my memory.

So, if you wake up next week to find yourself lying in the High Street, fear not (or fear less!). You might just have this wizened, quizzical face looking down at you.

I may not be terribly much help, but there will be either an ambulance or a cup of hot sweet tea on its way to you.

THE ARTIST

Roy Gebiv was a talented painter who specialized in oils, having a particular flare for colours and the abstract. He was a slightly shy fellow who lived for his work. He was not a religious man but was probably one of the most spiritual people I have ever met. His paintings, he would claim, bore a greater likeness to what he felt the scene conveyed rather then what the eye saw. Viewers and prospective buyers would nod uncertainly. He was not world, or even nationally, renowned nor did he ever express such a desire. He earned enough from the occasional sale of his work to pay for his materials, his food and his beloved wine.

I tended only to hear of him in passing or when reading reviews in local newspapers. We have one of his earlier works, in a chunky frame, in our dining room. Dinner guests often give their own interpretations of the splashes and smears upon the canvas and these usually start with the suggestion that it may be hanging the wrong way round!

As a patient, Roy did not darken (or lighten) the surgery door often as he kept in pretty good health. One afternoon, I was called by someone requesting that I visit Roy. Knowing such a request suggested a probable need, I took a few details and promised to call that evening. After bidding my last patient in surgery a good night, I drove out to Roy's cottage. The timber door was eventually opened by a girl, probably mid-twenties, wearing absolutely nothing other than a cord necklace and a slightly anxious smile. I've been met with few more memorable sights on my visits but could not help noticing her rather prominent appendicectomy scar. She did not seem bothered or even aware of her state of undress and, having never been introduced, seemed to make the assumption I was not attending to sell insurance. I confirmed it was me she had spoken with earlier and asked after the patient. Florence led me through to his studio and waved a slender arm, by way of apparent explanation. The studio was considerably tidier and better organized than when I last visited and suggested either a fastidious or absent artist. Not certain what was meant, I asked her to explain. "Can't you see doctor? Just look at his recent paintings." Donning my specs and stooping to study, I looked along a line of magnificent landscapes and a nude worthy of comparison to a Raphael. There was utterly no doubt Florence was the subject, further confirmed by the detailed representation of her appendicectomy scar; an operation unlikely to have been performed in early 16th century Italy. With a slight shiver, as though she suddenly became aware of her nakedness and imperfection, she reached for a chemise and slipped it on.

The final painting was one of the finest portraits of an older man I had ever seen. Every wrinkle and whisker was beautifully recreated and the shading was to near perfection. What was particularly evident though, was that the subject only met my gaze with one eye. His other was in a divergent squint and there seemed a slight drooping on that side of the face. Noticing my questioning look, Florence explained cryptically that Roy "was but wasn't himself anymore." His work had gone from the typically abstract to the stunningly accurate. Coarse daubs had evolved into fine details. Rather like Picasso's career, only in reverse.

I asked where Roy was and was shown through to the adjoining bedroom. He had apparently taken to sleeping for interminably long periods but when awake would talk and paint incessantly. Sitting up, he expressed both recognition and pleasure. With a dawning realization; I saw it was he who was the subject of the painting, a self-portrait.

I examined the unwell fellow and chided them a little for failing to contact me sooner, when something was so clearly wrong.

My fears were confirmed the following week with a scan. Roy

had a Glioblastoma, a rapidly progressing brain tumour. He declined any treatment, preferring to remain and work on in the studio. I did not argue with him, he was not suffering and was enjoying his last few weeks, with a vision and clarity he explained, he had been striving for all his life.

He left his entire estate to his model and companion, Florence. Galleries expressed an interest in displaying both his earlier and later works.

I sometimes look up from my roast beef and wonder if my guests were right after all, but it really does not matter. Art is for appreciating, not necessarily for understanding.

THE LION'S DEN

Leo Nynne missed his wife terribly. Her rapid demise at the end of last year left him bereft. He was truly lost without her.

Charm and good humour were not attributes Leo could claim as his own; he was not an endearing chap. I confess to having never found him the easiest of patients to deal with. He could be fierce, his bark and roar probably were as bad as his proverbial bite. His daughter once confided that he suffered a harsh and deprived childhood, by way of explanation I think for his behaviour. He didn't make friends easily and this added to the void, of which he was probably only too painfully aware. Acquaintances and neighbours passed on their condolences when Mrs Nynne died but after a few weeks they made themselves scarce. I always had sympathy for his long-suffering wife and felt it would have been more "just" had she outlived him. She might have enjoyed her twilight years without being subject to his constant criticism and negativity.

Aware that his house was too big for just one, he moved into a care facility weeks after the funeral. He almost moved south to be closer to his daughter but for some reason felt more comfortable remaining where he "knew people." I suspect Cleo was more than a little relieved at this decision!

The warden of the facility and others commented to me many times that Leo was "getting worse." His temper was even shorter and he was an exaggeration, as it were, of his former self. I felt the diagnosis of depression was straightforward, even in the context of his personality. I visited him one afternoon, ostensibly to enquire after his wellbeing, but really to discuss the "possibility" of a

– 150 –

depressive illness and the potential benefits of appropriate treatment. Offence was taken, he made that clear. How dare I imply he was "a failure and not coping?" I was not aware I had suggested either, merely that I appreciated the loss of a soulmate and wife of forty-four years would be a great loss and perhaps even a catalyst for physical and mental ill-health. I had known him for twenty years and spoke as his doctor. But no, his "religious faith and strength of character" had sustained him until now and would continue to do so, he informed me curtly.

I left both his room and the issue at that. Weeks passed but I could not ignore the continued expressions of concern at how he spoke to, and treated, other residents and staff. I wrote to him saying, as unpopular as it might make me, I would contact my colleagues in community psychiatric nursing to ask for their objective opinion. He sent them packing on the first occasion but interestingly bid them enter his den on their second approach. They concurred with my diagnosis of reactive depression and agreed on which particular treatment may be best suited to him. This "collusion" only reinforced his view that I had it in for him, apparently.

He took legal advice and soon a solicitor's letter followed requesting a copy of his entire medical records, in case I had "misrepresented him and lied in this fashion for years." Reading on I learned that I "may have defamed and besmirched our mutual client's good name." Leo himself sent me spiteful letter after venomous note and my considered responses and apologies, for "inadvertent offence caused," only sharpened his claws. This seemed to have given him a new will to live, but his over-reaction only reinforced my belief that he needed help.

I happened to visit his neighbour one day. After completing that call I stood outside Leo's room. I felt it might be an opportunity to pour oil on troubled waters. I took a deep breath and rapped the brass knocker. After several minutes, and as I was about to leave, the door opened slowly. He looked me up and down before snarling. He had nothing to say to me and was aware I had not come all this way just to visit him. (Quite how he knew this or why it was relevant I'll never know.) Before there was time to reply. I had two inches of solid pine closed on me. Even the brass face seemed to stare coldly at me.

I never saw or heard from him again. He died a few months later, never calling on medical services again. I suspect in his final illness he suffered pain, needlessly. I was rather sad. Sad that a professional relationship had been damaged beyond apparent repair. Sad that I acted in his best interests, as I saw it, but received only harsh rejection. Sad also that he went to his grave suffering and as bitter and resentful as he was.

Perhaps like Androcles, I only offered to pull the thorn from the paw of this injured lion.

GLOVES OFF

"You'll do the annual boxing match again this year again, I'm sure doc," declared Frank O'Raitor, our ever (and perhaps over) enthusiastic local fight promoter. Frank being Frank, it was more of a statement than a question, but most people know better than to argue with him. For the last decade or more I've agreed to be the ringside medic, there to administer: stitches, advice and the occasional declaration that a poor lad just cannot go on.

Many of my colleagues in medicine draw the line at boxing and other pugilistic or contact sports on the premise that being seen to condone, albeit mutually consenting fighters knocking ten bells out of each other, is not justifiable. Statistically, boxing has far fewer fatalities and serious injuries than, say, horse riding or diving but the prevalence of brain injury in later life is still being researched. I confess to having adopted a slightly more relaxed attitude about the "sweet science" and acknowledging that, as such events are going to proceed regardless, it would be better to have a doctor present to administer immediate assistance when it is needed.

Whether it is testosterone or just showmanship, many young men have an aggression that needs to be channelled. Most decent citizens would rather that it wasn't directed towards breaking windows, knocking policemen's hats off or worse and so the noble art of western boxing should be encouraged. If a chap would sooner study the works of Wordsworth, Browning or Auden then so be it, but should he wish to place a bookmark carefully between the pages and set such esteemed works aside for a while then he is welcome to don the leather gloves and release some of the passion and ardour that these great poets were inclined to engender.

So, once again that cold Saturday October night, I tied the bowtie tightly and set forth to the civic hall with my bag of bandages, smelling salts and other paraphernalia.

There is something about a darkened hall with floodlights focusing on the square (and oddly named) ring. Perhaps for me it some unachieved sporting dream or ambition, though I would not choose for my sons to enter any such arena. But could broken noses, fat lips and cauliflower ears be earned more nobly, except perhaps on a rugby field?

The Marquis of Queensbury made the rules; the same rule maker who ensured Oscar Wilde found himself in the dock and was sentenced to hard labour. Nonetheless, the black and white shirted referee makes instant decisions and, like Frank and the Marquis, there is no arguing. "Above the belt remember, no head butting and good cleaning punches, gentlemen. Break when I say and stop on the bell." Such absolute discipline and respect is surely an example to us all. Ding, ding. They're off. A customary, but sporting, initial meeting of gloves and months of training are about to determine a winner and a loser. But are there winners and losers, victors and vanquished? Is it not the very taking part that counts?

Such controlled, though naked, aggression (except for a pair of oversize shorts!) is something indeed to marvel. Walter Waite and his evenly matched opponent C. N. Starrs dance as if the skipping ropes are still rotating around them. Rather than be treated to the repetitive playground skipping rhymes, the cries of coaches and colleagues drone on with constant advice. Advice and barked commands that fill the, already adrenaline and aftershave-filled, atmosphere. For it is a male sport on the whole, one of the last bastions of chauvinism, I daresay. A few molls are present in their sequined low-cut dresses but the notion of Madame Defarge at the guillotine is an image I cannot rid myself of.

Already, despite the headguard and gumshield, Walter takes a direct blow to the face and blood oozes. I stand up ready to inspect. The referee gestures for me to remain seated while he assesses the damage and wipes away the blood with tissue in plastic gloved hand. I seem only to be here for more serious injuries and realise I am a mere cog in the workings of this well-oiled fight machine, but a cog the governing body insists upon. The first short round is over and a young lady, showing as much flesh as I suppose is appropriate for the sweaty conditions, displays a board announcing for the less well initiated that the next round is predicted to be the second.

Walter and C. N. are in the red and blue corners respectively having tactical instructions and cold water pushed down their throats. Grease to the eyebrow and a swab to the nose and in no time proceedings resume. Ducking and diving, lunging then shielding, they re-engage. The red-faced passion of those ringside causes me to check that my defibrillator is to hand should a blood vessel actually burst. A few more collective cheers, gasps and stoppages and before we know it the contest is over. The ever-smooth compere in a dinner jacket thanks the sponsors (surely he didn't just say the Women's Rural Institute, did he?) and, reading the judges' verdicts, raises a weary gloved hand aloft.

No Frank, it's an amateur sport, keep your fistful of banknotes. I'm glad these lads enjoyed themselves. They're better off in your back street gym than on the streets swigging cheap wine and reeling in a purposeless moral vacuum. I know Dr Bodie Aiken doesn't approve or agree with me but what I've seen again this evening I'm happy to support.

OFF DUTY

SHATTERED

We went up to the city last weekend. Perhaps I should have known better, but my son and his wife, for the urbanites that they have become, do cook a good game pie. After a pleasant evening of chat and a (strictly single) glass of Merlot, we bid our leave for the journey home. Sadly, a passer-by had taken it upon himself to ensure abundant and excessive ventilation for our vehicle. The brick lying on my seat and the thousands of pieces of glass scattered throughout were most unwelcome. "Dash, bother, tarnation, darn it all; this never happens in the country (but I know that it does.) Why do folks do such things?" It wasn't even for the vaguely plausible reason of theft, as nothing was taken. This anti-social and offensive deed was just mindless vandalism. The police, they were afraid, were occupied that evening with matters of damage to person, rather than just property. I couldn't argue with that, though momentarily felt like trying.

Our further misfortune was that it was the wettest, coldest night of the year. There was a sufficiently stiff gale to direct precipitation horizontally, into the vehicle. Even if the rain had been falling vertically it would have mattered little as occupants were going to be soaked regardless. Attempts to secure tarpaulin failed miserably, and even if successful would have caused a certain inability to see anything in a forwards direction.

I had to return home that evening as I was on duty early the next morning. Mrs Moody and I are now a one-car family, and what this gesture may have been doing to slow global warming was being rapidly undone by my rather heated demeanour.

Mrs Moody's hair was only newly permed, and I doubt even donning goggles and flaps-down deerstalker (as I had to do) would have prevented a hairdressing catastrophe. She wished me well, found a spare toothbrush in the glove compartment and returned to the warm hearth.

The city may have more windscreen companies than we do in the shires, but Sunday evening is not the best time to call upon them, I discovered. Answer phones promising "resumption of normal service" at 9 o'clock Monday morning are not what one wishes to hear. After leaving numerous messages, I was eventually called *en route* home. My next task was to convince the good lady that my predicament was indeed an "emergency." Being rather a pedant with the use of this particular word, having heard it so often misused in a medical context, I found myself reassessing the semantics. Of course I "needed" my window replaced as soon as possible. Neither did I wish to pick fault with her use of the word "repair," as I had little doubt this severely damaged pane was well past actual repair, and that nothing short of replacement was required. Mindful also of Aesop's fable promoting gentle persuasion, and glancing once again at the inclement climatic conditions, I felt a polite request for reasonably prompt service was what was required.

So, if I could make my way home a "repairman", who was covering the whole region single-handedly and had three pending calls, would call me. There was no saying when he would ring but, when he did, could I please make my way back to the metropolis?

I duly returned home, changed into dry clothes and waited. My garage had piled in it two tons of logs, chopped earlier that week, so the car had to remain outside in the rain for a few more hours. Total upholstery saturation as opposed to partial, and by now a complete belief that the elements and fate had it in for me.

True to their word though, the call came at 11pm. I set off, weaving around felled branches and flooding on the road, appropriately listening to Wagner's *Ride of the Valkyries* on the radio. I soon found myself standing in a fluorescent-lit industrial unit in the early hours of Monday morning, drinking machine coffee. I chatted with Miller (his friends call him "Windae"!) as he expertly levered out the remaining fragments and retrieved from a gallery of thousands of windows and windshields, the very one I required.

Elsewhere in the garage there were five, more severely damaged cars than mine, waiting for the regular crew in the morning. Miller seemed in no rush and, after asking what I did for a living, proceeded to compare his job to mine. It may have been just blether and perhaps, like the glass he selected, he adjusted the chat to fit the occasion but I did not mind. I had nothing better to do. I learned about the benefits and dangers of laminated glass and which cars have windows that are especially difficult to replace. Amusingly, he said, some people think they have such high specification cars that the press of a hidden button will instantly reveal a replacement window. I heard that stranded motorists may take their anger out on the first person they see, usually the poor old windshield chap. I know that many patients and relatives become agitated and abusive when illness, accident or assault occur. While it may be their usual manner when confronting difficult or new situations, it never endears them to, or gains favour from, the listening ear. Everyone seems to think that their car, journey or predicament takes priority over others, and nothing but immediate attention will do.

Miller was right in many ways; our jobs are not too dissimilar. Services and professionals are always there, ready to assist, and we see the best and worst in people and in society.

Emergency workers don't seek praise but just do a decent, honest job, which gives satisfaction and pleasure (and is hopefully appropriately remunerated!)

There is a sense of achievement in helping people when they find themselves at their most vulnerable and, I daresay, that I was that night.

After an hour the job was done, the customer satisfied. I paid my insurance "excess", expressed my gratitude and drove wearily, dryly and carefully home.

KEEPING IN TOUCH WITH OLD COLLEAGUES

"You've been invited to a medical school reunion, Dr Ken", announced Mrs Mona Lotte our practice manager. I've come to accept her opening my mail on the premise that I have no skeletons in my closet (other than the one from my Anatomy days.) She also manages to shield me from unsolicited mail sent by the pharmaceutical industry and filters the computer-generated literature from the Health Board and numerous other agencies.

It is usually fun meeting old friends after years apart but reunions, especially at my age, can be poignant or even sad affairs. Some friends have already been through divorces or suffered illness or loss. Others sadly have gone from us altogether.

One might argue though that if you have had no contact with people in the last ten years you really can't have terribly much in common at all. Like Christmas cards, friendships can whittle down to a signature without so much as a comment from year to year. But effort should be made, if only to recall the "old days" and to take stock for a while.

I recall our ten-year reunion. Mrs Moody was in an advanced state of pregnancy at the time (I know better than to describe her with an adverb such as "heavily", in any context!) About half of our number appeared, most of the others were on-call or could not be contacted. Some had made their excuses, never being ones to "socialise." It was a dinner and black tie (or kilt, of course) affair. The food and wine was pleasant and the chat was amusing and varied. Although people tend not to change, many colleagues had frayed and greyed around the edges a little (they were too polite to pass comment on my appearance) and most had settled into comfortable positions throughout the country and beyond. Many had already achieved consultancy or some sort of status in the medical, or even real, world. Some colleagues had left medicine altogether, perhaps only attending out of curiosity or to confirm for themselves that they had made the right decision. I was tickled that one or two colleagues commented that they laughed at a remark or article I'd had published in the medical press (even at the funny ones!)

We were keen to share anecdotes about cases and voice our frustrations at the "interfering" government of the day and at the Health Service that we know and love.

I would never say our student days were innocent but we were undoubtedly naïve to the pressures, demands and responsibilities of working life. We were also very fortunate to study before student loans were introduced and when beer was not taxed out of sight. Hospitals were run by lofty consultants and wards by starchy matrons. A hospital manager was little more than a clerk and the species had not yet multiplied as fast as bacteria do on a hospital floor. "Management speak" was not a language in the curriculum and we did not work in a compensation or supermarket culture.

I remember my three closest friends at medical school. We spent much of our training together, often in far-flung district general hospitals. On our final evening before graduation, we dined out together (a rare treat). We were literally heading East, South, North and West. The East was home to Hong Kong for Victor and the South was to London for Sam. Martin headed to Grampian and I went to the Hebrides. It did seem, and was, a "parting of the ways." We have managed to keep in touch and email is an effective, though impersonal, way to do this.

I'll need to dust off my final year photograph to see how many faces I can still put names to.

Yes, Mrs Lotte, drop the medical school secretary a line. I will go to the reunion but send in the next patient first, there's work to be done.

THERE IS NOTHING LIKE A DAME

It's curtain down on panto season once again. Oooooh yes it is, I'm afraid!

I believe that was my tenth year treading the boards and the fun never wavered. From mid October rehearsals stepped up to twice weekly. I suppose you could say in the latter part of each year I assumed the role of a grotesque figure of fun who was jeered and laughed at, and that's often before my inclusion in the cast was confirmed!

It was really by default that I first found myself donning the greasepaint and garish costumes. It was only a minor role, but one of the trees in the woodland scene, ironically "fell" ill. Elma Forrest sat feverishly in surgery late one afternoon, clearly concerned that she would never make curtain up in little over two hours. Before I could find an excuse to be elsewhere she thanked me. All I had to do was spruce myself up, plant myself on stage, wait fir my cue and I'd likely twig what was going on. If I was no good, she duly informed me, I would be swiftly axed. (This clearly was only the start of a week of groan inducing j-oaks!) Once inducted, I was duly asked to stump up the obligatory membership fee for the Peeblesshire Amateur Noël Thespian Organisation (not only "amateur" but actually paying for the pleasure!)

So, I pitched up at the theatre that evening only to be met with some rather incredulous looks and comments from the more seasoned performers, some of whom doubled as patients. What on earth was I doing backstage? Had someone, true to the customary bidding, actually broken a leg? When it was learned that Dr Ken was filling a gap in the forest my fellow thesps rallied round. A costume was found (little more than corrugated cardboard and a massive green wig) and I was to take my cue from neighbouring arboreal board-treaders. Nothing could go wrong and nor did it. But I was bitten, not by Dutch Elm disease but by the acting bug. Thereafter, it became accepted that my evening surgeries throughout December became a rarity, as I was performing.

From second tree on the left, I progressed up the shaky ladder to: villager; shopkeeper; back-end of panto cow; front-end of panto horse; stepfather; stepmother; ugly sister; village idiot and finally to the dizzy heights (in those dizzy heels!) the dame herself. And in the immortal words of Oscar Hammerstein, there really is nothing like her!

From a non-speaking part I was soon strutting about on stage like the best of them. Indeed I was described "like a man all at sea" by the *Peeblesshire News* theatre critic a few years ago when we put on *The Pirates of Zen Pants* (a corruption of the great G&S musical about Cornish miscreants.) Praise indeed! This year my Scots accent (and girth) broadened and my rollers in a ginger mop peeked out from under a wide-brimmed hat. The bust verged on the impossible and was supported by tightly folded arms as I bustled about. My make-up took a good hour to be plastered on and the lipstick was applied minutes before curtain-up. Over the top? Of course it was, it's panto.

I take my ribboned straw hat off though to real actors. You can get away with so much in this form of variety/vaudeville, call it what you will, but those who learn copious lines and have a real grasp of what the scriptwriter intended are the ones who deserve the loudest applause. You cannot ad-lib to Shakespeare, nor should you try. I am not such an actor and never will be. I need the occasional prompt and my sense of timing can be a little (woops!) off.

Writers, directors, lighting crew, musicians and producers are often overlooked but deserve great credit for creating, ushering, highlighting, introducing and enabling us to be there at all.

I now always go to see a "serious" play or musical when performed locally, as I know the considerable work and effort that goes into each production.

Perhaps the greatest aspect of being in this troupe, however briefly each year, is the camaraderie that there is. The after-show parties are memorable and there is much unwinding that takes place. Anecdotes and aperitifs aplenty and a chance to laugh at all the audience reactions, silly blunders and missed cues during the week.

Pantomime, from its possible Greek origins and certain Italian *Commedia dell'arte* influence has come a long way. Many highbrow critics have pooh-poohed it as an art form but some acclaimed actors have recently donned costumes, come panto season. They, and countless drama groups up and down the land, breathe life into this peculiar brand of entertainment.

There is humour at all levels. Whether it is the innuendo that flies over the heads of the Brownies in the first four rows or just slapstick, all generations split their sides. Not for the prudish perhaps, but few fail to be entertained.

Support your local panto folks. Hiss the villain, boo the witch, cheer the hero and laugh at the dame and the man in the gorilla suit.

I've served my time on stage though and have been asked to co-write next year's production. The best bit is, I'll be able to sit front of house and see and appreciate quite how funny the whole lark is. Panto's an escape and, unlike real life, always has a happy ending.

GLORY BUT NO POWER

We had a pleasant enough Christmas, thank you very much. No matter how much older and wiser we get, it's usually a bit of a rush in the lead up to the day itself.

I always enjoy the Watchnight service. The colder it is outside the merry little kirk the better, and traditional hymns bring back warm memories of childhood.

On Christmas morning I like to drop in on a few of the older folk in the community. Old neighbours, Stephen Feest and Agnes Fontagne, have no one else left in the world, and I'm only too happy to take them each a sack of coal. The cottage hospital is always a jolly place at this time of year and a prize in the raffle is practically assured.

I should have known though that things were not going to run smoothly when Mrs Moody came to unwrap her present. I thought it would have been safe buying a perfume, but discovered that nowadays men are as vain and varied in their tastes as women. Well, I know now, I'd bought her an aftershave. The scent has been sent back.

Relatives, old and young, started arriving just after noon. After I had taken all the coats and ushered Mrs Moody's innumerable aunts through to the drawing room for sherry, a slightly flustered Mrs M appeared from around the door. We had no power, she said, in something approaching an hysterical whisper. Not a sausage, and by implication: not a giblet, breast or leg either. The lights, refrigerator and, most pertinently, the electric oven were out, warming and cooling respectively. Oh dear. The weather was reasonably clement, this was no Act of God and we haven't had a power cut here in years. Our goose was only partially cooked and images of food poisoning sprang to mind. No point in asking to use our neighbours' oven. The Swans would be in the same pickle and would only have room for their own part-cooked bird. I've always resisted microwave ovens, and of course one would be no use either, having no volts at our disposal. My suggestion to finish off the main course with my blowtorch did not get the reception I was hoping for. The look I got back was a good deal frostier than the bird's. There was no alternative; we would have to raid the pantry. It was cold meat and salad all round this festive season.

After lunch we gathered round Aunt Joanna at the piano. She hammered away on the keys as we belted out carols and Gilbert & Sullivan numbers. Lit candles sat on every surface, the baubles on the tree glistened and I stoked the fire. The aunts were the ones who coped best and seemed to have the most fun. The kids' DVDs naturally wouldn't work and they didn't want to play boring old board games, they said glumly. It was just like old times the aunts chorused, just like the ones they used to know. Charades and trivia quizzes are good fun, if but once a year, and I still don't accept you can see the Great Wall of China from the moon.

Did I know that only 3% of Christmas cards this year feature the Nativity? Did I know experts have calculated the average family fall out on Christmas day at 4.17pm? (Quite what Her Majesty says that inspires animosity within an hour of her going off air I do not know!) Fortunately we had no such arguments after the most improvised and hastily arranged Christmas meal we've served to date. By late afternoon more senior members of the family where either in animated conversation or snoring loudly (funny what a glass of wine, to the unaccustomed, will do!)

The chimes of the longcase clock sounded ten and it was time to disperse. Apologies again for the situation; beyond our control, of course. Yes, I suppose it was like the last war, though I wasn't actually there. No doodlebugs overhead, just errant kids with party-poppers to make you jump.

As I went to retrieve Aunt Ginger's slightly fusty coat from the hall cupboard, I realised what had happened. Fox fur? Faux pas! The wretched thing had slipped off the hanger, tripping the mains switch. I gathered my composure and, coward that I am, only switched it back on again when my better half had gone to make a start on the dishes.

Still, this time of year is very much about tradition. We take a lot for granted, as those who have survived wars will remind us. We often lose sight of the true value of Christmas and the difficulties others did, and do, face. We are victims (or suckers) to the trappings of consumerism. We rely so much on heat, light and power at the flick of a switch (worse luck!) and our energy needs seem to ever rise.

You won't tell Mrs Moody about what happened, will you? It was an accident. You know, the fox that snatched the goose from right under our noses, and both long dead too. A sort of posthumous Aesop or a part humorous sop? Read into it as you will.

I write this (increasingly candid) column without Mrs Moody knowing. I'd hate for her to discover what really happened that day. She's best left in the dark (and perhaps will be used to this now!)

HOLIDAY SNAPS

"I think the readers may be interested in where a doctor takes his holiday Ken, and perhaps what reading material he takes with him."The editor put this to me during one of our regular meetings. In truth, I've always felt these sessions a little like the ones that occur between the prime minister and Her Majesty at the palace. The offices on Northgate admittedly are marginally less opulent than those at postcode SW1A 1AA but otherwise the proceedings, I suspect, are conducted in a similar fashion.

This year, as many before, Mrs Moody and I spent our vacation in East Anglia. On this occasion, two of our grandchildren accompanied us. My son, Guy Moody, and his wife remain extremely busy, simultaneously running an ostrich farm and the South of Scotland Space Programme, or SSSP (not a million miles away from the Soviet CCCP emblazoned rockets.) Mrs Moody and I maintain a dignified silence about both their occupations, believing sadly that neither will really get off the ground. Ever supportive though, we packed both ourselves and these two extra little Moodys in the old converted Bedford ambulance, and headed south. Our hopes of a peaceful journey and stay down there were patently naïve. No Mr Mozart or Karl Jenkins *en route,* rather we found ourselves singing along to tapes such as *Endless Jungle & Farm Animal Songs.*

Our destination, as ever, was the pleasant little Georgian town of Funn–next–the–sea. In fact it is a full seven miles from the coast but the town elders, in their wisdom, are mindful of the severe coastal erosion in that part of the country and anticipate themselves indeed to be subject to tide times in less than a generation from now.

There certainly is plenty for the young ones to do in East Anglia. Crab catching, seal watching and just messing about on the sands whiled away the days. Reliable old grandpa was there to tend and patch the scrapes, purchase tickets, pick sand out of sandwiches and toes and ensure hats and suncream were always applied.

I have to say that the traffic there is becoming a major problem. Quaint towns with higgledy-piggledy houses placed cheek-by-jowl were never intended to have four–wheel drives or any other vehicle driven along their cobbled streets. Picturesque places naturally attract tourists, ourselves included. On occasion, we found it simply impossible to park. I would never stoop low enough, of course, to deposit the charabanc in a space reserved for doctors or ambulances, regardless of how plausible she looks.

For the second half of our holiday, perhaps against our better judgement, we stayed with Mrs Moody's sister and her husband. Mr and Mrs Pryor-Booking never pretended to like children and indeed shipped their own off at the earliest opportunity to boarding school.

We never seem to learn from past visits and again forgot to take groceries and provisions, not only for ourselves but our "hosts." Clearly all their previously arranged engagements were of greater importance and we saw very little of them. When they did return to the house they were so worn-out from their social excursions that they would require peace and quiet. On rising, I would mischievously offer them a "hair of the dog" or to take the phone off the hook to gain their undivided attention, but I think the irony was lost. Frankly, we have little interest in their closest chums, heirs to a spicy food empire no less, Lady Mildred and Sir Horace Raddish. How they spend their time or curry favour is up to them of course, but children aside (as would be their choice) we left feeling just a little estranged.

Regrettably too, I had little time to sit down with the novels and paperbacks I had taken with me. *Bus stops of Selkirkshire*, by O.Clapham Ryder was even less gripping than one might imagine. I confess to some bemusement with modern bestsellers. Dull, dark esoteric works or myriad variations around the murder-mystery theme abound. Some authors, whether particularly original or not, seem to tap into the public's imagination and achieve great popularity and success. Very little literature tries to be, or is, overtly funny. Numerous authors, with their copious writings, may have stirred many emotions in their readership but rarely raise even the corners of one's mouth. I think this is a pity as life is often hard and dreary enough without having to read of more misery. My choices are anthologies of quotes or books by the likes of: Spike Milligan, Stephen Fry, Winston Churchill, Groucho Marx, Oscar Wilde, Douglas Adams, Dorothy Parker, Tom Sharpe, Mark Twain and Jonathan Swift. Cartoons by Giles, Larson or from Punch are often enough to have me falling off my fireside chair (ideally away from the hearth.)

I am not a complete giggling hedonist with my reading tastes though. I am easily absorbed by national and local newspapers. With the latter, it is interesting to note that this rather under-utilised resource has many similarities with other weeklies the length and breadth of the country. Letters to such newspapers are almost invariably ones of complaint, which perhaps says more about human psychology than most other things. People do care though about their schools, health services and use of their taxes. Crime is a prevailing blight and fatalities on the roads are as common and needless as they are tragic. The sense of community is not dead but society is undoubtedly becoming increasingly selfish, aggressive and fragmented.

After two weeks of paradoxical bliss, aggro, relaxation and stress we returned home. I managed to acquire a genuine Captain's chair after years of searching. The old Bedford was so laden with "stuff" that the said item had to be strapped to the roof. Quite what other road users thought of an ambulance with an upright but vacant chair salvaged from the *SS Norwich,* strapped where the blue light used to be, I'll never know.

I do hope the readership appreciate my holiday experiences

and musings Mr Editor, sir. As I'm sure they rediscover for themselves each year, spending so much time with our families is not necessarily of our choosing or liking. Holidays can be anything other than relaxing. I'll spare you the dozens of photos we took and respectively ask others to do the same.

LETTING ONE'S REMAINING HAIR DOWN

"Was that you in *The Goose* last night blethering with your buddies, Dr Ken?" asked Phyllis Glass one Friday morning. I was surprised she even had to ask as we've met there regularly for years and, now that the air is free of smoke and piped music, my profile and laugh are anything but ambiguous.

Once a week, after I've bolted the storm door to the surgery, devoured a steak pie, exercised the Labradors and my mind with a crossword (the dogs are not so good at anagrams!), I'll don the windcheater and head down to *The Goose*. Mrs Moody and I have an understanding; we each have an evening when we spend a few hours in the good company of respective friends. She to the Borders Ladies Arts and Handicrafts (BLAH) or the Intermediate belly dancing class (as if there would be more than one!) and I to the tavern for all too brief an interlude of ale, cheer and a conviction that we may have saved the world each week.

If it were suggested that we are a varied and talented group I would have to admit my contribution is slight. Comparisons with the regular meetings of CS Lewis, JRR Tolkien and friends in Oxford's *Eagle and Child* in the 1950s are perhaps fanciful but then the writer of this very column attends, does he not? These great authors wrote about magical, mythical creatures and I accept the notion that the good people of Peeblesshire, of whom I often and fondly write, may be heavenly but themselves likely find my musings and jottings less than fabulous.

The landlord, Harry, is a friendly and tolerant chap. He is of course quite literally accommodating but we've never yet had to shelter there for the night, always managing to find our ways home after last orders. He kindly lays on a spread of cold meats, humus, olives, cheeses and other welcome fare. This tends to materialize when he's aware that our conversation has become particularly animated.

But what of the jolly party itself? Whether we are a veritable collection of ne'er-do-wells or e'er-do-wells is perhaps for others to judge. Amongst us we have a rather comprehensive knowledge of the Arts, biology, botany, Information Technology, religion, ecclesiastical architecture, railways and canals, philosophy, etymology, history and politics (local, national and international), physics, literature and music. As for me, I have a passing knowledge of sport, current affairs and, to my eternal cost and ribbing, popular culture (I am in fact the youngest (or least senior!) of the assemblage and like to remind the others of this!) Increasingly the discussions are about the environment. Until recently, if asked whether I am doing enough to save the planet, I would have innocently enquired as to which one my efforts should be directed. Furthermore, carbon rationing, to me, meant only the need to scrape the burnt bits off my toast.

Logic would suggest we would make a fairly formidable quiz team but on the occasions we have put ourselves forward our performance has been dismal. This is largely because, even if an answer is within at least one skull, it will be argued and debated out again and an increasingly impatient quizmaster rushes us into supplying an erroneous compromise. Any self-respecting quizmaster will have lost both patience and sympathy after our repeated querying the validity of questions and the accuracy of his given answers.

Sometimes, evenings are given over in part to music. Amongst us we have a mandolinist, flautist, guitarist and squeezebox maestro. To say I am a percussionist may be overstating things but I can toe-tap, knuckle-rap and bang an Irish drum as well as the next man. In the absence of instruments one time, the spirit led us to sing

Victorian hymns with a resonance and enthusiasm reminiscent of a Borders' revival. Whether other drinkers thought they had stumbled on a temperance meeting I'll never know as the place was strangely empty by the time we departed.

Despite being tucked away in the Snug, other patrons of the establishment are often curious and are encouraged to join us. Ours is no clique, at least not by commission, and further views and contributions to debate are naturally welcome.

Sectarian and racist: never. Sexist, intemperate and controversial: occasionally. Challenging, politically incorrect and funny: always. "Boring? Us sir? Never. Be reminded that the most boring person in the world is a drunk. Ponder that sir and be aware you can sit elsewhere." (Usually said with the gesticulation of a hand holding a metaphorical or unlit clay pipe!)

"T'was me you saw last night, Phyllis. I've come to rely on this band of brothers, these comrades, kindred spirits and ale house scholars. It doesn't detract from my work as your doctor and I'm prepared to argue it makes me a better one for it."

THE ANNUAL SMOKER

In previous years I always found a reason not to attend the local Annual Smoker.

I never was as obvious as to suggest that I wash my hair every second Friday in November, and latterly such an excuse would have worn as thin as the strands themselves. I am certainly in favour of a few hours of exclusively male company and am usually amused to see other sides to normally taciturn and polite farmers, rugby players and other patients. I enjoy hearing local characters being ribbed or even lampooned and know that in my absence I've been the butt of this too. Comic legend and local anecdote are often the best themes for humour and it is fitting that stories are embellished and remembered down the years. But the main reason I previously declined, to the point of losing further invitations, was that I just don't like thick, acrid smoke polluting my clothes and the substance of my lungs. I only have one pair of bellows and choose to keep them functional and soot-free. Besides, I felt there would be an air of hypocrisy or a sense of tacit approval in my attending. High vaulted ceilings perhaps, but scores of chaps puffing solidly for several hours was never my idea of fun. I'm led to believe that some non-smokers felt obliged to enter into the spirit (in all senses) of the evening and light up, stifling their coughs and splutters like experimenting miscreants and teenagers.

As a doctor, I am aware and reminded daily of the catastrophic effects that smoking can have on one's health. I was a supporter of the ban in public places when it was first debated. Now that the ban is in place and widely accepted and respected, would it be hypocritical of me, even now, to attend this event, I wondered? I decided for the first time to accept the invitation from the convener, Ashworth Stubbs, and thanked him for it. I admit I went partly out of curiosity. I was curious to see whether two-hundred hardened and newly initiated puffers would be huddled at the exits between courses and during speeches. Would the after dinner speakers fail to raise a laugh from an empty hall, save for the few waiters present? I knew there would be no dissenting smokers lighting up in the hall as the committee know that their license would be revoked as quickly as a nicotine addict tears the cellophane off his packet of cancer sticks. Mischievously, I felt I should attend to canvass opinion and witness whether gents can indeed enjoy an evening of side-splitting (and occasionally dubious!) jokes, while consuming a beverage or two, but this time in a smoke-free environment.

I have to say I was a little disappointed. Not at the food, as the caterers drafted in from *The Goose* surpassed themselves once again. Not disappointed at the wine, as our award-winning local vintner produced some corkers from grapes that could only have been crushed by angels; and certainly not at the quality of speeches and heckles, for they were top class. No, I was somewhat disappointed that the evening passed off as if smoking had never been a factor or ingredient in its obvious success. There is even talk of changing the moniker to that of "Speakers' Evening." As you know I am a lover of tradition and even the occasional cigar, but it was as if history had been extinguished and a hundred years of this gentlemen's gathering had gone in a puff of, well, smoke. But what am I saying? Smoking surely should be eradicated, whatever the cost and sanctions it takes? Yes and no. Stringent measures are often needed for the greater good of the public. Some objected in the nineteenth century to the then government's insistence that people drink only fresh water, and so it is with this latest "clean air act."

This massive and sweeping legislative change, as contested as it was by some, is undoubtedly one of the greatest public health advances we will see in our (consequently ever lengthening) lifetimes.

But I do believe that the Annual Smoker should remain so named, and not submit to political expediency. The title is already a bit of an anachronism and I suspect it will eventually be rather quaint and thereby remain part of local history.

I will be attending the Smoker again next year. This is not just an assumption on my part as Ashworth has already asked me to dine at top table, as second speaker. A perfect opportunity, I think, to get my own back at the wags who gave me such a hard time at this and previous meetings.

WITH LABELS AROUND
THEIR NECKS

The front door bell rang one autumn Sunday afternoon. Rising, a little begrudgingly, from my comfortable armchair, I kicked on my slippers and shuffled through to answer it. Standing there was an elderly gent looking both a little anxious and emotional. Knowing religious sect cold callers tend to arrive in pairs, I unclenched my teeth and asked kindly, in what way I could help. Glancing over his shoulder I noticed sitting in a car, looking up the driveway, two middle-aged ladies. The old fellow apologised for interrupting my day and requested to know how long I had lived in this late Victorian villa of modest proportions, and whether I knew the previous owners? It emerged that he and his brother had been evacuated to this very house during the Second World War. I had heard it said by the previous resident that she indeed looked after two young brothers, sent from Glasgow, at the outbreak of hostilities. Mr Clyde Bank, now clearly in his twilight years, had implored his family to take him back to the place he thought of almost every day for the last sixty years and more.

I welcomed in Mr Bank and his daughters. Mrs Moody slipped off to prepare tea and to butter scones. He was really quite overwhelmed; not I think at the mess of scattered newspapers or our choice of decor, but at the memories that were evidently flooding back.

Life and childhood in these days were rather different from those of today. The Anderson committee in 1938 had divided the country into three zones: evacuation, neutral and reception. This, more rural, area was clearly in the latter category and the little Bank brothers and some 800,000 other school-age children in 1939/40 were dispatched out of the cities. Many mothers with infants were also evacuated; as the genuine fear was that urban areas would be targeted and flattened by the Germans. Reports describe this enormous migration of people as having been made in quite high spirits and without serious accident. I have also read however of rather chaotic situations and some children simply being placed on the most convenient train, rather than on ones going to intended destinations. I can imagine propagandists may have conveniently overlooked personal anguish, trauma and even the abuse that likely occurred.

Young Clyde and his brother had been anxious but excited. The journey by steam train to our, now non-existent, railway station had been their first trip out of the city and their first on rail.

He remembered a brass band playing on the platform, there to welcome the train. Amusingly, he had at first assumed the band was a permanent fixture. His mother warned him "folks in the country arc different." Several stern ladies had checked the cardboard labels on string around their necks, before one with a tightly tied bun, showed some recognition. She took them by the hand, threw their satchels and gas mask boxes onto a horse drawn cart and ushered them to clamber aboard. The adventure was unfolding but the obvious question had been; where are all the trams? They remained here for close on two years.

I was happy for him to walk from room to room. The gas wall-lights were gone, as was the dinner gong at the foot of the stairs and the carpets, he observed, made the house seem warmer. The Westminster chimes had the very same resonance, he was delighted to hear. The clock was one of the few items we inherited when buying the house. There only one fire burning and he remembered there were often five or six in the old days. It had been one of their many chores to clean the grates and prepare them for the next lighting. Their hosts had treated them well and fairly but made them work hard for their "keep."

After a couple of hours of chat, laughter and tears his daughters commented on the time. He knew this was his first and probably last visit back to the house and the poignancy was apparent. As they were leaving he reached inside his jacket pocket and carefully pulled, from between the pages of his diary, an old piece of brown card. "I would like you to have this, sir," he said. It was his actual evacuation label. I was vaguely embarrassed but realised it would have been ungracious to decline and, besides, he insisted that I take it. It was destined for here, he told me firmly, and here it should return and remain. He and his late brother had been the "delivery" and they had also been safely delivered home to the city, when Mr Churchill had ensured it safe for them to return.

By chance, I had recently acquired from a patient a sepia Valentine's postcard of the house, which even pre-dated his wartime stay. Equally forcefully, I insisted he took it as a gift.

I have little doubt he treasures it still and saw it as a fair, if unexpected, exchange.

GOLDEN COUPLES

"You are cordially invited to celebrate the fiftieth wedding anniversary of Mr and Mrs Bell." I passed the gold-rimmed invitation card over to Mrs Moody, asking if we were able to attend. Dewar and Dora had reached that remarkable point in their lives. Knowing them to be humble folk, shying away from any fuss, I suspected the family had insisted the occasion be marked in this way. At least it wasn't a surprise party, for the RSVP was to the Bell's address. Dewar's heart certainly did not need shocks of any kind.

But of course we should, could, and certainly would, be free. A half-century, my word, what a length of time. What an achievement. Mrs Moody and I are still a good few years short of that particular milestone but top hats off, indeed tossed in the air, for such an occasion. I once knew a chap who celebrated two Silver Weddings after the untimely death of his first wife. That may be more unusual, but a Golden anniversary is something special. Quite often, in the pages of this newspaper, we see happy couples surrounded by grandchildren, and even great grandchildren, cutting a cake or raising a glass. Surely a prouder moment than some fluke win on the lottery. This generation of golden couples may not have needed to survive the Second War (witnessed it perhaps, but not from the front line) but nevertheless, they will have overcome political, occupational and even domestic adversity to get where they are today.

Today's statistics make rather disappointing reading. They suggest that fewer people forge formal unions, and those that do are more likely to end in separation or divorce. Public health and life expectancy have improved so much though that there are legions more older people than ever before. But that is not the same as remaining together for these two score years and ten. Couples enter marriage in a rather different frame of mind than what they did back then and the gender roles are somewhat less distinct. Women's magazines generally no longer recommend that a wife place a fresh ribbon in her hair for the arrival home of her husband each evening. The size of the family is smaller and pressures, expectations and finances are altogether different. Divorce laws are laxer and society and even the churches' attitudes have changed.

When Dewar and Dora tied the knot, weddings tended not to cost her father the proverbial two limbs. Celebrations were smaller; sincere but not showy. There tended to be only one sepia photograph taken, when calling in at the local photographer's gallery en route from the church to the hotel. The bride's posy was always in bloom (being plastic!) and the background, a set. Funnily enough, I sometimes see the same Doric columns in framed pictures, on sideboards across the county. The honeymoon tended to be to near flung destinations like Saltcoats in the west, or North Berwick in the east. Hotel bookings were top secret and the real fear was that the Best Man would play havoc and do all he could to upset plans for their first night together. Nowadays, couples tend to boast of their all-expenses-paid resort vacations; swimming with dolphins in the Caribbean or swimming with penguins in the Antarctic (admittedly only for hardier Borders types!)

It was back to work soon after the nuptials, for Dewar. The office relied on him, after all. Dora, like many others of her day, started to feather the nest in preparation for the arrival of the honeymoon baby. Further issue followed soon after. For some, the cradle was never filled and infertility medicine was (paradoxically) just in its infancy. This was often a cause of great sadness, with feelings of loss; for others, relief at the prospect of relative peace and freedom from worry and expense. Children then were seen more as a privilege than a right.

If the stork did land on the chimney (and for all father knew that is how the bundle arrived, being banned from the delivery suite,) the top tier of the cake was brought out from the larder for the Christening. The white wedding gown, provided the moths hadn't got there first, was dusted down and from it the Christening robes were cut.

Off to school went the kids, long carefree summers, then into employment and the arms of suitable partners (one partner each, and hopefully enough to go around!). Mum and Dad, for that is what they called each other long after the offspring had sprung, never moved house. The Beswick ducks and brass sunray clock on the wall are not unique, nor antique, and give away the era from which they came. Theirs, though, is one of the most welcoming homes I ever visit, for coffee or matters medical.

We did go to the party. Their old bodies survived an entire Orkadian strip the willow and Beau, their eldest, succeeded in having the entire hall in stitches at his anecdotes and slides of family holidays, with the fashions and hairstyles of yesteryear.

It was a lovely evening. If we are spared and Mrs Moody continues to tolerate me, I'd be fair chuffed if our evening passed off half as well as theirs.

BEING A TEAM PLAYER

"I didn't know you used to play rugby Dr Ken," Jim McPatient chuckled as he studied a photo on my surgery wall. Rather than object to his certain use of the past tense, I beamed with pride. It had been taken by a press photographer on the day of my greatest sporting moment. I worked several years ago in a Maori community in rural New Zealand. Living there, I had no option other than to lace up the boots again having not played since school. That particular day, despite having the precision and dexterity of a startled giraffe, I managed to score two tries.

I recall also another time when, one Friday afternoon, a chap in his forties visited surgery with a worsening of his asthma. I prescribed steroid tablets and a change in his inhalers. Steroids, as you may know, can have a euphoric or disinhibiting effect in some people. The following day I was taken aback to see he was refereeing the match we were playing. As the game kicked off he winked at me saying how much better he felt and how grateful he was. As the game proceeded he complimented me on every touch of the ball I made and all refereeing decisions went in our side's favour. Needless to say we won. My team mates were incredulous, and the opposition was fuming, at the sway I seemed to have over the ref.

I learnt that year the social cohesion rugby can bring, from the youngsters tearing around playing "touch" to the Golden Oldies being penalised for trying too hard! Everyone in the town knew the individuals in the team and the game itself, intimately. It was a tremendous privilege for me to be welcomed in so graciously. Rugby clearly gave meaning and structure to life for several of the lads who I am sure would otherwise have drifted into trouble, having no other outlet for their aggression, energy and passion. I have seen this happen too here in Scotland with our local team, where even fathers and other followers of the game experience an "inclusion" they have never known before. I believe local sport should be encouraged, not so that youngsters can emulate their prima donna heroes, but can run, kick and breathe fun and sportsmanship for all it is worth.

THE SHOPPING EXPERIENCE

They are often just opportunities to exchange pleasantries but shopping queues can also be rather informative places. Shopping locally, as I believe we should, means that I get to see what my patients eat and drink and, of course, they may glance at my chosen items. I try not to be too Orwellian by chiding fellow shoppers for less than wholesome provisions in their baskets and trolleys, but may do so jokingly. If I am standing behind Seymour Butts at the kiosk and I know he is trying to give up the dreaded weed, I might suggest that I understand cigarettes are now "past their sell-by date." I don't fear being hypocritical as I have never bought a cancer stick in my life (only accepted the odd cigar!) but I do watch what savoury snacks and confectionery I place in my basket.

The main confession I have to make is that I occasionally visit a supermarket. Asmortesbury's is both rather a mouthful and bellyful, I've always felt. As ashamed as I am about knocking another nail in the coffin of local traders, I realize this is the way society is moving. I am old-fashioned and old enough to remember and rue the day the first ones opened. Mothers would enjoy queuing just to gain entry to these food emporia, and would leave legions of babies in prams at the entrance as they freely wandered the broad aisles. Within a few years there was somewhat of an uproar when shoppers learned that items where strategically placed on shelves based on psychological research. Warm granary smells were piped adjacent to the bakery section and rich coffee aromas filled the store elsewhere. Shopping became an experience for (or an assault on!) all of one's senses. The multi-billion pound grocery (and now clothing, insurance and electrical goods) industry is more competitive and sophisticated these days. Everything is bar-coded. We are drawn into loyalty card schemes where our every purchase is recorded and "special offers" are tailor-made to our perceived or predicted preferences. The more you spend the more you save, madam! We are cleverly coerced into buying items we don't really need and, if we think about it, don't really want. We buy and consume ever more and our nation grows ever fatter, yet estimates suggest that up to one-third of all purchased grocery items are discarded.

I am a little saddened when I hear many children's weekends are spent visiting retail parks. They understandably become bored, sitting in the back seat, while dad's temper shortens in the frustrating effort of finding a parking space. Once the weekly ritual of piling the trolley to the physical limit and loading the car til the suspension groans is completed, the treat is to go to the adjacent burger bar for fried food and fizzy drinks. These enormous retails units are generic obscenities to customer choice and creativity.

I firmly believe as much of our food as possible should be organic. At present there is still a significant cost difference, but if market forces increased, prices would come down. There are many who cannot afford to pay four times as much for organic as opposed to "ordinary" chicken but, as there is a reason for this differential in terms of quality, it is all the more important that consumers dictate the methods of our food production.

I see the best and worst of people in shopping queues. I once saw two stout ladies squaring up to each other at a checkout. It was an "eight items or less" queue and one lady had nine. Rather than turn a blind eye to her fellow shopper's presumed oversight, she attempted to nudge her to an adjacent, longer, unlimited-items queue. It emerged that two of the items were identical and, yes you've guessed it, were: "two for one."

Mrs Moody and I no longer shop together. Rather than being a reflection on the state of our marriage, I'd like to think it demonstrates the diversity of our tastes. She got rather fed up with me returning to the shelves almost every second item selected. I tried to persuade her that, just because the word "healthy" appears on the label, it doesn't necessarily tell the whole story. "Reduced fat" or "reduced sugar" is meaningless, I argued, without further qualification. She, in reply, helpfully suggested I stay at home and cook my own meals.

I sometimes lapse, out of laziness or convenience, but I could live off the wealth of produce in the shops on the High Street. Give me a delicatessen, greengrocer, butcher, baker and monthly farmers' market any day in preference to the alternative. But please don't ask to see in my canvas reusable bag, as I chink my way home from the wine shop.

BADDERS

I recommend to my patients, on an almost daily basis, that they take more exercise. Occasionally, a more argumentative fellow will look me suspiciously up and down before questioning whether the ready giver of such advice indeed dons the baggy shorts and plimsoles himself, more than once in a season. With as much pride as a humble medic can decently muster, I declare firmly that I am a regular and keen badminton player. I confess (but only to you!) that I possess a degree of armchair inertia and, without the discipline of organized sport, I suspect turning the pages of a newspaper would be the extent of my after-work exercise. It was for this reason that, shortly after moving here many summers ago, I enrolled in the local badminton club. One weekday evening, I make my way enthusiastically, with laden canvas bag, down to the sports hall. The sound that could be mistaken for a collective groan, as I step through the doorway, is in fact the grunts of the concentrated efforts of players, deep in athletic and mental combat.

These two dozen townsfolk and other acquaintances are already leaping, bounding or simply shuffling about the court; thrashing, smashing or deftly dropping shots over the net. I say two dozen but, unless you are entirely unfamiliar with the rules, you will know they cannot be stampeding, twelve to a team. No, there are fortunately six courts and simple arithmetic will determine that, playing doubles, means twelve chaps and twelve ladies are breaking into a sweat simultaneously. (Some more than others, and the latter group only perspiring, of course!)

I am rather a traditionalist in many regards and this extends to the equipment I use. I feel that; if the wooden-framed, catgut-stringed, slightly warped racquet was good enough for previous generations, it is good enough for me. I confess to accepting compromise about using original style shuttlecocks. This was really at the request of cleaning staff, though. I admire the craftsmanship in these corks with twelve overlapping goose feathers. The trouble was, the timing rather than the force of my attempted smashes caused them to disintegrate at an alarming rate, and the court soon resembled the aftermath of a fox's rampage through a chicken coop.

Badminton, I believe is the prince of sports. The concept was brought back from India by British army officers over 150 years ago. The net and court measurements and the playing rules were adapted and formalized at Badminton House, Gloucestershire, in 1873. Our local and endearing euphemism of "Badders" does sound rather "public school" I daresay, but is used and loved by all. The game is played in a very mannerly and sporting fashion. Tempers are never lost, overtly at least, and there is a customary handshake over the net on conclusion. Most of our matches are mixed doubles; that is a gentleman and a lady on each team, rather than skillful players and those of my standard. Games start with a brief tactical discussion about who shall cover the net and who'll be at the back of the court. It may be that playing "sides" is preferred. Any dubiety about line calls is settled with a simple replay of the point. Should a point be won by the shuttle falling, as a fluke, over the net an immediate good-humoured apology is proffered. A good partnership can lead to intelligent, strategic play and there can be few better feelings than wrong-footing one's opponents or winning a hard-fought rally. Unfortunately, wrong-footing one's own partner can occur too. Clashing racquets and smashing the shuttle into one's mid back or upper thigh region can leave interesting bruises. Accidentally whipping an ear with an ill-timed swipe is particularly sore. Playing this sport really ought not to draw blood.

To keep games as varied and interesting as possible, we never play with the same person twice in an evening. One particular lady instructs me (in effect) that she shall be rooted to the spot while I dart hither and thither about the remaining 90% of the court. Her repeated, invariably late, bellowing of "yours," even when the shuttle lands at her feet, and tutting when I breathlessly fail to reach it, raises my hackles a little. I am too gracious to comment, of course.

Badders can be played all year round, practically regardless of the weather. I am not absolute in this, you will notice. Before the sports hall was erected, we used to play in various church halls. One in particular, had a less than watertight roof. During rainstorms, various pails and receptacles were utilized. There is a limit to the number of water containers one can negotiate, while attempting a forehand return, and once or twice rain, indeed, stopped play! Interestingly, even in the official rulebook, there is no mention of minimum height requirement for the ceiling but, I suspect at Olympic level, an absence of the elements is taken for granted.

I look forward to my hour and a half of Badders each week and know it does me good. It is not about winning or losing. It is sporting and good-natured exercise and easily beats most other recreations or lazy evenings.

RHUBARB

"What a load of old rhubarb," muttered the delegate sitting next to me. I don't attend many medical conferences these days and am bitterly disappointed when the quality of lecturer and his material is poor and of little practical use. I agreed with my colleague, the professor from the Infirmary was blethering monotonously, as if his audience shared his fascination with minutiae and esoterica. We didn't and, being an audience of down to earth general practitioners, didn't need to. As Professor Cardigan continued phlegmatically, with evermore figures, tables and formulae, I confess my mind wandered to matters gastronomical. I pondered on what my fellow sceptic had said. I chewed on his choice of term. I ruminated on rhubarb.

In a general sense, "rhubarb" means superfluous or irrelevant chatter. That was indeed what we were being subjected to, but were too polite to leave our seats in the front row and make for the exits. This meaning probably derives from the use of the word in acting circles where extras, not contributing directly to the script, are expected to create realistic noise. Simple random repetition of this particular word apparently creates the illusion of background speech. Even though he was centre stage, the Prof may as well have been speaking thus, judging by the yawns and heavy breathing within the darkened auditorium.

In a medical sense, doctors sometimes talk about checking one's "serum rhubarb." More junior laboratory technicians might question our sanity were we to actually request such a measurement though. It tends to refer to a search for blood constituents of a more unusual nature, after standard tests have failed to find anything conclusive.

As tasty as the rhubarb stalk is, the leaf is poisonous. In theory, if someone inadvertently or foolishly ingested (in jest?) large quantities of this part of the plant, we could not be criticised for asking the hospital to check serum rhubarb levels. The more precise request for serum oxalic acid levels would be more helpful though.

Avoiding the dangers of consuming the waxy leaf, like many others, I have a penchant for the stalk of the vegetable itself. (Contrary to popular belief, it is not a fruit.) Mrs Moody and I like little better than the stewed, sweetened form, in a crumble, sprinkled with ginger and served with warm custard. There are over sixty varieties of rhubarb worldwide. For some reason, as a plant, it seems to be regarded as a bit of a joke in kitchen gardening circles. This may be because it requires very little attention and flowers effortlessly year after year. Snootier gardeners seem to prefer plants that require diligent attention.

At the bottom of our garden we have a patch of *Rheum x cultorum,* and most summers I am happy to have a few friends and neighbours round to sample the season's wine. I doubt Moody's rhubarb wine will ever seriously compete with finer French grapes, but I can vouch for memorable evenings sitting watching the sun go down, sharing a few bottles of our house plonk. The proportion of the crop that I don't use my better half commandeers, and over the winter months we are treated to jam, chutney and other preserves. You may have sampled some of these, purchased at local coffee mornings.

One holiday, when the family were much younger, we strayed into the Rhubarb Triangle. This inland region, I believe, is somewhat less treacherous than the Bermuda variety, and infinitely tastier than salt water. Within deepest Yorkshire there is an area where the cash crop is none other than the crunchy red stalked vegetable. The finest form, I learned, is grown under candlelight (probably no brighter than our lecture theatre!) How this was discovered I don't know, but I understand Yorkshire folk are famed for their thriftiness.

Other than the gastronomic and alcoholic options as

mentioned above, rhubarb is loved and recommended by this physician cum gardener for its therapeutic and medicinal properties. The longer I practise medicine, the more I appreciate that ancient remedies still have much to offer, and often are preferable to the synthetic pharmaceutical alternative promoted by multinational companies. For centuries rhubarb has been recognized as having laxative and general cleansing properties within the body. It is said to be an astringent; that is it reduces secretions when one suffers a cold, in the nose and airways. But my sense of smell and taste are not impaired right now. What a wonderful crumble that is Mrs Moody. I'll have another helping, thanks.

Oh dear, I must have dosed off, and there is still no end in sight to the dullest lecture I think I've ever attended.

STAG WEEKEND

Being of the age and generation in which I now find myself, I assumed my days of male bonding with high jinks and partaking of refreshing beverages were well behind me. This proved not to be the case recently when Anthony Lerr, the son of a good friend, invited me to join his pre-nuptial celebrations. I tried to make my excuses, for fear that this silver haired old goat might embarrass the lad; and even more likely, himself. But Ant's insistence seemed genuine enough and, after finally ensuring Mrs Moody's approval (oh, how much I'd have to warn the poor lad!) my name was added to the list.

Last Saturday lunchtime, a party of some sixteen lads (and two pre-pensioners!) congregated at one of Scotland's better kept secrets; a certain country house hotel right here in the Borders. The cricket sweater and rugger shirt clad lads arrived, somewhat less than quietly in their sports cars and oversized motors. They clearly were expecting a jolly good time. In days gone by, I might have said they arrived with gay abandon, but I kept this archaic observation to myself.

Introductions, reintroductions and reunions over, we only had time to find our rooms before being whisked away by rangers for a spot of clay pigeon shooting. I confess to finding the bird and its cousins easier to hit. Perhaps like my patients, I expect the unexpected and not for them to follow a straight predictable path. (Before reporting me to the authorities, please be assured that I take aim, other than verbally, at precious few patients in practice!)

To my shame, as a country man, I was declared as officially the worst shot. I was not representing the older generation particularly well, thus far.

After muddy quad bike circuit racing we found time for a beer before making our way to the paintball compound. I had nowhere to hide. My word, what a technicoloured, splattered mess I was.

The physical activities over, we showered and dressed for dinner. Venison seemed appropriate and a case of (not so) vintage wine from the year of the young man's birth had been ordered by his father. A splendid meal it was and as I was preparing to settle for the evening in front of the fire, malt in hand, the Best Man declared that a fleet of taxis was waiting to take us up to the city. I believe I slept on the way but found myself downtown on a Saturday night for the first time in years.

City centres these days seem to be given over entirely to alcohol and hedonism. Numerous churches, civic buildings and banks have been converted into theme bars, restaurants and clubs. Almost cocking a snoot at the history and discipline of religion, hard work and money, all for the pursuit of pleasure. We found a pleasant little jazz club in such a building, with the apposite moniker, *Bank Notes*. The sultry soul singer, with more than a passing resemblance to Billie Holliday, captured my attention and the moment well. The beat did not seem fast enough for the young bucks in our group and they sought pastures greener, or perhaps I should say bluer. Across the road there was a former rival bank which had been renamed *The Blue Bank Note*. Some of our party seemed eager to go there, to what they called a stag show. I had a fair idea what they had in mind. More thongs than songs, as it were. I see more than enough flesh than I necessarily want each week in surgery and Mrs Moody, herself, is very dear to me (I meant emotionally, but certainly financially as well!) Anyway, the moody jazz reminded this Moody fellow of earlier days and I was happy to stay put. Ant's father and I remained there until the wee small hours.

The taxis took us back to the hotel and we slept for what remained of the night. A marvellous full Scottish breakfast, black pudding and all, greeted the survivors of the night before. The canoeing trip was unanimously vetoed as being too much for any of the heavy-headed and red-eyed party. Perusal of the Sunday papers over pots of coffee and blether about the exploits of the night before was a welcome alternative.

Other obligations were remembered and the jaded revellers started to leave with bearhugs and handshakes before departure. The wedding is next weekend and the Best Man has even more anecdotes for his speech. "You're a good sport, Ken, but hope you're a better doc than you are a shot," teased a departing lad. I had not needed to be a doctor to any of the lads this weekend, and appreciated the break and the chance to unwind. A few scrapes and bruises in the party perhaps; a few sore heads certainly, but one ageing medic had been graciously allowed a glimpse of how the younger generation think, live and celebrate. And it wasn't at all bad!

BOUNCE, BOUNCE, BOUNCE

Tam nearly broke his neck on one. Pauline has the biggest in town and it blew right over the house in a storm. It seems hardly a day goes by in the surgery without some reference being made to that modern recreational and sporting phenomenon, the trampoline.

There are several theories as to the origins of the trampoline. One is that the Inuits used to toss each other about on a stretched walrus skin. Lacking classical literature or even a TV, they may indeed have done this for an evening's entertainment, but the more plausible explanation is that the modern trampoline originated from an early 20th century circus act. It seems, clowns jumping about on a springy surface covered with blankets resembling a bed, was hysterical to audiences at that time. Naturally, the bed sheets didn't stay on and the firm elasticated surface was soon exposed.

It was discovered that the trampoline, as well as being rather amusing, was a great form of exercise and required a certain skill. Pilots during the second war and NASA astronauts used the device for fitness and weightless training. It took until the 2000 Olympic Games in Sydney before trampolining was recognized as an individual discipline in Gymnastics. It seems now that no self-respecting garden is without one and the bigger the better. I am all in favour of this popularity as this on-the-spot aerobic exercise may be a means of slowing the obesity epidemic plaguing this country. Unfortunately though, I have seen some rather serious injuries and would advise that, at all skill levels, a protective fencing or guard is placed around.

What is of concern though is when fat dads at barbecues, having consumed rather too much white wine or beer, relent to the chants of the kids to join them on the trampoline. "Come on dad/uncle/mister, bounce us higher." Challenged by this invitation, fat dad hands his glass to the nearest wary mum, pulls off his shoes and rolls onto the canvas. He finds the spring to his liking and as the burgers and booze are thrown around inside, he feels both nauseated and young again. After cheers of encouragement, he thinks a few bottom-bounces and splits will raise a laugh amongst the onlookers. Dad's jeans and general stiffness only lend themselves to little less than a 45-degree parting of the legs, but he is undeterred and only further exhilarated. So keen to please, he has forgotten the eight pre-school kids sitting cross-legged at the side or frantically trying to bounce as high as he does (by virtue only of his weight!) What happens next I saw in agonizing slow-motion. You can probably visualize it too. Dad, after his 43rd breathless bounce, fails to see wee Tibia Brayke crawling beneath him. With a bone-crunching, deadened bounce onto the 3-year-old, the fun is over. Tibia's shriek could be heard well beyond the safety net, garden fence and possibly the estate itself. I could have kicked myself for not telling the fool to stop, mindful of the danger he presented. He probably had imbibed no more than I and our body masses were fairly comparable, but my guilt would have weighed a little less heavily that evening.

A wide, enclosed, well anchored and secluded trampoline is hard to beat. We acquired one, ostensibly for the grandchildren, but on a summer's evening I slip off the sandals and sneak down to the bottom of the garden. There, next to the rhubarb patch, carefully out of sight of neighbours and dogwalkers, I spring into action. Working up a rhythm, to the point of seeing beyond the Leylandii, I bounce and bounce 'til my beating heart's content. Trampolining is all about fun and, boy, is it ever?

GETTING PUBLISHED

This column has now been running for some two years. Several readers suggested I approach publishers so that my "advice, humour and most individualistic style" might be available "to others and even for generations to come." After letting the flush of modesty drain from my cheeks, I suggested that my website would surely suffice for those curious (or daft!) enough to look beyond the pages of this newspaper and my weekly offerings herein. One reply was that: "There is nothing like a book. A book you can touch, hold and smell. A book whose pages will absorb your tears and can be turned deliciously at leisure. A book you can slam shut in disgust or hold passionately to your breast." (I did wonder if this bibliophile gets more out of books than I do!) I was enthused by his imagery, though, but doubted whether anyone outwith my circle of long-suffering friends would wish to read me for reasons other than as a cure for insomnia. It was one of these friends who implored me to grant him permission to select and edit my better offerings and find a good publisher to bind my words, between covers.

When the project did get started, I was intrigued at how slowly the wheels of the publishing world turn and what it takes to oil them.

I assumed, naively, that getting published and attaining an ISBN number was a mere formality. How wrong I was. I should have remembered that even authors of classics, like Thomas Hardy, almost gave up trying to get published. Then we discovered the role of the literary agent. He or she seems to have muscled in on the scene, uninvited I daresay. Like a dodgy doorman, he demands his cut for liaising with the party upstairs, such is their tightly-knit little fraternal society.

One can submit a book to publishers without an agent but "unsolicited manuscripts" are sniggered at or frowned upon in the main. Authors are informed that only one-percent of such submitted works are ever published. As 100,000 new titles appear each year in the UK, a mind-boggling number of manuscripts, solicited or otherwise, must be churned out. My friend helpfully suggested that, as there is so much dross written, there must be room on shelves for one more title. How persuasive and encouraging he is!

Despite this bulk of pulp, the publishing world is not as large as it seems. Many different names and logos appear at the foot of book spines but we learned many are simply "imprints" of larger publishers. An imprint is where a publisher trades under a different name, perhaps the name of a smaller company gobbled along the way. There are not many companies behind today's best-selling works. It is a highly competitive business, and quality and originality of writing are not attributes given particular priority. Books are published to make the publisher money, nothing else. If publishers had a fraction of the imagination that budding authors do, the literary world would be considerably enriched and the better for it. I was saddened to learn that even decent published authors receive only a small percentage of their book's cover price. Most established authors do not even earn enough to live on. Famous authors who achieve megastardom and wealth are few and far between and will admit to their own good luck. There are plenty writers of similar skill and prolificacy who never hit that rich vein of success.

Several of our rejection letters praised me for the articles and their editing but suggested they would be "a tough sell" in the popular market. Admitting that I write in an original way, I "lack controversy, intrigue and abstraction." Modern readers apparently "expect profanities, innuendo and gritty urban culture." I couldn't even pretend to be able to supply any of these.

If an author remains determined to be published (for reasons of self-belief, a refusal to accept rejection or simply by having fun) there is always the option of self-publication. This does not involve glue, staples and a large pair of scissors, but rather that he finances the project himself. The publishing house (heaven forbid!) runs no financial risk. The author has to be more involved with the production and promotion of his book, but that of course will be more satisfying for most.

I admire authors whose lives' work are in the written (printed) word. I always try to attend book signings and talks by local authors. Whether their books are of aerial photographs, quantum physics or romantic fiction (I purchase the latter as a gift for Mrs Moody, though it arrives suspiciously creased at the spine!) I admire the pride an author has in her finished work. I enjoy hearing the story *behind* the book, as much as I do reading the one contained within.

So, as you may have gathered, *View from the Surgery* will be deciphered, abridged, bound and hand-stitched any day now. It will not change the world, literary or otherwise. There is no surgery-rebuilding book deal being drafted and no trendy literature prize awaits me at a glitzy London hotel. There is little prospect of a film studio buying the rights (what Hollywood star would forfeit his stellar career by playing a tweedy old duffer like me anyway?)

But, I'd love to sign you a copy and to endorse it with my good wishes. As ever, if I raise a smile on the face of a reader now, or after I am gone, every minute spent on this venture will have been worth it.

A RETIRING PARTNER

"What shall we get Dr Aiken for his retirement present, Ken?" asked Mona, our ever-efficient practice manager. I can hardly believe it Bodie, after more years than we could count, is finally hanging up the stethoscope, switching off the examination lamp and saying goodbye for the last time.

What we give him is not really important. A carriage clock is unnecessary. *Tempus fugit?* He knows time flies and has flown and, besides, he probably has the finest collection of antique chiming clocks this side of Edinburgh. A little replica timepiece would just get lost atop the large oak nineteenth century mantel in his drawing room.

His suggestion of a complete collection of Scott's (first edition) Waverley novels, we hope, was tongue-in-cheek, for he will be disappointed. Such a purchase would bankrupt the practice though, ironically, would be similar to how the great novelist ultimately found himself. I plan to give him Sir Walter's novel *Kenilworth* (1821) to remember me by. Kenilworth is of course my Sunday name and how I am known to university chancellors and maiden aunts. The volume I found Bodie is rather heavy, fusty and foxed. It utilises language from a different era, is overly long and is splitting slightly at the seams. In case he forgets who gifted it to him, I'd better include a note.

Bodie may be a "retiring" partner but he is anything but shy and withdrawn.

In truth, he has been a crotchety old devil these last few months. Rather than being demob happy I do believe he has been a little demob sad. Perhaps like free-falling in slow motion he has seen his life pass before him. I have a few years left until my lump sum, but I think we all reach a point in our careers, or indeed lives, where it is easier to look back rather than forward. Jobs or careers for life are much less common these days as people tend to be hired and fired; seek greater or different challenges or are head-hunted by rival firms.

Some people believe that you should do a job for only ten years or so and then seek pastures new. They argue that this is the optimal time when, what you have to offer, has reached or passed its peak.

Patients are often saddened by the retirement of a long established GP. He is often so much part of the practice, and indeed the community, that "the practice will never be the same without him."

I recall the introductory drinks party when I succeeded Dr Leigh Scheur. Lady Agatha Pettit-Lippe, taking it upon herself to be the spokesperson for patients and, whose outspoken ways were as yet unknown to me, appeared to be sincere in her long-winded welcome. She concluded her oration, not just with a hiccup but by stating that if Dr Aiken was absent and nobody else available then she would probably attend me. What I took to be her dry sense of humour, I later discovered, had long since withered on the vine.

Sadly, doctors do not have a particularly good record for enjoying long and healthy retirements. Whether it is because we work frantic and long hours for forty years or more and simply cannot settle into a more sedate pace, or because we generally retire later than most, I do not know. A rather more worrying possibility is that, despite years of dealing with the sick, we just make bad patients ourselves. We may fail to notice warning signs of illness or are poorly compliant with medication and treatment, when prescribed by more junior colleagues.

We are currently at the interview stage for finding Bodie's successor. Who will replace him? How could Dr Aiken possibly be replaced anyway? It will be frankly impossible to fill his tan brogues and, as it's looking increasingly likely that it will be a woman, unless she has a preference for large flat shoes, this will never happen.

Regardless of what gift we choose for Bodie, what he takes from the practice are our warmest wishes. What he leaves is a healthier, happier populace, a wealth of memories and, frankly, a bit of a void.

QUESTIONS PATIENTS ASK

SHOULD DOCTORS ARGUE
WITH THEIR PATIENTS?

"I thought you would be angry with me doctor for not taking my pills," a relieved Walter Cation said when I merely reinforced the need for his medication, rather than lambasting him for expressing doubts.

I used to frequently get into verbal tussles with patients but notice that I no longer get quite as heated about things. There may be several reasons for this. Times have changed and doctors are less paternalistic and authoritative generally and accept that patients are less inclined to receive instructions unquestioningly. We are not the fount of all wisdom and knowledge and, although some doctors acted like it, we almost certainly never were. The news media and internet are ready sources of information and patients do not generally sit in surgery, mouth agape, committing to heart every messianic word we utter.

Don't mistake me though for some compliant, passive prescription and sick note machine. There are certain things that I still find extremely irritating and will say so. I may not turn green and burst out my tweeds but I'll challenge certain requests, demands and behaviour when appropriate.

Some patients play "musical doctors" and will attend each GP in search of the answer they wish to hear. One patient wanted all reference to his violent temper (and its consequences) removed from his records. He was applying for a new job and felt this would count against him. We initially had a modicum of sympathy for him but erasing one's "unfavourable" history simply cannot be done. He was not happy at our unanimous response and his insistence and intemperate manner cast any doubt from our minds that we were correct in our stance (or that he had reformed.)

Hearing patients bad-mouthing colleagues is a guaranteed way to rub my hirsute flesh up the wrong way. Quite how someone feels that tutting and melodramatically raising his eyebrows, while relating how my colleague of twenty years "missed my (trivial) diagnosis, fool that he is," will curry favour is beyond me. Whether there is some perverse notion that Dr Bodie Aiken and I are locked in a game of one-upmanship I do not know, but I tend to let the patient spew forth. I will then suggest that if my colleagues are of such poor quality he should be disabused of the idea that I will be any better and I'll then invite him to challenge the neighbouring surgery with his expectations.

Patients asking for second or third opinions are not too far removed from this scenario either. I am not suggesting that we are perfect or do not err. Even if we diagnose 99% accurately that means we still get it wrong about twice each week. That is a sobering thought, but when patients seem dissatisfied with a considered opinion such as:"Dr Aiken said I have an iron deficiency anaemia with low MCV and ferritin levels and prescribed 200mg Ferrous sulphate three times each day, but I just wanted to be sure", what can one say?

Furthermore, people who are the perpetrators of domestic violence, inveterate malicious gossips or needlessly rude to our reception staff and then the essence of friendliness and politeness to me, raise the hair follicles on the back of my neck. I cannot challenge them on alleged behaviour nor when confidentiality may be at stake ("please don't tell my husband I showed you the bruises he gave me") but frank hypocrisy stinks and if the receptionist is in tears as we speak I shall "discuss" this with him before proceeding with the consultation.

So, Walter Cation and I did not have strong words that day but if he comes back to tell me he flushed his tablets down the loo, we just might!

SHOULD DOCTORS TALK
TO JOURNALISTS?

"There's a journalist wanting to speak with you, Dr Ken. I think it's about that article you wrote." After studying her business card I agreed for Rae Porter to be shown in.

Doctors have a rather uneasy relationship with the media. The public likes to read about medical breakthroughs or survival against the odds and these make for heart-warming stories. But despite this, studies have shown that the news media as a whole much prefers to report cases of blunder, failure and fraud. Doctors who fabricate evidence, abuse their positions or their patients and those who make grave errors are far more likely to find themselves on the front or middle pages than those who save lives. The lower (quality) end of the press is particularly keen to report on these subjects.

In my early years doctors were either despised like Dr Crippen or revered like Dr Livingston, there was little in between. The media (if it was even called that then) was very forgiving towards doctors and occasionally even to politicians. Our trainee informed me that medical students are not taught how to handle a feature-hungry journalist who, as the cliché goes, often isn't necessarily prepared to let the facts interfere with a good story.

A medical equivalent of the unanswerable "Have you stopped beating your wife?" would perhaps be, "Have you stopped molesting your patients?" Both an affirmative and negative reply would condemn oneself, and even "no comment" would invite the headline "Doctor refuses to deny he is a continuing risk to his patients."

Most journalists are genuine people with more than a modicum of intelligence. They are usually keen to represent stories accurately, but sometimes from a different "angle." Doctors reading lay interpretations of medical issues are sometimes frustrated by inaccuracies, misinterpretations or erroneous conclusions. Reputable newspapers and other organs often have a "resident doctor", not so much to administer smelling salts to faint-hearted news desk reporters but to provide an inside take on topical medical issues. (*The Peeblesshire News* wisely overlooked this wag for the role due to his near pathological levity and flippancy!)

My first brush with the media was on the other side of the world. When practising in New Zealand, I was consulted by a teenager and his mother. His school banned smoking and the lad claimed that, being addicted to cigarettes, he was unable to attend. Kiwi doctors are asked to sign sick notes confirming whether a given condition would "physically prevent" the student from attending. He asked for such a certificate. Rather taken aback by the ridiculousness of the suggestion, and never having met the weedy child before, I decided to join in the silly little game he was playing. I wrote, in as non-committal and unhelpful a way as I could: "I can confirm that Seymour Tellie told me that he is addicted to tobacco. This would, by your sensible rules, seem to prevent him from attending school, if he has neither the will nor the willpower to stop." At the end of my sabbatical year I wrote a veritable epistle of my work experiences in that noble, proud and beautiful country. I described poetically and anecdotally the cultural differences, from my perspective, and detailed the cases of fortitude and suffering I witnessed there, but common to people the world over. I submitted the article to a "National." Of all the events I described, the one that was singled out and published was, you've guessed it, that silly consultation. "School a real drag for teenager" was what New Zealand woke up to one Sunday morning. A spokesperson from ASH (Action on Smoking and Health) was wheeled out declaring, "This doctor's attitude isn't helping anyone."

I was stung. My supposedly bland, read-between-the-lines note had been twisted and made me look a bit of a dumpling.

I have that front page framed and hanging upside down in my study as a reminder of my year down-under and how *I* was metaphorically framed and held upside down by the bootstraps and shaken until the dollar coins and golf tees fell out my pockets.

But I write this column don't I? Might I not be misrepresented, again? Perhaps I should write under pseudonym, but am a bit late for that now. After I pedal frantically each week with the draft of Friday's article penned on a cancelled prescription pad, I barge into the editor's office and shake him by the lapels or trouser leg until he gives the article the nod. I am pleased that he leaves my ramblings largely unaltered, albeit transposing them into legible typed form. He sometimes, though, censors the names and details of my favourite luxuries, I think for fear of unremunerated advertising. By way of example, my best fawn corduroys cost £(expenses deleted), my preferred tipple is (aperitif deleted) and my choice coffee is (expresso deleted). Come on Ed, you're taking this too (expletive deleted) far!

I don't think doctors or other health care staff should approach newspapers with sensational stories, other than in exceptional circumstances. Where negligence or institutional mismanagement goes unchecked or unpunished occasionally a whistle-blower, providing he has the correct motives (and this certainly does not include money) should be applauded for approaching a responsible publisher. Modern infirmaries have trained spokespeople to deal with the press and to issue appropriate statements. These statements may be in sterile management-speak, but any further details before "appropriate enquiries are made" may just not be, well, appropriate.

If doctors do agree to speak to journalists, it should be in general terms. Patient confidentiality must be maintained. This might be very difficult, especially if a patient has made spurious allegations and "gone to the press." In that case, one ought to remain silent. There are worse things than finding oneself in court. There, confidentiality is over-ridden and "the truth will out", at least in theory. Better to have trial-by-law rather than trial-by-media in this democratic society with its incorruptible legal system, as I am led to believe we enjoy.

So, yes, come in Ms Porter, but I'll ask you to explain exactly why you're here and I'll be very careful with what I say. What, a photographer too? No, that's a bit much. Your readers don't deserve this ugly mug staring out at them. Sorry, no...well at least let me comb my hair.

DO DOCTORS ATTEND THEIR PATIENTS' FUNERALS?

"Will you be coming to mum's funeral on Friday, Dr Ken?" asked Bea Reeve. I had known old Mrs Reeve for many years. She had been at school with my mother, Mrs Effie Moody, and had remained a friend of the family. It was my intention to be there, work permitting.

Doctors though cannot, and generally do not, attend the funerals or memorial services of all their patients. If we did it could be legitimately argued that we either had precious few patients left or were not leaving sufficient time for "the living." With a list size such as ours we could be at a service once or twice every week.

My own feeling on the matter is that, for largely practical reasons, I ought to pay my "last respects" to patients who were also friends or those well known to me.

There would be a danger otherwise of course, that by finding myself seated in the pew at one service, I would be expected to be present at them all. That being the case, my failure to attend one could be taken as some form of slight. As with many aspects of general practice, I often have to do what I feel is right or what I feel most comfortable with. Occasionally offence is caused but this is unavoidable.

I have probably only been to about a dozen or so patients' funerals in all my years out here in the shires. One I did attend was perhaps out of a sense of regret or even guilt. Not guilt that I had made a "grave" error, but that the patient had died while I was away on holiday and I hadn't managed to see him through his final illness. In truth, occasionally we feel that aspects of our patients' care could have been different. As I'd be prepared to argue, to my own grave, doctors are not perfect, so consequently (and regrettably) not all care we provide is optimal. We may feel drug or surgical treatment could have been given earlier, or even withheld, or that a diagnosis could have been arrived at, or acted on, sooner. Some factors are entirely outwith our control. There are unacceptably lengthy hospital waiting lists, infections and other surgical complications may set in and not all patients can be given all "available" treatment. The ever-surprising idiosyncrasies of the human body and its response to illness and treatment make life and the practice of medicine unpredictable.

Funerals themselves are widely variable. When an old person, after years of frailty, decline and chronic illness dies, few would claim their demise was a tragedy. On the other hand, when a child or young person dies, whether expected or not, the loss and despair this brings can be beyond words. Doctors are sometimes said to become "immune" to the trauma and upset of death. While it would be wrong and no favour to our other patients if we shed tears at the loss of every patient, some deaths move us deeply. If this were not the case it would probably be time to move on and get a job in, say, accountancy.

Funerals these days are increasingly "celebrations of life" rather than mournful ceremonies. While many still include Psalm 23 and uplifting and reassuring Victorian hymns, popular music tracks with lyrics that had significance to the deceased are often now played. Some of the words of contemporary ballads and anthems may in fact be a bit dubious but perhaps are more appropriate if the deceased was unfamiliar with "I to the hills will lift mine eyes; from whence doth come mine aid."

Funerals, I believe, are very important as a focus for the bereaved, whether religious or not. I have known relatives who felt too grief-stricken to attend and have regretted it later. They can also be tremendously informative affairs. You may think you knew someone well until you hear an eulogy from a colleague or old friend and achievements, talents or acts of generosity become apparent which had humbly gone unmentioned. Hilarious anecdotes retold can leave the "mourners" in stitches and this can only be a good thing. If *I* wished to be remembered for one thing it would be for having a good sense of humour. (Readers of this column may feel that, this being the case, I should perhaps start demonstrating it soon!)

It's certainly not inappropriate to laugh at funerals but they should be a commemoration according to what the deceased would have wished. People often say they would like to go "out with a bang." Heart pacemakers should be removed before cremations occur, or it could be a send-off for more than just the intended! I knew a pyrotechnician whose life was celebrated with a fireworks display and an entertainer whose hearse was filled with colourful balloons. Respect and respect for one's wishes must surely be what is foremost.

Although a visit to the home is usually much appreciated, I do not think relatives, or for that matter patients, really expect their doctor to attend funerals. If asked, as I was on this occasion, I would certainly make every effort to go.

I'll have to decide whether to wear a black tie or my more informal striped one on the day.

DOES THIS DOCTOR
ENJOY HIS JOB?

"Do you enjoy your job, Dr Ken?" asked Mrs Nessie Parker. General practice is nothing if not varied and part of the variety is that we never know what or who is going to walk through the door, or what we are going to be asked, next. It was a pretty broad question she was asking me but, glancing at the clock, I saw that I did on this occasion have time to ponder.

My job now is not what it was when I started out many years ago, nor what I ever envisaged it would be. Originally, I was on duty several evenings each week and one or two weekends in a month. Surgeries were relatively leisurely affairs and visits often included coffee and chat, when the business of diagnosing and treating was done. There was plenty time for patients but less for family and leisure pursuits. But all this has changed, not suddenly but gradually. This occurred through short-sighted, self-interested interference by successive governments; increasing litigiousness and consumerism in society and by some misrepresentation by our own GP "representatives." (This wasn't quite the answer I gave Mrs Parker though!)

Part of my job of course is listening to people describe their own employment, which may be under rather Dickensian conditions with unreasonable employers or colleagues. I hear the devastating impact workplace bullying and physical or sexual harassment has on people. I witness the effects of the constant threat of redundancy or of ever increasing demands with ever decreasing colleagues. I pity those with appalling hours and pressures where there is the effective absence of decent union representation. I cannot fathom how some people make ends meet with houses full of children, unemployed or absent spouses while trying to live off the minimum wage with no pay for days' leave or sickness.

I cannot put myself in any of these positions, so with such relative job security, decent pay and pension provision and reasonable employers (GPs are technically self-employed) I should have no reason other than to be content. But it is not always quite as straightforward as that in life. Just because one's lot may be better than another's does not mean it is necessarily good.

I have been criticised for having little to do with the present out-of-hours arrangements. For the first time in my working life I do not, and do not need to, work in the evenings and at weekends. For this very reason I've chosen to take advantage of this, at least for now. It was once said to me by a senior colleague: "no one ever looks back on their career and says: gosh, I wish I had worked harder and spent less time with the family." To this end, I never will.

Currently I work up to 50 hours each week and spend a couple of evenings in the surgery catching up with the paperwork, which often simply cannot be done during the course of the day, without interruption.

Yes, I am happy with my work Mrs Parker. I enjoy contributing a little, and sometimes a lot, to the quality of people's lives. I can feel supreme pleasure with certain things that happen and can laugh until my waistcoat buttons pop. My family life does not suffer much as a result of my work and Mrs Moody and I can watch the fire together most evenings until the embers burn low. What more could one ask?

ARE DOCTORS JUST TOO NICE?

"I think Dr Bodie Aiken and you are just too nice to patients, Ken," our practice manager Mrs. Mona Lotte informed us last week. Whatever could she mean? Could that be a bad thing? Most consultations are indeed polite affairs. The patient leaves feeling, and often is, that little bit better. But there are consultations that leave us feeling angry and frustrated. The ones where patients make unreasonable demands, have totally unrealistic expectations or insist on being seen at the drop of a hat, often at the expense of less well patients.

I've had a few consultations that left me feeling that I am (or my training has made me) just too darn polite. (If that's the strongest language I can come up with you'll start to see what I mean!). I suspect few doctors have, or want, confrontations all day long. It would drain us of the will to live, let alone work. But, I believe the occasional confrontation with a patient is necessary. The interests of the genuinely sick are paramount and can be trodden on by people who demand disproportionate amounts of our time. Of course patients are not medically trained, but surely everyone knows that a simple runny nose does not *have* to be seen urgently. In our practice we try to keep to 10-minute appointments, but can spend more time seeing long-winded and hypochondriacal patients than genuinely sick ones. Why is that? Why can't we tell these self-important people "your odour problem and crinkly toenails will have to wait for a routine appointment"? And it might not be tomorrow or the next day. Why do doctors indulge overweight dyspeptic, flatulent patients who scoff at colleagues for suggesting they first "exercise more and eat less"? Why do we indulge a patient who insists on an urgent referral after he cancelled the last one due to "business commitments"? Why do we indulge patients who fail to attend most appointments and when they do attend it's for what would qualify as trivia in even the most seasoned hypochondriac's book?

It's perhaps because we are not brave enough. We know that if we bark at or dismiss a recently investigated patient presenting for the umpteenth time with tummy pain, that she may have a malignancy this time. "I told you so" is on the tip of her tongue and the ink on the lawyer's letter will not yet be dry. Besides, we'd feel thoroughly rotten for it.

I think Mrs Lotte is right, we should be more confrontational with misusers of the system. They are unlikely to forget the "advice" offered. It would be in the best interests of all patients and doctors would certainly feel better for it too.

DO PATIENTS NEED
SO MANY MEDICINES?

"Do I really need to take so many blinkin' pills, Dr Ken, I'm nearly rattling?"

By "blinkin'" I wondered if Ray Maddy was subconsciously telling me he only takes them in a very "on, off" fashion, but it was not an unreasonable question he was asking. I have no doubts that patients' prescription lists are ever lengthening, that doctors are prescribing more medicines generally and that the NHS drug budget is heading skywards. Why should this be? Are people less well than they used to be? Are people living longer and their need for medicines increasing or, are doctors just suckers to the lures of the pharmaceutical industry?

I believe the treatment of blood pressure, diabetes and raised cholesterol has a lot to do with the current situation. My more senior colleague (in age alone!), Dr Bodie Aiken, recalls the days when doctors were less "aggressive" in their treatment of these and other conditions, tending to treat just the most extreme cases. Consequently, scores of patients were left severely disabled from strokes or died tragically young from heart attacks and haemorrhages. Sadly these still occur, but undoubtedly to a much lesser extent, and appropriate prescribing has been the difference.

We (try to) practise more "preventative" rather than "curative" medicine these days. In other words, we work to prevent major events (strokes etc.) occurring rather than just picking up the pieces when they do. It can be difficult convincing people that they may be walking time bombs when they "feel fine." Like winning the lottery, "It only happens to other people", but they play it anyway, yet the odds for illness are much greater. Others take the more fatalistic view: "Well, you've got to die from something." Yes, but would you rather not put off your final illness for another thirty years?

High blood pressure (hypertension) is a common condition. Just because it is common does not mean it's not worth treating. As you get older, your blood vessel walls become less elastic and your blood pressure therefore tends to rise, making the need for treatment greater. It is also a complex condition and sometimes three or even four types of anti-hypertensive medicines are required.

Most patients who are on loads of medicines do not pay for them. If you are treated for diabetes, an underactive thyroid, epilepsy, are aged over 60 or in lower income brackets you are not charged for *any* prescriptions. Fewer than 20% of prescriptions in Scotland are paid for by the patient and some politicians are calling for this to extend to every single prescription. I cannot subscribe to this view, as medicines have to be paid for at some level, whether in general taxation or in the pharmacy.

If I felt morally comfortable (which I don't) about taking shares in particular medicines, it would have to be in the cholesterol lowering drugs, the statins. They are increasingly prescribed and it seems you will soon need a good reason not to be on one. Perhaps they will be added to the water supply!

But scanning Ray's repeat prescription I saw that, as our computer lists items in alphabetical order, his first page had six medicines starting with the letter A. Following this sequence, did he have one-hundred and fifty-six medicines, finishing with the letter Z (most sleeping tablets appropriately start with this letter)? No, not quite. A greater proportion of drugs start with the letters A, S and P. (Oddly enough, the spelling of the snake which delivered the poison that killed Cleopatra!)

Something that concerns me is that patients often really don't know what their medicines are for or why they are taking them. One smart (and award winning) doctor elsewhere always has printed beside each prescribed medicine the reason for taking (or needing) them. So simple and yet so effective and his patients demonstrated that they are much better at taking their tablets, given this basic information.

Drug companies and doctors are aware of the problems with this modern phenomenon of "polypharmacy." By taking more medicines you are more likely to suffer side effects and the problems of drug interactions. Taking so many, you may also simply forget (or choose not) to take some. Efforts are being made to simplify things. One current area of research is where some patients, who were put on a standard five-medicine regime after suffering a heart attack, are now given a "polypill" (a five-rolled-into-one medicine). Such "combination therapies" prevent adjustments to individual components though.

Once established on a medicine, there is no reason why it cannot be issued on a three-monthly basis. One of our gripes (and admittedly usually of our own making) is when prescriptions finish out of synchronisation with each other. We like to "review" patients' prescriptions every six months and this can be a good time for ensuring medicines are all "in-step" with each other and that all medicines remain necessary.

Older patients, or those likely to have trouble co-ordinating so many medicines, can ask their pharmacist to "pre-package" them in one tray and to have them supplied weekly.

Finally, contrary to belief, GPs are not paid according to the number of prescriptions we write. We are paid according to the health of our patients. Sometimes this means prescribing, sometimes making adjustments and sometimes in fact stopping medicines altogether.

SHOULD DOCTORS FRATERNISE WITH PHARMACEUTICAL REPRESENTATIVES?

"There's a drug rep through in the coffee room, Dr Ken, I think she may have some sandwiches", Mrs Mona Lotte called through. No matter how busy duty days can be, when my stomach starts complaining I have to down tools and eat. If I am up early enough in the morning I will have filled a flask with broth but, failing that, I am wont to raid the biscuit tin or ask our receptionist to pop out for rolls and scones.

The invitation of an easy sandwich, savoured (or even wolfed) between consultations, can be too much to resist. But what is there to "resist"? It is often said that there is no such thing as a free lunch. The reps who visit the practice do not expect the exchange of silver coins but do expect to bend my ear for a few minutes. I am usually happy for a friendly person to chat about issues other than themselves. I am not being disingenuous to patients, but listening to medicine promotion, perhaps wrapped in anecdote and humour, is fine by me. Some doctors feel that by allowing ourselves any direct contact with the pharmaceutical industry we are compromising, or even "prostituting", ourselves. They feel that all advertising works in a subliminal way and that merely talking with reps will compromise our care of patients. We will be, it is asserted, partial in our prescribing and will not necessarily be acting in our patients' best interests all of the time. On the next occasion we prescribe a cream for, say, eczema we will be more likely to select the one Fern Massey discussed over a chicken and mayonnaise sandwich.

All doctors have a relationship with the industry whether it is to be rude and refuse all contact or, at the other extreme, to be wined and dined at every opportunity. As a younger (greener?) doctor I erred towards the latter category. The changing factor was a St Valentines' dinner which I surprised the new Mrs Moody with. We went to a favourite restaurant and enjoyed a delicious four-course dinner with wine. It was only when we got home that I discovered the cause of her displeasure was the fact a rep had accompanied us. I had noticed her dissatisfaction was matched only by the rep's apparent discomfiture and realise now he was wearing a gooseberry green jacket (another subliminal message? I now wonder). Yes, we were the only table-for-three in the restaurant, but only spent little over half the evening listening to company propaganda and talking shop. I have never considered myself average in any way but Mrs Moody did suggest that evening that I was "particularly mean."

After three weeks of the cold shoulder (and cold dinners) I learned my lesson and resolved to never let the industry play as large a part in my social and professional life again. I had published in the esteemed *British Medical Journal* a letter pointing out differing standards between the pharmaceutical industry and my own profession. When doctors publish information about, or photographs of, patients we have to declare that signed consent has been obtained. In contrast medicine adverts can show models with digitally perfected bodies and enhanced smiles declaring that their lives have changed immeasurably since discovering this new–better–than–all–the–rest (but often more expensive) laxative/anti–epileptic/anti–reflux/HRT (delete as appropriate).

On another occasion, I wrote to the ABPI (Association of the British Pharmaceutical Industry) complaining that a company sent me an unsolicited advert for a product, marking it "urgent." I noted the package had arrived second class. I argued that a bone-strengthening drug for many patients may be of great benefit but "urgent" correspondence designed to attract the attention of busy GPs should never be a mere advertisement.

This little David has only fired these two shots at the Goliath of the multinationals but I still scrabble around for pebbles to sling when I feel representations need to be made.

The Industry seems a little more aware these days of criticism and allegations of being "too friendly" with doctors. Evenings now are supposed to include an "educational component", but I wonder if sponsoring a speaker to favourably present the company's flavour of the month is really that educational.

I am never rude to reps. They are usually over-dressed/groomed/scented new graduates and sales-people. They mean well, are enthusiastic and are doing a job to pay the mortgage, one that I could never do. (My slightly fusty tweeds would probably never see me through an interview anyway!)

Some doctors have been "lured" by the pharmaceutical industry but I can only assume this is by big bucks rather than job security, and perhaps a certain disillusionment with wall-to-wall patients (in the same way I suspect some doctors go into academia.) When our medical students leave after their two-month stints with us we arrange a rep-sponsored meal in one of the country house hotels nearby. A stone bleeds more easily than the university reimburses us for our time and teaching, so the occasional perk seems justifiable.

I believe life is too short and work hours too long to decline all contact with drug reps. Sandwiches on duty and venison and ale off duty are always welcome. I assure my patients that I'll be as impartial in my prescribing as possible and promise Mrs Moody I'll be a little more romantic and generous in future.

ARE DOCTORS ACCURATE WHEN DESCRIBING THEIR PATIENTS?

"I hope you'll describe me in your letter in a nice way, Dr Ken," said Vanessa Peacock. I was only referring her to a surgeon for a simple augmentation procedure, but she was keen that I described her in favourable terms. Quite why this mattered I did not know. I did wonder though how we describe our patients in letters and what they would think should they ever read them. So, in an idle half hour, I looked at letters in our archives that had been written, to and from the Infirmary, over the last few decades. I was amused to see how the nature and style of correspondence between consultants and GPs has changed.

Clearly, in the old days consultants were only one rung on the ladder from God; clinical cases were a form of "sport" and the GP had done jolly well to get his patient seen at all.

I was interested as well to see how patients, attending hospital clinics, are described nowadays. Glowing adjectives are frequently employed to describe them. "This delightful chap", "this lovely old lady" or "this most attractive 35 year old lady was seen by myself in clinic today" (had the specialist engineered it that way?) All of these may have been accurate, but how helpful are such subjective comments? We may of course know the mutual patient a good deal better and struggle to recognise him, described by what may simply be a cliché, saved on a standard letter. The words "gentleman" and "lady" seem in danger of being hackneyed to death. I would argue that anyone who keeps his baseball cap glued to his head or her chewing gum between tongue and cheek, when having her tonsils examined, relinquishes the right to such descriptions, in all but the most liberal of minds.

I suspect the rights patients now have, of access to their medical records, has a big impact on the way patients are described by doctors. All consultations now can be viewed as potential court cases (how negative and defensive is that?) This probably tempers what and how doctors write. Several recent studies have shown that, of patients offered copies of their referral letters, only about twenty percent take it up. When patients do ask/demand to see their records we can still remove reference to third parties or material we feel may be harmful, but "censoring" all reference to patients may, rightly, make the inquisitive patient more than a little suspicious.

Now, I don't think that medical letters should be as sterile as lawyers' letters, heaven forbid but, by being gushing and obsequious, we risk meaninglessness creeping in (or creepiness replacing meaning.)

I feel that: "This plethoric, Pickwickian, unkempt, tar-stained, suspiciously intoxicated, reputedly retired race-fixer" sets a better scene than: "This delightfully engaging and charmingly fragrant lady was seen today in clinic."

Perhaps all this is just an anachronism. Increasingly our local hospital departments issue us formatted forms to be completed and faxed back. One such clinic form stipulates that: "Unless at least 2 out of 5 boxes are ticked your patient will not be seen." (These criteria incidentally are not that she is lovely, decent, delightful, nice, pleasant etc!) The Breast Clinic form has standard issue glands already sketched and we are asked simply to append an X to indicate the area of concern, along with a few other details.

Hand-held records are another anticipated development, where patients will be able to carry a bar-coded card that will contain their entire medical records. Perhaps patients will then be able to access their own records and amend them to their liking, scrolling down lists of adjectives and superlatives to describe themselves.

Maybe we should just return to the days when a referral letter might simply say: "Dear Colleague, Please see and advise, yours etc."

"Don't worry Mrs Peacock, I'll let the specialist know what he needs to know. No more and no less."

WHAT SHOULD YOU
CALL YOUR DOCTOR?

"Do you mind that I call you Dr Ken, Dr Ken?" asked Mrs Hetty Kitt politely. I don't suppose that I do, nor do I really object to what patients call me at all? I prefer not to get called derogatory names though, but I probably do out of earshot (or within earshot if I lay down the law to a drug addict or blatantly unreasonable patient).

Perhaps how patients address us is relevant and can give away much about them.

Age has a lot to do with it. I am not called "son" by older patients nearly as often these days, but I love it when I am. I still have patients old enough to be my parents but my weathered, greyed, whiskered, mildly fatigued look makes that whole concept somewhat less plausible.

Some patients, particularly those of my own age, can be a little over-familiar and insist on calling me just by my Christian name. Annoyingly, this can be in almost every sentence, but if they feel at ease with this then I am never going to draw attention to it.

Not all names have abbreviations. When I am called "Kenilworth" I expect what follows to be a scolding but I suspect few in the practice know my full name, at least not until now. Mrs Mona Lotte, our practice manager, often asks (read "demands") if she can "have a word" and starts this with my Sunday name. I suppose this informs me that I have erred and prepares me for the lecture that will follow. She may, of course, have just read this weekly column and its references to her (she rightly never declared a sense of humour on her CV!)

"Dr Ken" is, of course, friendly and only semi-formal at best. When I think about it, "Dr Ken" is reminiscent of a children's TV character. There already is a friendly eponymous postman and fireman, so why not add a cuddly and reliable doctor who gets into all sorts of muddles and adventures but wins through in the end?

"Dr Moody", in truth, is probably my most common address in correspondence and in the surgery. It is my correct title and what I am paid to do. If I am meeting patients in a social setting I will ask them to drop the formality, especially if they are buying the next round.

I have never been comfortable when called "Sir." I am not landed or gentry and do not assume (or have) any superior status. I notice that most people who call me this are rather nervous, new to me or are looking for a favour of sorts. I'll ask them to drop the "sir" bit unless I suspect that this will make them even more uncomfortable. If military people, current or retired, find it rolls off the tongue so be it, they have my attention, but I'll remain seated.

Of course, how and what we call patients is relevant too. I address many elderly gents as "sir." They probably called their seniors that so, in some way, they have "earned" the right to it. I have never found "madam" quite as natural, but will use it if it seems appropriate.

I call most patients by their first name if they age with me or are younger. Those older than me, particularly if not familiar, I call by their title and surname.

Polls have shown that about a fifth of patients prefer to be called by their title and surname at all times. I have no objections and agree that it is wrong to assume an older patient will be more comfortable when called by her Christian name by younger staff. This occasionally needs challenging and can be a loss of dignity to some people. Simply asking what patients in surgery, hospital wards and nursing homes wish to be called can be much appreciated.

But then there are the truly titled. Whether I would call "one" in from the waiting room by the formal title and name is another matter. I did try once: "Lady Elizabeth Hermione Eucalyptus, Duchess of Upper Gumtree, please." The waiting room hushed and the canned music seemed to magically change from 1980s pop anthems to Handel's Zadok the Priest. But despite this, once in my room, she said: "I don't need that entrance doctor, just call me Betty." Thereafter, I always did.

Of course Mrs Kitt, call me Dr Ken if you wish, but what should I call you?

DO WE NEED OUR COTTAGE HOSPITALS?

"Can you take Annie Moore?" I asked Sister Kate down the phone. "Annie Moore or any more?" she rightly asked me to confirm. Old Annie is an increasing burden to her long-suffering husband, Nye, and any chance of a bit of peace (or respite) is always welcome. We count ourselves tremendously privileged to have the use of our cottage hospital out here in the hinterlands. Without it and its like, the city hospitals would quickly fill up with such cases and elderly relatives would simply not be able to travel to visit.

There is something a little quaint about the term "cottage hospital" and also the long-forgotten dignitaries they are often named after. It would be wrong to suggest that they just serve as respite facilities as they are also good stepping stones for patients after surgery or illness, where they are too well for the main hospitals but not quite ready for home. Physiotherapy, occupational therapy and ever-professional nursing care are on hand and the confidence this can give patients is immeasurable. Larger hospitals, I feel are becoming increasing blind to the needs of individual patients and are discharging folk alarmingly early. "Out of sight out of mind" seems to be the maxim and GPs are left to pick up the pieces.

Patients are sometimes admitted to cottage hospitals for terminal care. We do not pretend that we can provide the same level of expertise as hospices, so we may call upon palliative care specialists for advice. Patients and families consider it important to be close to home, if not in it, as the end nears, and we try to accommodate this wish where possible.

The trouble with cottage hospitals is that they are constantly under threat of closure. As the purse strings tighten, justification for existence is demanded annually. The money men at the Health Board see that there can be quieter periods, when our bed occupancy can be as low as 50%. This does not compare favourably to the Infirmary where occupancy runs at no less than 120%, if you include trolleys in corridors!

Unfortunately, some of our patients feel that their cottage hospital does not provide everything it should. We no longer, for instance, have radiology facilities. Previously, if a patient had a suspected fracture, an X-ray could be taken and a diagnosis made. Unfortunately, modern machines cost many thousands of pounds and require regular maintenance. There also needs to be appropriately trained staff on site. In these smaller communities we could not even start to try to justify a return to this facility, at a financial level anyway. The medical cover of cottage hospitals is provided entirely by GPs, often nipping over between patients in surgery. We have no particular skills in interpreting X-rays and, as with everything else, would be subject to litigation if subtle fractures or other problems were overlooked.

A cottage hospital is not a nursing (or care) home, to the disgruntlement of some relatives, but can be a staging post before transfer to one.

We do provide a minor casualty facility during working hours and can suture and dress wounds, when they are of a less serious nature. We can also admit patients to monitor changes to medication, run certain tests or if we just have a feeling that closer supervision is required.

Some of our older patients recall, that many decades before, they had their tonsils extracted or children delivered in the same room in which they are now ensconced. Safety and modern techniques and practises prevent our return to these days when cottage hospitals really functioned as smaller versions of their city counterparts.

So, we got old Annie into a bed for the rest of the week while

Social Work had bathing aids and other appliances fitted in the house. Nye will be refreshed and looking forward to her return again soon.

SHOULD DOCTORS ACCEPT GIFTS FROM PATIENTS?

"...and you'll accept this wee gift in good faith of course, Dr Ken," said Mrs Bess Towe.

I am nearly always touched to receive gifts from patients but this comment set me wondering: why do patients offer gifts; why am I receiving one at this particular (I almost said present!) time, and should I be accepting gifts at all?

I have received many things over the years from patients, but I expect many doctors, particularly those of us working in more personal, rural practices, will have too.

I believe patients give wine, whisky, cheese, chocolates, fruitcake, pheasant, duck and other luxury groceries (not necessarily in the same hamper!) out of genuine gratitude and, very occasionally, by way of apology. This may seem obvious but there have been instances where the item was clearly meant as a bung or a bribe of sorts, with the expectation that preferential treatment would be the result. I would return the item if this was the stated wish, and would think very deeply about it if I felt it might be. Returning a gift of course could cause great offence but that would be better than leaving Freddie Pettit-Lippe with the mistaken belief that I will visit him and his family, or even see them in surgery, at the drop of a fedora.

Christmas naturally is the most common time of year to find a bottle-shaped, gift-wrapped object sitting on my desk. Sometimes after making a diagnosis from an observation worthy of Sherlock Holmes, but more usually for simply doing my job, a patient or relative feels it appropriate to express their gratitude by way of a gift.

Whether we should accept is another matter. If it is money, I draw the line. I once received a cheque from a patient who had mental health problems. She declined its return, so I had no choice other than to shred it, witnessed by Mrs Mona Lotte our practice manager. As doctors we cannot accept money from NHS patients anyway, even if told to "buy something for the children."

Knowing my liking for preserves and pickles a patient, having removed her urine sample from her handbag, proceeded to retrieve from its depths a jar of home-made gooseberry and pear chutney. It was dropped in the bin as the door closed behind her and my taste for these particular fruits is only just returning. But the strangest gift of all has to be from a patient, attending after an operation, who produced a travel sweet tin. Rather than the contents being coloured sweets dusted in fine sugar, there sat his recently extracted gallstones. With earnest enthusiasm he requested I show them to future patients suffering from gallstones who "will then know what the wee devils look like!"

Of course I enjoy a graciously gifted bottle of Merlot or the like, but in truth the warm smile, handshake or modest card from a patient is what means the most and perhaps what keeps me going.

ARE SOME PATIENTS MORE EQUAL THAN OTHERS?

"We do treat all our patients the same, don't we Ken?" asked Dr Bodie Aiken with a rather anxious expression. Whatever did he mean? Of course we do. We treat them for the illnesses they've got, no more and no less. But Bodie was wondering if we spend more time, or are more thorough, with certain folks because of who they are. There is no doubt that our poshest family, the Pettit-Lippes, are very demanding of our time. Despite each member's wishful opening gambit: "I won't take up much of your time doctor," they proceed to trot out numerous symptoms, interspersed with updates on the salmon and pheasant season. I'm really only remotely interested if they can be consumed with a good wine (the game rather than the family that is!) I think there is the presumption that, if one's family has owned the surrounding land and employed locals for hundreds of years, what then is another half hour of the community's time? But I don't see it that way. I'm no socialist, lowest-common-denominator sort of voter or practitioner, believe me. We are all living, breathing (some not so easily) folk, medical school taught me that. Being self-important, loud and a dreadful bore should not muffle the cries of the silent suffering ones. Heaven and my conscience forbid. But there is the danger of this scenario occurring. Perhaps my biggest fear in medical practice is that I miss the wood for the trees. I mean overlooking, due to distracting trivia, a serious illness because, either a patient with her symptoms has been pushed to the back of the queue or because the foliage of bureaucracy has taken my eye off the balsa, spruce or pine.

Lady Agatha, matriarch-elect of the Pettit-Lippe family, just last week ticked me off for keeping her waiting a few minutes (during an emergency surgery) with only a boil on her behind. It did "not do" for her to be saddle sore but if etiquette, diplomacy and the GMC did not forbid, my size 10 brogue may have made her just so. She did come very close to being "ticked off" my list with the warning that if it is private medicine she wants she can seek it and pay for it elsewhere.

But this is not a swipe at the gentry. Ned Capp attended surgery with a sore throat. I knew better than to expect him to remove his reversed skip cap, when I examined his tonsils, but am I too old-fashioned to assume he will have already digested his crisps and chocolate bar? Despite the confectionery coating resembling that of a partially swallowed hedgehog, I explained that his was a viral sore throat which, given time and aspirin gargles would improve. "Aye," he said with another swallow, "but what are you going to do about it? I'm off on holiday tomorrow. Should I no have antibiotics?" "Nothing, big deal and no" were the correct and abbreviated responses but he seemed to need fuller and repeated answers and this further delayed evening surgery.

Some people seem to need lengthy explanations for all given suggestions and diagnoses. I am happy to discuss such issues, which allows for shared decision-making, but not when everything is questioned to the nth degree.

We try to keep consultations to the standard ten minutes but appreciate this in not always possible. Some of our patients were allocated, based on their previous lengthy consultations, double slots. We noted though, that such extended consultations were often for patients who were not particularly unwell. For a while we felt this was getting out of control as "doublers" rolled into triple appointments and we ran behind for the rest of the day. One workable compromise, other than: limiting problems to single figures; cutting one off mid sentence or holding the door open suggesting the cleaner needed access, was to allocate Mr Art Cinque and family the last space on each list. This ate into our (and domestic staff's!) time and, boy, did I miss my coffee breaks. Refreshment and relaxation are essential. I relay this sage advice daily to my clientèle, so surely ought to practise it myself? There also exists the law of diminishing returns. When applied to the GP consultation, it might mean that half an hour and the first dozen problems out the way (and with no end in sight) your doctor's concentration and empathy may be starting to wane.

Surgeries cannot be allowed to run interminably and merge one into another. Therefore, occasionally (even rude) interruptions are necessary. Doctors cannot always sort all problems at the one sitting and less pressing issues may just have to wait. Some may even resolve themselves, the body being the great natural healer that it is.

So, if you feel your doctor is winding up the consultation, when you seem to be in full flow, it may be because it's in your (and everyone else's) best interests.

TONICS AND REMEDIES

DOCTORS ARE NOT NECESSARILY FOLLOWERS OF FASHION

"You do look smart today Dr Ken", commented Emma Flyrtt in surgery last week.

I'm never particularly comfortable with folk volunteering comments about my appearance, whether flattering or not. I feel it suggests over-familiarity on a patient's part. (If, of course, my flies were undone I would be grateful for a subtle prompt so I could quickly recover my dignity!)

I was once informed by a female patient that my eyebrows were "striking and intriguing." It was an entirely inappropriate comment. Quite what my thick sweat catching sunscreens did to provoke such a reaction is beyond me but they were probably raised to such a level on hearing this that they took on a whole different architecture.

By chance I recently read an article in a medical journal about the influence doctors' appearance and dress has on patients and how it may influence the consultation. The findings were that, even nowadays, patients prefer doctors to be conservatively and modestly dressed. For men this implies long sleeved, collared shirts and non-denim trousers and for women: a skirt and blouse or trouser suit. Interestingly, and perhaps predictably, items not inspiring such confidence were: facial piercings, dangly earrings, tattoos, copious make-up, dyed hair and T-shirts. I can only claim ownership of the latter mentioned item. Shorts were also on this list but, the good people of Peeblesshire would likely fill the letters pages of this august newspaper should my hairy mutton shanks ever be exposed in surgery.

As tempted as I have been, I have never worn my kilt to work. (Moody is affiliated with the Stewart clan and on formal occasions I will wear the red Royal version.) I recall one Highlander who worked at the Infirmary. He invariably wore his beneath his white coat. Unfortunately, as the coat was longer than the kilt, from behind it looked as if he had simply forgotten to don his breeks (although with our constantly disturbed sleep in these training years he could almost have been forgiven).

I still try to wear a collar and tie in surgery and when out on calls. In truth, ties are a nuisance. They are also carriers of germs, being the least washed item of clothing, unless a dollop of jam and cream should fall from my scone as I take tea at the Hydro. I have lost count of the number of times I have nearly garrotted myself by trapping my tie in my desk drawer.

It has never happened to me, but a colleague after performing an intimate examination, discovered the end of his tie remained in..... *situ*! Bow ties are more practical, but are a bit professorial for me.

I am not a wearer of novelty ties either. At Christmas time I might humour the children by wearing a silly tie but would be wary of not being taken seriously, especially when breaking bad news, if I wore one adorned with large cartoon characters.

When my collared shirts are both at the laundry I sometimes wear a dark turtle-necked sweater under my jacket. The receptionists tease me though by suggesting I look like the chap from the milk chocolate advert, but my belly belies the fact that I am more likely to have digested said chocolates, rather than have parachuted in to present them to the lady, while raising one thick eyebrow.

Of course, doctors pay attention to what patients are wearing too. I personally have no problem with farmers attending directly from the fields. Dried manure is usually tolerable but when the steam is still rising I try to keep the consultation brief (and find subsequent consultations are somewhat shorter too!). It is more important that patients don't wear a dozen layers if I need to examine them as these will each need to be laboriously unpeeled and corsets, stockings and long johns shed (not usually from the same patient though!).

Patients often dress according to their peers or (dare I say) class, whether it is the white shell suit and obligatory skip cap of Ned Capp and his pals or the corduroys, checked shirt and wax jacket, of Hugo Pettit-Lippe and clan.

So, you can expect your doctor to be smart-casual but he'll wish you to be appropriately dressed to.

TIME AND TIME AGAIN

"Procrastination is the thief of time, Dr Ken," chirped Norman Waites, our collection and deliveryman from the infirmary. I was dithering about what particular specimens to send and he was keen to move on to the next collection point. Proverbs and philosophical advice about the fourth dimension are not always welcome on busy Monday mornings, but Norman's permanent cheerfulness and sense of proportion are hard to criticise. "Time waits for no man either, but Norman Waites!" I responded, without missing a beat.

I lose count of the number of occasions in a week when patients and staff refer to a certain lack of that precious commodity.

We live in this age of communication but rather than making life more straightforward and pleasurable, it's had the opposite effect. The fact we can text, fax and email demands of others instant responses rather than the more dignified and respectful "by return of post" or "after due consideration."

Having too few hours each day for too much work, or too many commitments, leads to stress. Stress pervades like a cancer and can cause or worsen almost any medical condition. "Could my headaches, blood pressure, depression, heart attack, stroke and insomnia be brought on by stress doctor?" "Yes, six-times over ma'am."

"My kids hardly know me, my wife and I never speak and the office won't leave me alone," are all commonly heard complaints.

Some people take pride in, or like giving the impression of, being busy. The ubiquitous mobile phone is their best friend and how they love it to ring. Travelling by train is an education in modern etiquette (or lack thereof!) I remember a chap who apparently failed to receive a call while travelling through a tunnel. Unable to determine who it had been, he proceeded to ring all possible callers without managing to solve his query. Such people are often keen to inform their colleagues exactly where they are, possibly as a form of gloating that they too are not office-bound. Almost every week a fatuous ringtone emits from deep inside a handbag or jacket during surgery. My patient is, interestingly, either mortified at the intrusion or blithely proceeds to take the call. If the conversation is obviously trivial, I'll solemnly study my pocket watch or, should the hint not be taken, proffer the open door to the patient whose priorities clearly lie elsewhere. I recall an executive businesswoman who finally found a window in her diary to have an essential screening test done. Perhaps predictably, she was contacted mid-examination. Never one to let a phone ring out, she took the call and duly informed her office that: "doctor is doing my smear right now, but do carry on." I had to enquire whether this instruction was to me or the other subordinate. Such multi-tasking, however skilled, seems to be creating a society where attention span is becoming attention deficit and where efficiency gives way to indecision and impatience.

Hospital waiting times remain a political over-cooked spud. Outpatient delays are used as a ruler with which managers' and governments' knuckles are rapped.

Patients increasingly are discharged from hospital, often after major surgery, ridiculously early and more procedures are done as day-cases. Both of these practises may improve the hospital productivity figures but do nothing to save GPs' time, especially when the inevitable complications occur. I referred one patient to the city for his vasectomy, having decided that my colour-blindness precludes me from changing a plug and performing this similarly delicate, and potentially charged, procedure. He told me his father-in-law drove him to the hospital (I'd heard of a shot-gun wedding but this was new to me!) The car park was so full that my patient was back in the car before a free space had been found. Quite what this says of modern hospitals I'll leave to more enquiring minds than my own.

Like water and money, time seems never to be evenly distributed. People either have too much or too little. Unemployed or retired people may have too many hours in the day to fill and more people than ever are socially isolated. The rich, gravelly sound of Louis Armstrong's "We have all the time in the world" may strike a hollow chord and boredom snuffs out any remaining creativity and satisfaction.

Recently our old kitchen clock (salvaged from a long-gone Borders railway station), which ticked reliably and sagely for years, stopped. Our usual instrument repairer quoted me four months to overhaul it, being "so busy!" I suppose some things just can't be rushed. In the end a retired patient, who quite literally had time on his hands, took it and returned it in good working order the following week.

I feel those of us who are rushed should all just slow down a bit. Take stock and take time out if necessary. Tell customers, clients and patients, politely, to wait. The service will probably be better if they do. Take time to eat, pass water and kiss the kids goodnight.

Anyway, could you get this sample to the lab in good time, Norman; and you can spare the horses.

A SON OF THE BORDERS

It may not be seemly for doctors to have heroes (especially non medical ones), but that does not stop me from declaring one of mine to be the great Scottish novelist, John Buchan (1875-1940). I am not usually given to celebrate anniversaries either, but I note we are approaching the two-thirds centenary, next month, of Buchan's death. I suspect the poignancy of this may be lost on most but, to be honest, I could not wait another thirty-three years for the "full" centenary to come round before writing my tribute to him.

I think *JB*, as his admirers and family affectionately refer to him, epitomises for me all that is great in a Scotsman. As well as being a supremely talented and prolific novelist he was a law graduate, classicist, soldier, Unionist MP, journalist, biographer, diplomat and intelligence officer. He was a devoted family man and husband grounded, as he was, in the Presbyterian hard working tradition. By nature he was: humble, compassionate, articulate, erudite, intelligent, persuasive and remarkably influential. Some have described him as enigmatic or even complex, but if these were his most negative attributes that can't be bad. As Baron Tweedsmuir, the 15th Governor General of Canada, he signed the document which took that great nation in to the Second World War, though he died soon after hostilities began. In his five years in Canada he proved himself to be a progressive and hands-on governor who saw education and reading as being fundamental to the needs of the people. He established an annual literature prize that exists to this day. Buchan was said to have had a genius for friendship maintaining many good friends all his life. He was close to President Roosevelt and respected by the monarchs of his day. His memorial service was at Westminster

Abbey and the editor of *The Times* stated that he had never before received as many letters expressing grief at the announcement of a death.

Buchan published at an astonishing rate (over one hundred books), never letting up even during the busiest times in his illustrious career. He is probably best remembered for his fiction but this amounted to under half of his publications. He is regarded by many as having written, as Winston Churchill did for the second, the definitive history of the First World War. His most famous work, *The Thirty -Nine Steps,* was in fact just the first in a series of Richard Hannay novels. Like many others, characters were based on friends or acquaintances and set in various parts of the world where he had been posted or visited, but often right here in the Borders. Buchan lived to see the first film version of this novel, filmed in 1935 and directed by Alfred Hitchcock. His first dramatized novel was *Huntingtower,* starring another legendary Scot, Sir Harry Lauder.

One of Buchan's children, William, is still alive today. His daughter, JB's granddaughter, Lady Deborah Stewartby is a delightful person and will relate anecdotes and tales with an enthusiasm and in a manner which the great man himself would be proud. The John Buchan Centre continues to display a marvellous array of "Buchanalia." The building is the former church where JB's father, the Reverend John Buchan, met his wife, Helen Masterton and where JB worshipped many times.

This little museum lies immediately south of Broughton on the A701, Moffat Road. Deborah herself lives nearby and frequently pops in. She or any of the other volunteers would be only too happy to introduce you to the legend and memory of Buchan or reacquaint you if you have not read him since school. Not only that but the centre gives us an insight into a way of life, from not so long ago, when values and experiences were quite different to those of today. Personal tragedy was common and often colleagues, family and friends valiantly went off to fight on the battlefields of Europe, never to return. One of the most moving documents I read there was a letter from Churchill to Buchan in 1917, commiserating with him on the death of his brother, Alistair Buchan, who earlier that month had been killed in action. JB also lost a sister when she was five and the newspaper announcement of her passing was as heart breaking as it was common in the late nineteenth century.

Do find the time to manage along, it's here on our doorstep. The entry fee is very modest and it is soon to close again for the season. Honour, or at least acknowledge, with me this hero of our county and our country. Purchase there a reprint or early edition work (first editions can fetch hundreds of pounds or more!) and immerse yourself and your senses in an age gone by. Sixty-six years and eight months (or the "two-thirds centenary") is an odd one to celebrate I admit, but it's as good an excuse as any for me to sing and write Buchan's praises and to raise a glass to him on October 11th.

DOCTORS AND THE
INSURANCE INDUSTRY

"Oh no, not another insurance application to complete", groaned Dr Bodie Aiken, "this one's for Paul Hissey, it will take ages." I had sympathy with Bodie, no doctor looks forward to form-filling and insurance forms take tediousness to a different level. Like omnibuses they seem to come along in convoy rather than being evenly spaced. People often make several applications in the increasingly competitive insurance market and are at liberty to pick the best quote. As a consequence though, the rainforests are further depleted and our landfill sites (and in-trays!) bulge. We tend to distribute them in batches of a dozen in the practice so that we each are temporarily relieved of this drudgery. But forgive my flippancy and candour, such policies are of great importance to the "proposed." As mundane as they may be to general practitioners, we admittedly are in the best position to overview patients' records. We can succinctly list and detail relevant issues in as fair and accurate a way as possible.

When a person buys a house, changes occupation, gets married or reaches some other milestone along life's journey taking financial stock seems as ritualistic as the exchanging of keys or rings. Critical illness and life assurance cover are the applications that most commonly land on our desks but there are others such as mortgage and income protection plans.

It is my increasing (but perhaps mischievous) belief that the country and indeed the world is not run by governments, or even civil servants, but by the Pharmaceutical and Insurance Industries.

Of some reassurance, at present there is a moratorium against insurance companies insisting on the disclosure of genetic or AIDS testing. If a patient has been tested due to the prevalence of cancer within his family or was concerned that a previous partner may have left more than just memories, there is currently no obligation to inform a prospective insurer of this information, even if it may be in one's favour. Doctors, campaigners and other interested parties fear that, should this situation change, a "genetic subculture" could develop where a section of the community would become uninsurable or subject to prohibitive premiums because of their suspect or defective genes.

Several steps short of this nightmare scenario is a question that is legitimately asked at present. "Has your patient/the proposed had any tests performed recently?"

One of my patients developed strange sensations in his limbs and was promptly referred to a Neurologist. The specialist considered the possibility of Multiple Sclerosis (notoriously difficult to diagnose in early stages) but suggested there was nothing to be done other than wait and saw no reason to concern the patient with this "worst case scenario." I agreed with this course of (in)action. Several weeks later however, he came to see me disturbed at having been turned down by every insurance company "based on the Neurologist's comments." I had to be honest and discussed the consultant's letter with him but was seething at having our "hand forced" and at the prejudicial effect it was having on this young man's insurance and, perhaps even, credit rating.

This raises another issue of whether we should withhold information that could adversely affect a patient's chances of being "approved." There was a case elsewhere where a doctor was coerced into "overlooking" an unfavourable medical condition. When the patient later developed more obvious symptoms, which in fact led to incapacity, the company invalidated the policy. Undoubtedly worse than him being declined in the first place.

I notice a closing question on forms states "has your patient asked you to withhold any information?" I suppose a frankly dishonest "no" is more blatant than a "simple" omission. It also makes us a little more circumspect about what we write in records, aware that mere speculation rather than fact may have great implications.

Increasingly, people are accepted by an insurer, but with "exclusion clauses" attached, (I cannot say accepted with "conditions" as this may in fact be the very opposite!) The insurers may pay out to our Mr Hissey in the event of a claim, but not if it is for something that has been excluded. This selective/exclusive type of policy is often a feature of private medical insurances and may lead to some people being unable to obtain meaningful insurance cover at all. Most application forms in fact follow a standard format that would seem to have been drafted midway through the last century. Some have updated certain sections but occasionally, for example, there is no metric option for height and weight. Even this old Imperialist (in most senses) realises that metric measurements and calculations are winning the debate, in medicine at least.

It would be wrong of me to give the impression that there is no benefit to completing these forms. We often learn relevant facts about patients when trawling through their records, which may help or put into perspective, present day problems. We are also rewarded with a few guineas, which we toss in to the practice coffers. I still hand-write them (some comfort perhaps to those shocked at my metrification!) rather than simply pressing "print", although this is now an accepted option

Insurance applications, I'll be honest, will never excite me and the lancing of haemorrhoids or plain-old healing of the sick will always take priority, but I will endeavour to give them the time and attention they are due and not leave coffee mug rings or blood, sweat and tears upon them.

THE ENGLISH

And did the feet in ancient time.
Walk upon England's mountain green?
And was the holy Lamb of God
Oh England's pleasant pastures seen.

The words of William Blake's poem and the equally inspiring music of Hubert Parry echoed through my mind one afternoon, for reasons I could not at first fathom. Then, out of the blue (Saltire, Pantone 300), it suddenly struck me. This great English anthem had subconsciously planted itself, like a little acorn, in my fertile imagination. And from little acorns....well, great oaks grow!

Of course, that was it, every patient in my morning surgery, all 23 of them, was, or at least originated, from south of that stone and turf partition, properly known as *Vallum Hadriani*. One under two dozen was indeed a full surgery but was further coincidence, as that is the very day St George's Feast is celebrated each day in April.

I love the English. I've lived and worked down there and have more connections with that land than I'd probably be prepared to admit, for fear I might be mistaken for an Englishman! That land of some 50 million people, as it always was, is a conglomeration of many disparate (and often warring) tribes and peoples. The stereotypical bowler-hatted and pinstriped English gent who takes the Slough (as opposed to the fast!) train up to London always was a bit of a misnomer. Even now, people born and dwelling within these 50,000 square miles are from a multitude of cultures and beliefs and have little in common with each other. A Cumbrian quite probably feels he is closer and has more in common with a chap from Dumfries than he does with a Londoner. Inhabitants of Devon and Cornwall might deny close links with the Bretons and Normans across the water but, in truth, share greater similarities than they do with the Northern English.

I'd aver that there is no such thing as an English accent. I've always believed England, for its comparatively limited size has a greater variety of dialects within its borders than any other country or land mass, though having failed to master even one language, I suppose this may be difficult to confirm.

Sometimes I think we Scots can be just a bit too insular and rather enjoy wallowing in a perceived underdog status. An enthusiastic Englishman is often just what is required in some of our clubs, towns and businesses; breathing fresh life and new ideas. We Scots can shovel pessimism in spades: "Let's not bother, it's bound to rain." Grudges last ages: "Look what ye did to our Wallace." But, worst of all is ill-informed nationalistic pride: "Nobody can touch Burns, but all I can recite is something about a haggis and "A man's a man for a' that," and that hardly proves my point!"" I sympathize though with the mild resentment at certain pushy, loud Southerners who insist on informing us how much better things are "back home." An obvious suggestion to them may follow! They speak in a manner that no one can fail to hear, and with an unqualified confidence and assumed superiority. Nor would I argue with the notion that, what many such people have in verbosity and opinions, they lack in sincerity and knowledge. I do question the wisdom though of a few retired English couples who, when registering with the practice, have told me they always fancied retiring to Scotland. Despite never having visited this great land, they glanced at an atlas one evening after a few glasses of wine and simply placed a pin. Akin to the children's party game, they made rather an ass of themselves. Such naivety and belief in chocolate box, shortbread tin visions of Caledonia is almost asking for disappointment and disillusionment.

What really gets my goat though is when, during football tournaments and suchlike, children wearing English colours are assaulted by drunken oafs. Such Neanderthal thuggery deserves to have the racism red card brandished (and why not brand them with a red hot St George's cross as well?) These convicted criminals should have several months added for racially motivated crime, spent in an English jail of their choice. (My candidature for Justice of the Peace may have just gone up in smoke!)

There, I've written an article that if hurriedly read will probably succeed in alienating me from both my Scots and English colleagues, friends and patients. But it shouldn't: we're all Jock (John, George or Geordie) Tamson's bairns.

OBSESSED WITH NUMBERS

"Why are patients so obsessed with their numbers these days Ken?" asked Di Jitt our practice-based clinical researcher. I hadn't really thought about it, but I knew exactly what she meant.

Many patients have mentioned to me that, when out and about, they've popped into pharmacies or stores that are advertising blood pressure, cholesterol or diabetes checks. Can I possibly find fault with Juan DuFrey showing an interest in his own numbers? In this context, yes I can. Such patients, I notice, are almost always those already being treated or monitored for the conditions they are seeking further measurements. So why do they do it? The surgery already bends over backwards to accommodate them and what do they go and do on a wet Saturday afternoon but get a further test done, even at their own expense. One of my patients had a finger-prick cholesterol test over coffee and biscuits at a "health awareness meeting," the very week we confirmed her cholesterol was satisfactory on appropriate treatment!

I know of another who visited a pharmacy to get a blood sugar check. He undoubtedly excited the pharmacist by scoring a high reading, only for him to state that he knew he was diabetic but was just curious! Now, I am not suggesting that we should scoff at attempts to find the supposed "missing million" of undiagnosed diabetics and I am sure the odd case of serious hypertension, rampant diabetes or other problems has been detected in this fashion, but I do question both the motivation behind these drop-in facilities and the people who attend. One long-term hypertensive patient said she saw her pharmacy blood pressure checks as a form of "second opinion" and as saving the practice's time. Perhaps she should look elsewhere for her "first opinion" if we cannot be relied upon.

Doctors ourselves seem rather obsessed with numbers and statistics these days. In the British Medical Journal there is now a section entitled "The week in numbers." In this I learned that the average GP works 44.4 hours; 54 UK doctors were struck off last year and there are 50% more medical students than 10 years ago. These are all very interesting facts, I'm sure, but do not help me in my day to day work. GPs with our new national contact are now target-driven and as a consequence have become rather "unhealthily" obsessed with achieving these numbers. This may have worn off a little on our patients. While I was attempting to allay the fears a man had for his forthcoming heart surgery, his wife, quite inappropriately, walked across the room and stood on the scales. Sitting back down again she said " oops, couldn't resist." This was followed by an embarrassed silence. Perhaps that's it, we are just a number-obsessed society: the Lotto; interest rates; celebrities' bank-balances and now our cholesterol levels and weight.

My main fear is that there is a health paradox. The "worried well" worry themselves sick and the undiagnosed health time bombs, who never darken our doors, go on to suffer their heart attacks and strokes.

Resources, as ever, are a major issue and I would certainly argue that the NHS should not be paying for unnecessary informal "health checks" outwith the surgery setting. Private agencies can fund these if they wish, but I don't believe they are done for purely altruistic reasons. Results must be relevant and complement (not duplicate or confuse) our own ongoing monitoring, otherwise patients will ultimately suffer.

Doctors treat patients and not numbers and it would be a mistake to lose sight of this. Anyway, enough of such numerical pontification, I'm off to check my blood pressure after checking my lottery numbers.

FOUL PLAY

"Stool, faeces, pooh, manure, dung, job, night soil, mess, muck, effluent, number two, bowel movement, product of defecation." This was not the rather sanitised mutterings of a disgruntled colleague or the editor on receiving another manuscript but a few of the terms for…well, you know what!

It is interesting though to note that almost all expletives and curses are of an excretory or copulatory nature.

Consider also the toilet. Correctly, this is the "act of dressing and preparing oneself," rather than the porcelain bowl itself. One really visits the lavatory, but in common parlance this can be the: water closet (WC), khazi, loo, pan, cludgie, dunnakin (dunny), john, wash/powder/rest room, privy, conveniences or, if really caught out, the policies.

Recurring letters of complaint to local newspapers are about "ignorant and irresponsible" dog owners who allow their canine friends to foul in public places and make no attempt to clean up after them. Several readers contacted me to ask that I write an article condemning this thoughtless practice. I am happy to do so and to discuss the disease risks but shall broaden the subject to include other aspects of the pseudo-academic discipline of Scatology. As I promised these readers, I brought in examples from the surgery (anecdotes rather than physical evidence, you understand!)

It's said that skin complaints and coughs are the commonest presentations in general practice, but bowel issues must come a close third. One's visits to the lavatory are regarded as normal if they are between thrice per day and once every third day. In other words, a nine-fold variation between individuals would not in itself give your enthralled GP any immediate cause for concern. I am not being facetious. I think I can speak for colleagues by saying bowels are an everyday issue for us in the surgery. Some people unfortunately are little short of obsessed with their own. Keeping a record of one's bowel habit for sixty years does not always engender praise from the GP and is unlikely to fascinate the average publisher either. Sadly, on the other (gloved) hand, many find it a great source of embarrassment and attend their doctors far later than they should have done. Bowel cancer in this part of the world is appallingly common and the development of the unexplained passage of blood or slime *per rectum* needs investigating. Bowel examination is also a common event for your matter-of-fact GP, so embarrassment need not enter into the equation. As a matter of fact, I'd sooner deal with a patient suffering actual diarrhoea than one with the verbal variety.

Living near a tourist town as I do, I believe first impressions matter a great deal. As I stroll with the Labradors for the Sunday papers (poly bags to the ready), the pavement and grass verge "art" from the week before would make even the most intrepid travellers jump back into their campervans and head to pastures perceptibly greener. They may have read of the rivers and mountains of Scotland in their guidebooks but surely not the yellow and tan varieties they stumbled (perhaps literally) upon.

If such fouling is regarded as littering it is certainly the most obnoxious type. Leaving dogs' dirt as a steaming mass in a public place is quite out of order, and now (since 2003) legally so too.

The great majority of dog owners it seems are good, responsible citizens and are usually seen carrying little bags, tied neatly and containing "chocolate drops." But it only takes one or two less thoughtful folk, or those who let their dogs stray and, when on a daily basis, the pile soon piles up, so to speak. Listing: Toxoplasmosis, Toxocariosis, Hydatid disease and even E coli as potentially fatal diseases transmissible to children may sound like scaremongering but they are a considerable risk for larking, stumbling, slipping kids and others.

The introduction of our sewerage system and fresh water supply were probably the greatest contributions to public health we have ever seen. Allowing exposure to waste products, animal or human, can lead to the re-emergence of serious illnesses.

Cats shouldn't be let off lightly either. Our particular problem at *chez* Moody was night-time visits from the neighbours' mogs. As territorial as cats are, the folks next door had a "fertiliser-free" garden and ours seemed to be *catus lavatorium*. The problem was soon solved after a visit to Edinburgh zoo where they obliged me with a sack of lion dung. Perhaps I was just replacing one dropping with another (albeit a more exotic) one but at least it proved who was king of our particular jungle and we never had feline trespassers again.

Most decent people would ask: why allow your pet to defecate in public places when you wouldn't allow her to do the same in your own house? I am mindful of one patient though who lived in abject squalor. The visiting social worker was stunned at the mess and (mainly dog) filth of the interior. She asked the old man, on her departure, if she should let the dog out. "If you like, dear," he replied, "but I thought it was yours."

There are always exceptions, but scooping your pooch's poop would not only look good but you should and it is the law. Leaving Rover's festering pile is puerile, hostile and unsterile. If you have no consideration or respect for others then, quite rightly, you'll get hit in the pocket.

DOC COM

There is a resurgence in the popularity of the book *Charlotte's Web* by E B White. That it is the best selling children's book of all time is perhaps neither here nor there, but it well deserves the accolade and success it has achieved. It is a beautifully crafted book and a delight to read.

When I first read it, only a few years after it was published in 1952, I was greatly moved and confess that I am to this day. Chapter 14, entitled *Dr Dorian,* is perhaps the most inspiring chapter in literature, as a doctor, that I have ever read. The story, for the few of you unfamiliar with it, or those who have forgotten, is about a little girl called Fern. She befriends several creatures on the farm, most notably the eponymous grey spider.

Her mother, Mrs Arable, fears for her, as she seems to have no human friends of her own age. Furthermore, Fern delights in the stories her arachnid companion tells. Her mother is disbelieving, particularly when one such tale involved a fish getting caught in a web, strategically spun across a small stream. On the basis of this, she decides to visit the wisest counsel in town, none other than the old, bearded Dr Dorian. It may have been Dr Dorian who inspired me into general practice, I cannot quite recall, but his sage advice and the marvellous line: "Dr Dorian leaned back and closed his eyes," remained with me for some time. Whether I ever mistakenly thought doctors had the time or inclination to be so *inclined,* I do not know. I daresay the effect would be rather sedating, should I do this forty times each day, as I consider each case presented to me.

Charlotte has attracted great interest within the neighbourhood by writing certain words in the webs she spins and weaves. People travel from miles around to see these adjectives describing a particular little pig named Wilbur. (She is in fact doing this to save his bacon.) Mrs Arable is puzzled and confesses to not liking what she doesn't understand. Dr Dorian advises her that none of us do. He admits to neither comprehending how the spider integrated text within its web nor how she spun it in the first place. Mrs Arable sees no mystery in this feat as she can crochet a doily, having been taught by her own mother. But there lies the real wonder, points out the wise medic, for the spider never received tuition. Its intricate creation is entirely innate as it starts, untutored, shortly after emerging from the egg sac.

He does not fear for young Fern's sanity. He is unsure if animals indeed talk to each other or to people, as perhaps one spoke civilly to him but, rudely, he wasn't paying attention. He suggests the day will come when Henry Fussy, or some other boy, will make a chance remark, catching Fern's attention and affections. In the meantime, the animals would innocently provide the best company for her.

But it is the closing two sentences to this chapter that are the real inspiration. Not that a doctor should set out to please all his patients, all of the time, but when we do it is greatly rewarding. "Mrs Arable said goodbye and thanked Dr Dorian very much for his advice. She felt greatly relieved." Like any good counsellor, he had not really answered any questions, merely helped his patient see things in a rather different light.

I have never seen a spider's web containing a word. Perhaps I have just not studied one closely enough nor am I sufficiently fluent in languages to recognise necessary patterns and symbols. The arachnid creates this object of beauty for its very survival. Like all other creatures, it requires nutrition. Flies and other insects would not be my first choice of sustenance, but she sets her trap for them. This near invisible net entraps the unsuspecting aphid and when it does its number's up. Out from its hiding place scurries Charlotte, or one of her cousins, along the radials and circumferentials by the shortest route. She quickly wraps her prey in further silk strands, administering the fatal injection as she goes. The web is designed to allow her to travel from any one point to any other and this, I suspect, is why our modern day wonder, the internet, is so named. The Web is rapidly enabling all those online, (not necessarily of the silky strand type) to get and remain in contact with others elsewhere. Fortunately, it is rarely for the purposes of seeing off our contacts, but there is undoubtedly a shady and malign aspect to this technology.

Readers have contacted me, expressing regret at having missed an article. I am happy to oblige and dig out a copy from the archives but was heeded by suggestions to either write a book or create a website. I shall mull over the former but the latter I discovered, though certainly not innate, is easier than ever to establish. So dear readers, you now have free and ready access, should you choose, to thirty or so of these Dr Ken articles. Most are back numbers and some are, as yet, unpublished in the paper form. I shall keep rotating (and of course writing) them, highlighting the one that features that particular week As ever, your comments and suggestions are most welcome.

So here it is, here is my website. Fly into it at your peril.

CLEMENT BRYCE GUNN

Sitting proudly on my shelf is a little book of just under two-hundred pages. Some of you may be familiar with this humble publication, but for those who are not I thoroughly commend it to you. *"Leaves from the Life of A Country Doctor"* by Clement Bryce Gunn was first published in 1935. A second edition appeared in 1947 and it was republished in 2002, complete with archive photographs. It is mainly his diary and reminiscences but is edited and annotated by Rutherford Crockett. For me, it is a priceless book and I frequently revisit it for inspiration.

Dr Gunn (1860-1933) was a general practitioner in Peebles and surrounding district. He was a true all-rounder in both the medical and general senses. As a GP living and working in Peebles in the late nineteenth and early twentieth centuries, he practised in a way that is long since gone but I cannot help comparing the way I work now to how he did. He chronicled in the most beautiful and archaic of prose the sheer hardship of life and acceptance of death so long ago. Sometimes I feel I can just lift from the page what he is saying as though he were speaking directly to me. In 1892 he wrote: *"May not my own successors in this place be interested one day-say a hundred years hence-in reading of the daily professional routine of their nineteenth-century predecessor? Will they laugh at his equestrian adventures with a flesh-and-blood horse, while they are whirled from patient to patient in their electric carriages? Will they perhaps ridicule his ancient diagnoses and medical theories?"* I may laugh with fascination Dr Gunn, but not with ridicule.

Clement Gunn practised at a time when death was often just around the corner and no great fuss was made. Infections, so common then, could decimate families within weeks. He often marvelled at the charity of neighbours who sat with dying mothers or their children, in what he described as "practical religion." He wrote touchingly about a visit to a rather chaotic household of children and animals while a little child lay quietly dying from diphtheria. Some of my patients complain that their tetanus jags are combined "unnecessarily" with the diphtheria immunisation.

Being so distant from Edinburgh, all cases and accidents, no matter how serious, were dealt with by him. A girl once got her long hair entangled in machinery and was literally scalped. He sent people to retrieve the four pieces and proceeded to stitch them all back again. Miraculously she went on to make a good recovery. As happy as I am to suture wounds, if there is any suspicion of more serious underlying problems, to the infirmary they will go.

Reading about his maternity cases was perhaps the part from which I felt furthest removed. Dr Gunn was on-call all of the time. He was often juggling four or more simultaneous labours in different parts of the county. As soon as one babe was delivered, alive or dead, he would rush to the next bedside to begin the whole process again, or occasionally find himself arriving too late. (Being tethered by bureaucracy as we now are, I would venture to say that my nearest analogy is rushing from one life assurance policy form to another disabled parking application!) In one incident a child was stillborn. He took the body away by horse and trap, only to hear minutes later a "punchinello" cry from beneath his seat. The movement and cold within the carriage had achieved resuscitation. Gunn returned the now hearty baby to the hitherto heart-broken mother. We tend to see expectant mums at booking and post-natally, with midwives having muscled in on the entire interval in between, unless complications occur. Proposed home-deliveries are rare and generally something advised against. Like any other practise, the less one does the more de-skilled one becomes.

For all his hard work Dr Gunn took the occasional holiday. He had to find a *locum tenens* to cover such absences (at the princely sum of three guineas a week.) I laughed when I read that his locum was "half-killed" by the work, but in fact had visited a hundred fewer patients *in a week* than Dr Gunn himself would have done. In order to optimise our time, visits now are very much the exception and reserved for the frail, elderly or particularly sick and may only amount to a couple of dozen or so each week. He often had to reach distant farms by trudging through deep snow or wading through rivers. He was reliant on his trusty horse and at least once was thrown from his cart. No mobile phone could inform him of his next case and he would rely on messengers or have to make his way home to *Lindores*, in Peebles, to discover where next he was being summoned. Even on his wedding night he had to leave his bride in the company of his mother as he had half a dozen visits to complete. A harsh introduction indeed, for Mrs Gunn, to being a rural doctor's wife.

Social services at that time were non-existent. One mother of ten died of cancer in her thirties. Dr Gunn managed to find work for the older children and placements for some of the younger ones. All efforts were made to keep people from the poorhouse, but this was not always possible.

His place in history is quite poignant too. Arthur Conan-Dole was a contemporary of Gunn's, and one of his lecturers at Edinburgh University was Joseph Bell, the inspiration for Sherlock Holmes. "*Thus he trained us, his amateur Watsons, the habit of observation.*" He described in 1901 the death of Queen Victoria. He saw the "great Hydropathic fire" from his house in 1905 and cycled rapidly there with his children to rescue posh residents and their jewellery (I believe in that order!) The First World War of 1914–18 meant he visited recently bereaved women who were trying to keep a semblance of normality in their proud households. He saw children "gleefully playing" with postcards sent from the Front by their, now late, fathers. Belgian refugees somehow found their way to Peebles and were warmly welcomed by the Gunn family and other Peebles residents.

Dr Gunn's diary is interrupted soon after the war as he

concentrated for seven years on cataloguing and publishing, in five volumes, the details of "the unreturning brave." This was information or "portraits" of every man from Peeblesshire who perished on the battlefields of Europe during that dark time.

Dr Gunn was the first person in the town to acquire a telephone, but soon discovered he was the only one. After a full year, the local pharmacist learned of the benefits of such technology and their medicinal hotline was established. Gunn claimed also to be the first person in Peeblesshire to use the "new fangled" automobile.

He remarked on the nephew of a great friend who showed promise in the literary field, one John Buchan. (He, of course went on to become our nation's finest novelist in recent times!) Buchan, in fact, wrote the foreword to this very book, in which he described Gunn as having "a stiff sense of duty and a rich humanity" and as being "an old and much-esteemed friend."

His great, tireless and often unpaid work did not go unnoticed or unrewarded. As a mark of appreciation for his work detailing war victims, in 1922 along with Earl Haig, he was granted "The freedom of the Royal Burgh of Peebles."

When he died his coffin was carried "on a farm cart garlanded with holly, through streets (of Peebles) thronged with weeping crowds."

If ever I was invited on BBC Radio 4's *Desert Island Discs* and was asked to choose my favourite book, then surely this would be it.

Leaves from the Life of A Country Doctor, Birlinn Press 2002, ISBN 1841582387

DOCTORS AND (OTHER) CRIMINALS

"If that's Ms Creant in for an appointment you'd better keep your eye on her", warned Mona Lotte our practice manager, "or she'll be off with the chair from under your…fundament."There is often a certain prejudice against people who have acquired criminal records. Sometimes such wariness is wise but often it is unnecessary and unfair.

General practitioners during their training will have dealt with patients who would be classified as "criminal" and will still do so whether working in asphalt inner city, or leafy rural, practices. To earn this moniker one has to have been convicted of an offence, but it also applies to a person who "commits crimes for a living." Of course such crimes may range from petty theft to mass murder so such a term is not particularly helpful other than to indicate that one has strayed, at least once, into the chastising path of the law.

My first experience of criminality (second-hand you understand) was having to assess and treat, in hospital, patients handcuffed to police or prison officers. Of course, confidentiality is at risk under such circumstances but is less important if one's own well-being is under imminent threat.

It is sad though to see people descend, for whatever reason or none, on a slope from mischief to murder by way of malevolence. They often spend years in prison or are in and out of porridge, hardly ever "passing Go." Through unemployment and "unemployability" they drag their dependents down the social ladder faster than an escape party sniffing freedom.

I was once asked by a lad facing further charges if I could

prepare a letter excusing him from court on the basis of a recurrent ear infection. I respectfully pointed out that he had not sought any medical advice (inside or out) for over two years; so such a "problem" would (unlike the defendant) probably not stand up in court. Realising his predicament he asked if I could think of "anything else then" that might get him off.

I need only read elsewhere in these pages (*The Peeblesshire News*) each week to learn of the latest drunken brawl or driving offence Mal Factor, Miss Dee Meanor or other patients are being charged with.

Work in Accident & Emergency led to me appearing in court innumerable times. Not, I am pleased to report, for a catalogue of errors but as a professional witness to the effects of, and injuries from, assaults (always "alleged" assaults of course, until guilt is proven!). About a year after I finished that particular post a man, whom I did not recognise, approached me in a restaurant. He shook me vigorously by the hand and thanked me for helping him "get off an attempted murder charge." I had certainly never wittingly stated anything other than the facts, as I knew them. His gratitude extended to him proffering me his "business card" for one of the building trades. "No job too large or too small", may have seemed inviting but my DIY skills, or lack thereof, became eminently preferable.

Some doctors dedicate their careers to prison medicine or forensic medicine. I have practised a little of both and found them rewarding experiences. Being a police surgeon (Forensic Medical Examiner) is not as glamorous as an Agatha Conan Dexter mystery and the bulk of the work is meeting the demands (and rights) of addicts to "see a doctor", late at night in custody. Drugs are a huge blight on and in our society. While (the love of) money may be the "root of all evil", drugs are the trunk and branches. There may be complex social, judicial and political issues but I firmly believe that all efforts to eradicate drugs from source all the way to the street must be made.

Of course doctors are neither above the law nor always on the right side of it. Complaints about GPs and other doctors are increasing and while indiscretions with patients and drug and alcohol addictions have always existed, it is difficult to say if we really are a less honest and trustworthy bunch. I honestly believe we remain the same, but you may not trust me on this. Dr Harold "Fred" Shipman, as a British GP, is likely to be unique in his despicable crimes. He was a mass murderer who happened, unfortunately, to be a doctor. He has not forever tarnished my profession but has certainly changed it. Much greater regulation, accountability and transparency is demanded of us. These are to be welcomed to a certain extent but we are currently buried under bureaucracy, ironically at the expense of patient care, in order to achieve these. I personally draw the line at the publication of crude unqualified league tables that do little more than scaremonger. They exist to score political points, for those who count such things.

So, even if Ms Creant does manage to make away with my creaky wooden swivel chair, I'll just pinch Dr Bodie Aiken's from next door.

THE DOG AND BONE

"Love or loathe its intrusion, the telephone has been the greatest contribution to Medicine since 1840. Whether to summon help (emergency 999 number introduced in 1937), request urgent advice or latterly to make contact wherever/whenever, it has been invaluable. My predecessors in general practice would visit distant farms or hamlets then return home only to discover the need to attend another labouring, haemorrhaging or seriously ill patient. Wasted minutes and hours frequently mean(t) the difference between life and death. Email and the internet are handy, but it is the telephone that contributes to the saving of innumerable lives."

This was my modest, and ultimately negligible, contribution to the whimsical debate a journal editor created for the edification and amusement of his readers.

Nevertheless, it can be rather fun and educational to consider things from a different and lighter point of view. On this occasion, as you will have gathered, we were asked to consider the "most important medical advances" in two centuries less a generation; when the journal was founded.

I daresay there have been a few retrograde steps in this time as well. Perhaps next year, I'll mischievously suggest a poll of such medical regressions. (Ward hygiene; the sense of vocation and the influence of pharmaceutical companies should feature highly.)

We were invited to submit proposals, in no more than 100 words, to an online forum where others could read and discuss them. These were streamlined to a "top 15" and the proposers were then asked to argue eloquently and passionately (if they so wished), with an outright winner selected from the greatest number of votes cast.

Before submitting mine, I chewed over what was meant by the "most important medical advance." Was it the discovery or invention of a product which, quite simply, has saved the greatest number of lives? Vaccines prevent deadly diseases, but trying to calculate their success numerically is a little simplistic and fails to acknowledge other factors. Other developments, such as antibiotics, may have cured illnesses but had very serious, sometimes fatal, side effects. (As useful as the bread poultice was, I suspect its influence has now passed its peak!) Anaesthetics, making surgical procedures considerably safer, have helped save many lives, but statistically would not compare to vaccines and antibiotics.

Some colleagues suggested: plastic; the contraceptive pill: anti-malarials, pacemakers and defibrillators and the discovery of DNA. Medical imaging, including X-Rays and ultrasound, also featured highly.

Thinking a little laterally (I find this easier than pondering in a forwards direction!) I decided upon and proposed the telephone. As you will see, it was my contention that this communication device has helped save numerous lives. I accept that Medicine cannot claim it for its own and it has advanced many other fields too, but doctors and their patients owe it an immeasurable debt of gratitude.

Perhaps because of this immeasurability, and rather curiously, I received no votes or notes of support–the equivalent, I suppose, of it just ringing out. We really do take "the dog and bone" for granted. We rely so much upon it and the benefits are enormous (and that's ignoring premium rate numbers and polyphonic ringtones–if only we could!)

Romantically, we like to think it was a Scot, Alexander Graham Bell with his wonderfully appropriate surname, who invented it. Bell, a naturalised American, was indeed involved in the upgrading of the telegraph system, but credit really ought to go to the Italian, Antonio Meucci. It was he who created a telephonic device, years before Bell. The battle for its patent was fierce and dirty. Poor old Meucci's application was "lost" and he could not afford to reapply.

The patent was eventually granted to Bell in 1876 and he and his investors proceeded to make millions from it. It was such a staggering success that it was confidently predicted that, one day, every large town in the United States would have its own telephone. Bell is also credited with the metal detector in 1881. He first used his invention in an effort to locate the assassin's bullet within the body of president James Garfield. Unfortunately he failed, having not taken into account the metal bed frame, on which the late leader lay. Not exactly testament to his engineering genius, I don't suppose.

I almost forgot, the overall winner? It was sanitation. The installation of clean water and the safe disposal of sewage from our towns and cities was considered the greatest development. Arguably, again, an engineering rather than a medical feat. But the greatest developments are often those where there is a blend of talents, ingenuity and a genuine desire for better health and well-being in fellow man.

TOKENISM

"My boss has accused me of not giving my all and he told me I was on my last warning," sobbed Minnie Mall into her tissue. It was true that Minnie had a rather romantic and vivid imagination. Her job as office clerk and deputy envelope-licker, probably lent itself to tangential thoughts and less than a concerted effort on her part. She is somewhat of a dependent personality too, and still writes me lengthy letters about: this, that and the next inconsequential thing. All her missives are addressed "To Ken," so if accusations of "tokenism" could be levelled at her I'd mischievously suggest they were more of the "to Ken-ism" variety, though I'd never ask a patient to stop writing to me. But I never promise to read every word.

My ever reliable dictionary defines "tokenism" as "doing no more than the minimum, especially with regards to a law." A common example in a working environment might be clock-watching.

I meet a lot of patients who fulfil the criteria, whether it is at work or at college. I pity those who have to meet sales figures and targets in order to justify their jobs, but for some such a work climate may be necessary to rid them of terminal inertia. Ready access to the internet is a great means of reducing one's productive hours. Sometimes employees need reminding whose time they are misappropriating and Mrs Mona Lotte, our practice manager, is quick to remind us of this.

Tokenism occurs in the home as well, of course. A chap doesn't usually make much effort to lift a dishtowel (unless his good lady has dropped it.) Nor does he willingly put up a shelf or decorate the spare room unless sanctions are threatened. If it is Saturday afternoon and the golf course beckons, I suspect not much more than going through the motions will occur and sometimes (especially with the likes of wallpapering) half a job done is probably worse than none at all. Signs of affection are few and far between, and gushing gestures on Valentine's Day are not so much an example of classic tokenism but a poor attempt to make up for 52 weeks of attention-neglect and affection starvation.

But it is health issues that obviously interest this old medic the most. Overweight folk and their token efforts to slim usually invite my comment. Perhaps this is because, what a supposed dieter says and what the scales and girth measuring tape show are often markedly at odds. I decline to prescribe "fat busting" drugs unless my patient can demonstrate the willpower and effort to shed several pounds for himself. In addition to limiting the food going down the cake-hole, weight reduction requires an exercise regime. All too often the response is that the dog requires walking. Indeed he does, but few calories are burned off if my patient shuffles along the road swinging a dog leash or when said canine is tied to railings outside *Tatti's* the Italian Fish Bar.

Like every other person who deals with the public, I appreciate honesty. Patients are good at telling me what they think I want to hear. All too often, I'm fed a few porkie pies (metaphorically, of course!). My patience is the only thing that wears thin when Mr Lardsworth insists he eats dry crackers, grapes and celery but still sends the needle on the scales round for a second circuit. While this menu may be accurate, it is likely on closer questioning that this rather unpalatable and implausible diet in fact commenced the previous day. Furthermore, some patients need reminding that dietary recommendations are to be consumed *instead of* their habitual pie and chips, and not *in addition to*. But enough of unhealthy food (if only it were!), smoking is another area where tokens seem to fit neatly into the respective vending machine slots. No cigarette is beneficial to the lungs: no level of consumption is acceptable health-wise. If only the vast majority of smokers indeed have cut down as they dubiously claim. I cannot recall any smoker telling me he smokes more than he used to. Two-dozen cancer-sticks each day is a little better than two score but might just mean the dial on the oxygen cylinder is set a little lower, as he constantly struggles for breath, in ten years time.

Alcohol, too, with its vice-like addictive grip, is subject to the truth being diluted as much as the drams should be. In cases of abuse, total abstinence is easier (or certainly less difficult) to achieve than reducing from a bottle and a half to a bottle each day. There is nothing wrong with a few drinks on a few nights each week but, all too often, this becomes a bucketful every night, at considerable financial and personal cost.

Perhaps we all are guilty of tokenism; whether it is at work, at home or with our loved ones. I don't really think though that this column writer could be accused of such. Gosh, I've spent 58 minutes and 13 seconds writing this article, that should be just enough to satisfy the editor and, you, the readership. No more, no less. Job done.

A FAMOUS PATIENT

As a doctor I have to be careful when writing about patients. Confidentiality, of course, is of paramount importance. I have to be particularly cautious when detailing one who is (or at least was) very well known and I exercise such care now. In an unusual twist, I shall refer to this chap by his real rather than his stage name, for you would almost certainly recognize him by the latter. Len Sayes was a household name in the Sixties, when he played bass for The Spectacles. (I use the band's lesser known and former name, again for fear of recognition.) Music in these bygone days still had a degree of innocence about it. It was not commercially driven but created for sheer pleasure and with raw talent. Groups of lads got together in sitting-rooms, somewhere in suburbia, and penned some of the iconic tunes of the age. The Spectacles were never quite up there with The Kinks or The Rolling Stones but were undoubtedly bigger than the likes of The Paperclips. They had hits that briefly occupied positions further up the hit parade than even the great bands of the day. On their marvellously popular "Focus on the People" tours, The Spectacles would gig right around the great cities of Glasgow and Edinburgh and then perform on legs taking in numerous towns down the newly opened Ml and M6 motorways. They could never work it out but this route seemed particularly appropriate. Their memories of these times were generally good ones but also a bit of a blur. Drugs started to take hold but, despite this, they shifted LPs by the barrel-load and the pre-decimalized currency, rolled in. By the late Sixties, as you may recall, it was unusual and seriously uncool for a teenager to be without a pair of NHS-prescription spectacles. As the Seventies dawned, cracks started to appear and the bond loosened. The drummer and percussionist felt they shared a different vision and wanted the band to head in a different direction. As a group, they stumbled on for a few months but there was no saving them, and they finally folded.

Len found himself in his early thirties with more money than he would ever need. He had no clear way in sight of how to spend this fortune, or the rest of his life. He always fancied settling in the south of Scotland and purchased, for cash, a large and rambling estate only a few miles from here. The royalties continue to pour in with each digitally remastered CD and the occasional Hollywood director adopts one of his songs for the title track to a blockbuster movie. (Len happily admits to never having watched any though!)

Len married Iris when they were barely out their teens. She had been a groupie and wouldn't miss a concert. There had been plenty of girls but he just couldn't see past Iris. They couldn't keep their eyes (or their hands!) off each other but, in truth, weren't really well matched. He now says that he doesn't know what he saw in her at all and blames the dark and smoky concert halls. In his thirties Len met a much younger woman than himself, Cornelia, and they remain a couple to this day. Journalists from the weekend supplements try to hide their disappointment when they discover Len's interests are principally philately and campanology and nothing more unconventional. His biggest mistake he says was agreeing to be the face of a high street optician's chain and he winces when he sees himself, even now, on afternoon TV.

As his doctor and neighbour, I have visited his mansion on many occasions. He converted one of the stable blocks into a recording studio and enjoys moderate success even now in the Japanese market. The brick walls are adorned with black and white photos of the band larking about and a framed platinum disc of their greatest hit, the much imitated and misinterpreted track "What's this thing called, love?" Other notable awards were for the singles "Love is blind" and "You caught my eye and I want it back."

I enjoy the conversations we share and after a wine or two have had the enormous privilege of strumming and humming with the maestro himself as he conjures up the melodic magic of yesteryear. Len never dwells on his fame or impressive wealth but often wonders how different things might have been without the good luck he enjoyed. He is prone to bouts of depression and melancholia and attributes this in part to the years of drug and alcohol abuse. He has no intention of reuniting with the surviving band members and hardly speaks with them year to year. He expresses concern at the pursuit of fame at all costs by today's young celebrities, particularly when their talent is still to make itself obvious. He worries that when reality bites they will have no way of coping with the real world. He dislikes the ease with which music is created and shared nowadays and feels its true worth and meaning have been lost along the way. To his credit, he has given of his time and runs masterclasses at his studio. Many of his pupils are already starting to make names for themselves.

I do not treat Len any differently from other patients who may not have enjoyed their moment in the limelight. He eats, sleeps, laughs, cries and hurts like the rest of us; though he is a living, breathing legend.

MRS MOODY

"Does Mrs Moody mind being married to a general practitioner, Dr Ken?" asked Marty Monie our recently engaged secretary over coffee. D'you know, I've never asked her or given it any particular thought. What could there possibly be for her to mind? The hours are pretty reasonable now, the remuneration is fair and, unlike our farming neighbours, I tend not to have the odour of my work about me (or at least I don't have any such excuse!) If she does have valid cause for complaint it may be for my mild eccentricities and general disorganisation, I suspect, rather than for my job itself.

So, that evening, more out of curiosity than consideration I suppose and as I poured the last of a passable Chardonnay into my fair spouse's glass, I enquired whether Mrs Moody indeed had any regrets about my chosen profession. Emitting a partially muffled belch (or eructation to more sensitive readers) and as she digested my question, I checked the label to ensure it was not a sparkling wine that I had served. When the last drop had slipped gracefully down her slender neck (on the inside) and with a reflective, or perhaps just glazed, look she licked her lips and started a most extraordinary speech. In all these years it had not gone unnoticed that I made the great assumption that it was her wish to move from the city to this green and fertile place. (It transpired I had been green and she supremely fertile!) I had also taken as read her vocation for being a doctor's wife. She had relinquished her ambitions for nursing; the then mushrooming field of atomic science and, her greatest love, vaudeville. I never doubted her ability or dexterity to juggle all three. She was fine looking and a (metaphorically) striking woman in her day (see photo, front cover) and I'd be prepared to argue that her "day" has only just reached late afternoon. I was attracted by her: looks and books; curves and loves and waist and tastes. She is of good stock; in fact her allergies lend themselves to the suggestion that she is too finely bred. Most shared and personal interests however have sadly passed by the way or been sacrificed for more pressing things. Visits back to Edinburgh dwindled and eventually only the galleries and an intimate wee restaurant off the Royal Mile ever drew us back.

In the early years down here, before mobile phones made their unbidden entrance, this hitherto unrecognised, behind-the-scenes stalwart was there as a mother, receptionist and unqualified (in only the formal sense) medic. She dispensed sage advice over the telephone in my absence and handled many an emergency with a cool head. Quite often I would return to our gloriously warm hearth after pushing the door closed against the blizzard outside. Once there she would dolefully but pityingly relay the message that I had another patient to visit in the far-flung village from where I had just returned. One of my greatest frustrations was once when, rather grudgingly, I had to retrace my Austin tyre tracks in the snow. On arrival I was informed that I had been spotted (on my first trip) and my calling might "save" me having to sign a sick note for Dickie Legg the next morning in surgery (or more likely save Dickie the trip!)

I have not been the best husband, father or even doctor to my family. In times of illness or injury my ability to under or overdiagnose the Moody clan is little short of legendary. Evening surgeries, lectures, conferences and dinners have taken priority over family events or other special occasions down the years and these times cannot be replaced. I never literally brought my work home with me, in the form of patients (unless they doubled as friends), but I have been distracted, preoccupied, occasionally irate and, dare I say, moody depending on what sort of day I've had. Confidentiality always forbids me discussing the reasons for such unattractive states though the retort of "just work" usually ends further discussion.

I've been poor at remembering anniversaries and birthdays, and as another decade of our union passed quietly by recently her patience and good humour remain firm.

Jings, she has been a tower of strength, a lighthouse, one that I've taken for granted during raging storms and calm seas. I must have a blind spot the size of the average fishing vessel. Doctors' partners whether: established; new; replaced; plural; same gender; medical or whatever provide the rock to their medical "other-halves."

I love you Mrs Moody and please let it be known throughout the Borders and in your heart that I am forever grateful (and if this doesn't make you chortle I'm an avuncular primate!)

MUSINGS FROM A LILY PAD

As I sit here on a large *Nymphaeaceae* leaf at the cusp of yet another new year, I ponder on what it will bring.

A new year often brings excitement and fresh challenges, and so will this one I have no doubt. The young particularly, with all their potential, should be encouraged and allowed to flourish under our protective gaze. (Sadly though only about 10 % of my spawn reach adulthood!)

Two problems weigh heavily with me, and these may come as a surprise to you. Not the diminishing dragonfly population or the creeping realisation that I am not in fact a prince with a spell upon me.

Global warming and international terrorism are what trouble me most. These are undoubtedly the biggest threats ever known to both the plant on which I currently sit and rather more seriously, the planet itself. Events in recent years have proven, if proof were ever needed, that we as a race and a species are not invincible, and certainly not immortal.

The former is of our own making and the damage done in the last few decades with carbon emissions and our consumer lifestyles is almost past the point of no return. Just the other day a fellow creature croaked to me "everything will be all right as nature always triumphs." But he misses the point, we are destroying that buffer. Nature is being rendered "unnatural" as we burn ever more fossil fuels and rape the earth of its beauty, natural resources and sustainability.

Global warming is the appalling consequence of "progress," through our ignorance, negligence and selfishness. It can be slowed and even reversed but only if radical action is taken. The trouble is, there is no global action plan, even when one is mooted superpowers "opt out." Governments, even in the so-called developed world, have other (and undeclared) agendas. Necessary capping of energy usage and, more broadly speaking, lifestyle excesses are unpopular, risk slowing economies and (heaven forbid!) lose votes.

Wars have always been fought and sadly always will be. Greed, power, jealously, tribalism and perhaps most dangerous of all; need, prompt military action. Many recent conflicts have been about declining resources such as oil, and some predict battles will increasingly be waged for the essence of life itself, water. Disease and warfare may slow the exploding global population, but not to a significant extent. There are ever more mouths to feed with ever less to go round. Unprecedented droughts in Africa and floods in Asia decimate crops, as their respective climates grow increasingly hostile. Technology to predict such catastrophes and to provide alternative food sources offers some hope but does not have all the answers.

Terrorism with the appalling potential it presents is even less predictable and just as much to be feared. It is beyond most people's understanding, whatever their culture and beliefs, that it can be someone's sole purpose to destroy others in as devastating a way as possible. That it should be in the name of religion is, for many, the ultimate perversity. Some religions may engender a certain self-righteousness but never, in my reading and understanding, a complete intolerance of the very existence of other peoples.

Forgive me if I appear a little heavy in my musings, I would not wish you to mistake me for my chubbier cousin, the toad. I should be offering you felicitations and glad tidings and I certainly do wish you well.

I do not pretend to be a big frog in a little pond or even a diminutive amphibian in a sizeable pool, but therein lies (or squats!) the problem. We often feel that the woes of the world are beyond

DR KEN B MOODY

our understanding and our influence. So we sit there motionless, mouth agape catching flies. What can I do in my little pond, in my little corner of the Borders? Globally, I suppose, not a lot. But, if more of us strove to live harmoniously, were more environmentally concerned and sought to educate ourselves on issues that baffle and worry us, it would be a step (or a leap) in the right direction.

Life is short enough. We amphibians don't usually exceed 7 years, and only then if we've successfully dodged predators.

Anyway, I wish you and yours the very best. May the year be all you deserve it to be. Ours is the future. I'll hop off now. I really must stop ribbiting on.